ABRAHAM AARON ROBACK

A DICTIONARY OF
INTERNATIONAL SLURS

MALEDICTA PRESS PUBLICATIONS · V

GENERAL EDITOR: REINHOLD AMAN

A Dictionary of
INTERNATIONAL SLURS
(ETHNOPHAULISMS)

WITH A SUPPLEMENTARY ESSAY ON

ASPECTS OF ETHNIC PREJUDICE

BY

A. A. ROBACK

SCI-ART PUBLISHERS
HARVARD SQUARE
CAMBRIDGE, MASS.

Library of Congress Catalog
Card Number 76-5696

ISSN 0363-9037

ISBN 0-916500-05-5

From the 1944 Edition:

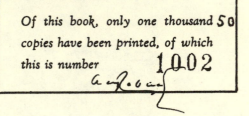

Of this book, only one thousand 50
copies have been printed, of which
this is number 1002

MALEDICTA PRESS
331 South Greenfield Avenue
Waukesha, Wisconsin 53186

Printed in the United States of America

To

GENERAL CHARLES DE GAULLE

THE CONSCIENCE OF THE ALLIED COMMAND

CONTENTS

Contents

A Psychoanalytic Hint . . . Sequence of Dislikes and Rivalry
. . . Dread of the Foreigner . . . Methodology . . . Break-
down of National Slurs . . . Americans . . . The British . . .
The Dutch and the Germans . . . The French . . . The Italians
. . . The Jews . . . The Moors . . . The Negroes . . . The
Osmanlis and the Turks . . . The Orientals . . . The Portu-
guese and the Spanish . . . The Scandinavians . . . The Slavs
. . . The Genesis of a Proverb . . . Is a Nation a *Tabula Rasa?*
. . . Associative and Assonance Factors . . . How Pernicious
are the Slurs? . . . Inconsistencies of the Law . . . The Logic
of Phobia . . . The Preventive Phase of Legislation . . .
Spectres of the Past . . . Imps of the Present . . . Bigotry as
a Disease . . . The Synecdoche Complex in Bigots . . .
Above all Nations Humanity . . . Not Education but Enlightenment Our Hope.

[2]

Contents

BIBLIOGRAPHIES

INDEXES

[3]

FOREWORD

It is highly fitting that Maledicta Press should be reissuing A. A. Roback's *Dictionary of International Slurs* in a handsome photographic reprint, for the original edition of this valuable work, published in only 1050 copies toward the end of World War II by a one-man firm, has long been extremely scarce and largely inaccessible. Some thirty years after its publication this book is still the standard work in the field, and what its author modestly regarded as an initial attempt to give a sampling of slurs (for which he coined the term "ethnophaulisms") and stimulate further research has never been duplicated, let alone surpassed.

The *Dictionary*, to be sure, is not without its limitations and flaws. In one of the few reviews it elicited, Raven I. McDavid, writing in *American Speech*, criticized what he regarded as the compiler's lack of critical apparatus and scholarly discrimination, his scant documentation and unsupported statements, his dubious arrangement of the material and his mingling of obsolete and current locutions. In response, Roback, an eminently polemical spirit, issued a challenge to other scholars to improve upon "the only work of its kind without guide or model." This challenge has yet to be met.

Roback pointed out that in his view a slur was "not a philological or linguistic entity but a *mental attitude*." Who will deny that in the last quarter of the twentieth century

[5]

such attitudes have proliferated and hardened? The author disposes of McDavid's charge that in his essay "Aspects of Ethnic Prejudice" he had written "against anti-Judaism, not against national slurs" by saying that if the Jews had received more space than any other group, this was natural in view of the fact that they have been "the world's scapegoat No. 1 for two thousand years." In this respect, too, the past three decades have exacerbated the problem rather than relieving it.

The foregoing exchange exemplifies not only Roback's penchant for polemics but also the philological, psychological, and broadly humanistic concerns that are so often combined in his writings. Two terms come to mind to characterize Abraham Aaron Roback: *Universalgelehrter* and *Streitbares Leben*. It is perhaps symptomatic that both are German, for Roback had a truly Prussian sense of duty and decorum and was in the German professorial tradition. The first term means simply "polymath," and it aptly describes Roback the psychologist, Yiddishist, folklorist, linguist, and cultural historian. *Streitbares Leben* is the title of the autobiography of Max Brod, one of the most eminent sons of the polemical city of Prague. *Streitbar* means "argumentative," "cantankerous," and "belligerent," but also "valiant" and "valorous," so the full phrase may be translated best as "a fighter's life." Brod called himself an "unwilling polemicist," and this phrase applies to Roback as well. During his lifelong championship of a variety of important but not always popular causes, Dr. Roback met with more that his share of incomprehension, indifference, and deliberate obfuscation, and everything he touched seemed to turn into polemics. (*Kritik un Kritzenish*, "Gritting as Greeting," is the title of one of his polemical pamphlets.) To have created an imposing literary legacy despite numerous obstacles is in itself a noteworthy achievement.

Born in Russia in 1890 and taken to Montreal as an infant, A. A. Roback attended McGill University and then pursued graduate studies at Harvard. He always fondly and proudly remembered the "golden age" of Harvard's departments of Philosophy and Psychology, marked by such luminaries as William James (to whom Roback devoted a study in 1942), Josiah Royce, and Hugo Münsterberg. Roback's publications in psychology run the gamut from his doctoral dissertation, *The Interference of Will Impulses*, to *Aspects of Applied Psychology and Crime* (1964). His *Psychology of Character*, first published in 1927 and repeatedly reissued and translated into several languages, and *History of American Psychology* (1952) are probably his most significant contributions in that field. Roback's books on personality and behaviorism are some of the other works which stamp Roback as an influential writer on problems of personality and character. These reveal him as a scholar *sui generis* who followed no particular school, a non-conformist with great synoptical ability and an eminently practical orientation. They bespeak great erudition and evidence a personal, idiomatic, occasionally idiosyncratic approach and a fascination with colorful biographical incident.

Roback's *magnum opus* in the field of cultural history is his book *Jewish Influence in Modern Thought*, published in 1929 on the occasion of the bicentenary of Moses Mendelssohn and Gotthold Ephraim Lessing and also commemorating the birthday anniversaries of Henri Bergson, Albert Einstein, and other Jewish luminaries. With *Destiny and*

Motivation in Language (1954), a thoughtful excercise in psycholinguistics and glossodynamics which offers, among many other things, a daring psychoanalytical exploration of "Shmoo and Shmo," Roback returned to his first love, the study of language. These works are scholarly in an unorthodox way and disarmingly personal—the kind of books that stimulate reflection, discussion, and disagreement. But Roback's most characteristic contributions in the Jewish realm were made to the Yiddish language and literature. In the words of Moshe Starkman, Roback was a *romantisher ritter fun mameh loshn*, a romantic knight of Yiddish, a tireless fighter against the psychology of *untergangism*, i.e., the conviction that Yiddish—the language and the culture— is moribund. Roback's lifelong love affair with *mameh loshn* was based on the conviction that Yiddish is "the most enduring medium of expression which the Jewish people, i.e., the masses, have had . . . . it contains nearly all the elements of other languages which the Jews have employed." *I. L. Peretz: Psychologist of Literature* (1935) was followed in 1940 by *The Story of Yiddish Literature* Two of Roback's later books were written in Yiddish: *Di Imperye Yidish* was published in Mexico and *Der Folksgaist in der Yidisher Shprakh* appeared in Paris, lending support to the author's abundant faith in the vitality, viability, and international dissemination of what many have for so long regarded as a parochial affair and a moribund jargon.

A dedicated and resourceful teacher with a number of endearing idiosyncracies, Roback used psychology as a fulcrum for the dynamic presentation of the broad spectrum of human culture. He held an instructorship at Harvard as well as professorships at Northeastern University and Emerson College in Boston, and he also taught at the Boston Center for Adult Education and in the University Extension Division of the Commonwealth of Massachusetts. However, he was not fated to end his life on the high note of an appointment at a major university. Roback's uncompromising devotion to his ideals and his almost Spartan mode of living caused him to be increasingly lonely in his last years. His death occurred at Cambridge, Massachusetts, his home for several decades, in 1965.

It is not generally known that the author of more than two dozen books and some two thousand articles appearing in about a hundred journals was also a one-man publishing firm. Founded in the 1920s to escape the caprices and commercial considerations of established editors and publishers, Sci-Art Publishers, operated by Roback from his apartment, issued not only most of his own books in handsome if small editions, but also published books by his fellow psychologists Morton Prince, R. B. Cattell, and Hanns Sachs. The Sci-Art list also includes the first selection in English from the writings of the German satirist Kurt Tucholsky and two volumes devoted to Albert Schweitzer, whose greatness Roback recognized well before the *grand docteur* captured America's imagination.

The *Dictionary of International Slurs* is here reprinted exactly as first published in 1944—in itself a remarkable typographic achievement and production job under the restrictions of wartime. (One ruefully reflects that Roback could not have issued this work under present conditions or been a "Dutch uncle," as he once put it, in his dealings with production people.) No attempt has been made to correct misprints and other slips or to update the bibliography. Although Roback would undoubtedly have made many changes in a new edition (including the dedication, for an updated version might well include some of Charles de Gaulle's own more recent utterances), such editorial work would hardly have been in the author's spirit and would undoubtedly have produced a book far less "Robackian" than the original. Maledicta's prime purpose here has been the renewed availability of this important work. Just as it is to be hoped that this republication will inspire scholars to improve upon and go beyond Roback's original compilation, this work will stand as a worthy monument to a man staunchly committed to enduring humanistic values and an uncommonly wide-ranging and venturesome spirit.

Brandeis University   *Harry Zohn*
July 4, 1976

PREFACE

These word-lists do not represent a dictionary of international references, of which there are many thousands in English alone. Each country has its own fauna and flora, its own modes of civilization, styles of cooking, for instance, and cultural forms peculiar to itself. The naming of an article in accordance with its provenance is only a matter of necessity or convenience, and might readily be expected. There is nothing either derogatory or commendatory about such terms as suede, romance, cravat (Croat), currants, sardines, italics, polka, japanning, turquoise (Turkey), etc.; but the moment a slang coinage is encountered, with reference to an Italian, Irishman, Jew, or Scotsman, we are immediately aware that we are no longer in the sphere of lexicography, but have skirted the realm of folklore and social psychology; for here we are studying *attitudes* of one people toward another. The moment a shrub or herb is designated by some humorous term, supposedly characteristic of another nationality, the purely objective approach is supplanted by the subjective. It is then time for the psychologist to step in and traverse the ground with his analytical divining rod.

Undoubtedly some lay person will interpose the question: Why confine oneself to slurs and not include also the complimentary allusions? The answer is simple. There are practically none of the latter. This question will be dealt with at length in the essay at the conclusion of the dictionary. It may just as well be asked why medicine concentrates on disease rather than on health.

As in individual adjustments, it is frequently more use ful to know what particular criticism is levelled against a person than to ascertain the points of merit which are re lated about him. At this stage in history, where a con certed effort will surely be made to coördinate (not as the Nazis have used the word) the nations, it behooves us to make a thorough investigation into the prejudices before matters could be righted. Common parlance is a vast repository of these prejudices, in their most natural state. When a cultured man of good breeding uses the word "jew-trick," he is betraying his inner state of mind, al though if asked then and there whether he really believes Jews to be craftier than, let us say, Yankees, he might answer the question in the negative, and might vehemently deny the charge that he is anti-Semitic.

A good deal of light may be shed on the personality of an individual who uses certain expressions of an objec tionable nature. Some phrases, it is true, are picked up in the environment and bandied about thoughtlessly, but even this excuse is, as the French would say, in itself an accusation. The chief problem before us, however is: How did these many prejudicial epithets and references arise? What truth is there in the majority of them?

It is with this purpose in view of helping to solve these problems, at least in offering the raw material, that this little work has been undertaken.

No doubt some of the phrases and proverbs will not seem to the reader altogether uncomplimentary. It was thought fit, however, to include even those which are debatable. Thus although *laconic* may have a favorable connotation to most people, there will be some occasions when the adjective will be used in the sense of brusque or scarcely civil. So it is with the word *bohemian,* which is known both in a good and a bad sense.

As an initial attempt, this dictionary is fairly complete in its proverbs and English terms, which, of course, con-stitute the body of the work. The foreign sections serve more as samples and do not pretend to be full lists. I can visualize, however, a future edition which would contain more extended inventories of the foreign disparaging allusions (or as I have named them, "ethnophaulisms") in a score of languages, as well as a section on striking quotations from important individuals, which come under this head. Naturally a comprehensive dictionary of neu-tral international references in English alone would fill a large volume, but what purpose would it serve? All but a few of such other-country terms could be found in any of the unabridged standard dictionaries. The compilation of words and phrases *critical* of another people, on the other hand, does present us with the material for studies in folklore, social psychology, and comparative prejudice.

Although the method of recording is fairly obvious in general, a few words may clear up a possible misappre-hension. In the first place, since the purpose of the volume is not primarily lexicographic, it was deemed unnecessary to separate the standard terms from the slang or cant, even if that were possible to accomplish satisfactorily. Not only are the gradations too fine in many instances, but a word which is definitely vulgar in one age may become standard usage in another, as a glance at F. H. Grose's *A Classical Dictionary of the Vulgar Tongue* would disclose, and *vice versa;* for some of the unprintable words today were employed in books a few centuries ago. The demarcation line between colloquial speech and slang, or between slang and cant, is at best a fluctuating one, yet where the usage is clearcut, labels have been supplied.

In the compilation of the foreign section, I have received some assistance in the less known languages like Hungarian, Polish, and Swedish from Messrs. M. Kligs-berg, E. Loeb, R. Vámbéry and Eugénie Söderberg, to whom I am grateful for the instances. Several of those who have glanced at one list or another of the foreign phrases, offering a suggestion here and there, have asked me not to mention their service as too slight. Dr. Nykl has translated four proverbs.

My obligations to the compilers of various reference works and source-books, as well as to writers of pertinent articles, will be inferred from the listing in the bibliography, at the end of the book.

It was only after the work was fairly advanced, that the thought occurred to me of presenting the sources, but even if I were ready to retrace my steps from the very beginning, the bulk of the documentation would have hampered the publication, particularly for the present. The citing of the proverbs in the original languages would have been a desideratum, but a luxury under the circumstances. Only a work subsidized by a learned body could be conceived and carried out on such comprehensive principles. At another time, too, all the foreign phrases would have been recorded in their original alphabet. Technical difficulties have made this infeasible even with the Greek and Russian expressions, with but few exceptions in the Greek, upon which the printers compromised.

It is only fair to remind the reader that even in normal times, a bilingual dictionary offers considerable problems in typography. When we stop to consider, in addition, the complications presented by a polyglot publication, with peculiar characters for some of the languages, with almost a dozen different sets of diacritic marks (accents) in several fonts, and with rules of capitalization, often at odds with each other, we must acknowledge the splendid coöperation of Cecil H. Wrightson, Inc. in producing the work at a time when ordinary typesetting is virtually being rationed. For a number of matrices with out-of-the-way accents (which have been on order for months) I am again indebted to Mr. Wm. Gallagher of the Boston Public Library.

In the English and American section, the many references to Grose's *Classical Dictionary of the Vulgar Tongue* (first edition only) have been included partly because Grose was a pioneer in this special field, and partly because we may thereby gain an idea as to the age of some of the locutions, since this first compilation to list national slurs appeared in 1785. Some of the other abbreviated references, to be found among the foreign phrases, are intended mainly as a mnemonic guide to the author, although some clue may be had to them, on the part of the reader, by consulting the bibliography of philological works and dictionaries in the present work.

In conclusion, while it is true that the work is by no

means as rounded out as I should have wished it to be, and while I anticipate the detection of slips and omissions on the part of specialized linguists, I feel, nevertheless, that unless one were to make the investigation a life work, and enlist the aid of a staff of collaborators, the gaps and lapses must be expected in the first attempt at a reference work of this sort.

The contingency of life being such as it is, it has seemed to me better that critics should find mistakes in a published book than that friends should find an almost perfect manuscript doomed to gather dust in some basement or attic and eventually forgotten, so that the arduous labor would have to be begun all anew by someone else.

Nevertheless, additions and corrections might easily be made in a subsequent edition; and with this in view, I should be grateful if readers would communicate suggestions toward a possible revision in the not too distant future.

A. A. Roback.

April 18, 1944.

PART ONE

ETHNOPHAULISMS IN ENGLISH

ETHNOPHAULISMS IN ENGLISH

A

Abraham: 1. "A clothier's shop of the lowest description (*cant*). 2. Penis, probably from covenant of Abraham. Of still lower usage is the phrase *Abraham's bosom* as pudendum muliebre (*low slang*).

Abraham man: A beggar feigning insanity.

Abraham sham: Any malingering or pretense of poverty.

Abraham store: A clothing store.

Abraham suit: An illegitimate lawsuit in order to extort.

Abram cove: "A naked or poor man; also a lusty strong rogue." [GROSE]. (*Cant among thieves.*)

Abram man: A thief of pocketbooks.

Abram work: Any sham or swindle.

Abrahamer: A vagrant.

Albion, perfidious: Treacherous England.

American devil: A very shrill whistle calling the workmen to their tasks (*English slang*).

American shoulders: Square cut of a coat emphasizing the breadth of the shoulders.

American tweezers: Tools burglars use to open doors.

Americanese: The locutions and modes peculiar to United States usage, especially of the lower classes.

Americanitis: Nervous tension resulting from the ceaseless drive associated with the inhabitants and civilization of contemporary North America.

amiral suisse: A naval officer who does not leave the shore. (Adopted from the French).

Apache, savage as an: Extremely fierce and relentless.

Arab, free as an: Very unbridled or undisciplined; untractable.

Arabs, wild as: Unruly in the extreme.

Aussie (ey): An Australian.

Aussieland: Australia.

Australian flag: "A shirt-tail rucked up between trousers and waistcoat" [PARTRIDGE].

Australian grip: A handshake that is a bit too cordial for the shakee's comfort.

B

Babylon: A state of glamorous vice, magnificent debauchery. Among Protestants, the concept is linked with Rome under the Borgias.

Badian: Barbadian [PARTRIDGE].

Balkan prince: A romantically adventurous prince from one of the small Balkan states as depicted in operettas and musical comedy.

Bananaland: Australia.

Bark(s): Irish people (*low slang*).

Barney: The nickname for any Australian.

Bashi-bazouk: A hooligan; a cruel lout; a churl.

bean-eater: A Mexican.

Beardie: A Jewish convert to Christianity. (Did converts all wear beards during the Victorian era?)

befritz: To dupe, manipulate (from *Fritz,* which see). "How M............ befritzed gas rations." Headline in *P.M.,* June 3, 1943.

Belgeek: A Belgian.

Bengal light: An Indian soldier in France.

Bengal scene: A highly spectacular or sensational display on the stage or screen.

biddy: A scrubwoman or charlady (from the Irish name, *Bridget,* which see).

Bimshah: An Englishman. Probably from *Bimshire.*

Bismarcker, bismarquer to: "To cheat especially at cards or billiards." The Bismarck policy in the '60's of the last century, which culminated in the forging of a telegram that precipitated the Franco-Prussian war, is the origin of this slang word.

black bean: A Negro (*slang*).

blackbird: A Negro (*slang*).

blackhead: A Negro (*slang*).

black teapot: A Negro footman (*slang*).

blackie (y): A Negro (*colloquialism*).

Blarney: Boasting, bluff, especially in the phrase "tip the blarney," later acquiring the sense of flattery, smooth talk. The meaning is derived from the numerous tales related by would-be adventurers about their having licked the Blarney stone, on the topmost point of Blarney Castle, in the county of Cork, Ireland. The stone-licking suggested also the bootlicking and fawning which is associated with the word mainly at present.

bleached ebony: A Mulatto (*American slang*).

Blemish: A mixture of Belgian and Flemish (*portmanteau word*).

Blighty: England.

blue bonnet: A Scotchman.

Blue-cap: A Scotchman.

Boche: A German soldier, especially in France during the first World War. "It is remarkable that the censor [in Paris] passed the term 'Boche,' which is as a rule forbidden in France since the Armistice." *Office of the Commissioner of Information,* October 3, 1942.

Boeotian: A stupid rustic. The Athenians regarded all the inhabitants of Boeotia as such.

Bogland: Ireland (*English slang*).

Boglander: An Irishman (*English slang*).

Bog-trotter: Originally an uncouth Irishman; then, any Irishman.

bohemian: A person of artistic inclinations, living an irregular and often irresponsible life, as Fedya in Tolstoi's *Living Corpse.*

bohunk (bohink): Czech, or other minor Slav language (*American slang*).

boogie: A Negro (*American slang*).

Bootchkey: A Czech. Apparently from *počkej,* (hold on) which the boys cry at play (*American slang*).

Borneo, the wild man of: A savage-looking individual; an uncivilized or uncouth fellow.

Borsht Belt: The sector in the Catskill Mountains where chilled beet-soup is served with cream in the summer resorts; thus indicating a Jewish clientèle.

bow and arrow: An Indian.

Bridget: An Irish servant girl. From the frequency of its occurrence as a name among Irish maids.

bridgeting: "The plausible acquisition of money from Irish servant girls, for political — or allegedly — political purposes." ex *Bridget,* a popular name in Ireland. Cf., *biddy* [PARTRIDGE-WARE].

bright mulatto: A quadroon or octoroon.

[22]

Brissotin: A Frenchman, particularly one who is a reformer.

British barilla. Crude soda ash made from common salt; black ash.

British brandy: An artificial cognac.

British champagne: Porter.

British Imperialism: The policy associated with Great Britain of spreading its rule to far-flung dominions.

British official: Unreliable (*newspaper slang*).

British treasury note: A blanket which New Zealand soldiers would find too thin to warm them.

broguen speech: Irish (play on *brogue* and "*broken*" English).

Bronx cheer: An oral sound of contempt, resembling that of high flatulence, allegedly originating in the Bronx. Sometimes also referring to the derisive expression "Rrazz-b-e-rr-ies."

buck: The male of any Indian, North or South American.

broom-squires: Gypsy squatters.

brownie: A Malayan or Polynesian.

browns and tans: Mulattoes.

brownskin: A Negro.

Buffalo: A Negro. [WESEEN].

Bug: An Englishman. The English were said to have introduced bugs into Ireland (*Irish slang*).

Bulgarian atrocities: "Varna and Rutschuk Railway 3% obligations." [PARTRIDGE]. Evidently a British stock exchange phrase.

Bulldog: The symbolic animal representing the character of the English people. See *John Bull*.

Burglar: A Bulgarian, probably *ex* assonance of two words (*military slang in England*).

burr-head: A Negro.

bush-cove: A Gypsy.

bushwhacker: *1.* An Australian. *2.* A Pennsylvania German. The word connotes a backwoodsman.

Butter-box: A Dutchman, because of the enormous quantity of butter produced and eaten in Holland (*except during the Nazi occupation*).

butter-mouth: A Dutchman, *ex* the amount of dairy products consumed in Holland. Cf. *butterbox.*

Buttinsky, Mr: One who interrupts or intrudes. A meddler. Ex *butt-in* plus Russian suffix (*American slang*).

C

Canada pest: A herb of the *Gentianaceae* family.

Canuck: A Canadian (*American slang*).

Celestial: A Chinese, *ex* the conceit that China constitutes the Celestial Empire (*journalese*).

Celestial Empire: China.

c(h)alder: To cheat, outsmart, impose upon. Possibly from Laban the Aramean, or Chaldean, who tricked Jacob into marrying Leah, and working in addition.

charcoal: A Negro (*American slang*).

chee-chee: A half-caste Eurasian (*American slang*).

chili-eater: Mexican (*American slang*).

China orange, all Lombard St: The odds are that . . .

Chinaman: "A left-hand bowler's leg-break" (*Cricketer's slang*). Partridge explains that it is from "the manner of Chinese script, right to left." But we were under the impression that Chinese is written top-down—*i.e.*, neither left to right, nor right to left.

Chinaman, to give a ↘ a music lesson: To go to the toilet; to go for a drink (*euphemistic slang* offered as an excuse to leave, like "to go and pick a daisy.")

Chinaman's chance, not to have a: To have a very slim chance; practically impossible.

Chinaman's copy: An exact copy, mistakes and all (*typewriting slang*).

Chinaman's shout: See *Dutch treat* (*Australian slang*).

Chinee: A Chinese (*jocose or illiterate*).

Chinese compliment: 1. A make-believe acceptance of someone's suggestion. 2. Exaggerated deference covering up some unsavory scheme.

Chinese fashion, to walk: to walk single file.

Chinese landing: A landing with one wing low (*aviation slang*).

Chinese potato: The cinnamon vine.

Chinese puzzle: An unintelligible situation.

Chinese Rolls-Royce: A Ford automobile; a flivver.

Chinese three-point landing: A crash landing (*aviation slang*).

Chinese wall: A barrier against enlightenment or the solution of a problem.

Chinese watermelon: The wax gourd.

Chink(ie): Chinese (*vulgarism*).

Chinkland: China (*vulgarism*).

chocolate drop: A Negro (*slang*).

Choctaw: Spanish.

Chosen People: The Jews. Sometimes burlesqued into *Chosen Pipples.*

Chow Meinland: China (*slang*).

Christ-killer: A Jew (*low usage*).

cinemagogue: A movie house owned by a Jew. The blend is obviously a play on *synagogue*.

circumcised ducat: A smaller amount than agreed on, or rather expected. Beethoven used the phrase in a letter to Carl Holz, with reference to his music publisher, Schlesinger, a Jew who rather indulged the composer instead of wronging him. Beethoven often insisted on advance payment while the proffered masterpiece was only an idea. It may be that the phrase did not originate with Beethoven but was in local use.

Closh: Dutch seamen. Abbreviated corruption of Claus from Klaas, abbreviation of Nicolaas, a favorite Dutch given name. (18th *Century slang*). [GROSE].

Cockpit of Europe: Belgium.

Colin Tampon: A Swiss.

Coon: A Negro (*vulgarism*).

Cropoh: A Frenchman. Derived from *crapaud* (*nautical slang*).

Corinthian: A debauchee, a gay fellow, a "sport" or "swell."

Croppy: An Irish rebel at time of the French revolution (ex *cropped hair*).

Czech: An unpopular superior employee (*post office slang*).

D

Dago: An Italian. Originally, a nickname for Spaniards, from *Diego* (James) (*American vulgarism*).

Dago's piano: An accordion (*American slang*).

Daily Levy: The *Daily Telegraph*, a London newspaper. The reference is to its former owner, Joseph Moses Levy.

Dansker: A Dane or Danish. Generally used collectively (*Sailor's slang*). Cf. *Polack* for "Pole."

darky (ey): A Negro (*colloquialism*).

ETHNOPHAULISMS IN ENGLISH

dear joys: Irishmen. The expression apparently originated or was heard most among them [GROSE].

Dee-Donk: A Frenchman (*English slang*).

Diggerland: Australia (*English slang*).

dink: A Negro (*American slang*).

dog-Latin: A juvenile code language, formed by generally putting the first consonant of a word last and adding *ay* after it (used in speaking only).

double Dutch: Unintelligible talk, gibberish, foreign speech.

drive French horses, to: To vomit (*slang*).

dutch: To clean and harden, as by dipping in sand.

Dutch act: Suicide.

Dutch auction: A bogus auction; an auction which is started at a high bid and then gradually reduced.

Dutch bank: The game of blind hooky.

Dutch bargain: 1. The ratification of a transaction by drinking to the event. Sealing a bargain with liquor. 2. A transaction with the advantage all on one side.

Dutch bath: A mordant composed of potassium chlorate and hydrochloric acid for etching purposes.

Dutch, beat the: To do something extraordinary, usually in an ironical sense. "That beats the Dutch" is equivalent to "Well I've never come across anything like this. Have you?" "That's the limit," "That takes the cake," "I'll be jiggered."

Dutch, be in: To be in trouble; to be on the carpet.

dutch book: A record or book of bets (*gamblers' slang*).

Dutch brig: A naval punishment cell (*American nautical slang*).

Dutch build: A squat figure.

Dutch cheese: A baldheaded person (*low slang*).

[27]

Dutch comedian: A vaudeville comedian depicting *German* characters (*American colloquialism*).

Dutch comfort: A state of mind characterized by the expression "Well, it might have been worse." See also *Dutch consolation*.

Dutch concert: "Where everyone plays or sings a different tune." [GROSE]. "Dutch Medley" was the phrase that came into vogue about a century later to denote the same thing.

Dutch consolation: See *Dutch comfort*.

Dutch courage: Foolhardiness, induced by liquor.

Dutch cure: See *Dutch act*.

Dutch curse: A daisy.

Dutch cut: A style of haircut showing the front of the head almost banged while the back of the head is almost close-cropped.

Dutch defense: Not a genuine act.

Dutch defense, to offer a: To offer no defense whatever.

Dutch, do a: To desert, "give the slip." Cf. *take French leave; filer à l'anglaise*.

Dutch, double: See *double Dutch*.

Dutch feast: "Where the entertainer gets drunk before his guests" [GROSE].

Dutch foot: A type of furniture leg suggesting the club-foot, in an outward turn.

Dutch gleek: Liquor of any sort.

Dutch gold: Tombac rolled into very thin sheets and used for decorative purposes.

Dutch honors: In whist, the 10 and 9 are often called *Dutch honors*.

Dutch-hound: A dachshund.

dutch it, to: To cross the suit at euchre (*card term*).

Dutch jawbreakers, (high): Words that are very difficult to pronounce. (The duplication of vowels and semi-vowels often gives this impression).

Dutch-kiss: Sexual intimacy.

Dutch liquid: Ethylene chloride.

Dutch lottery: A game of chance in which the prizes are arranged according to series and classes, the values increasing accordingly.

Dutch medley: See *Dutch concert.*

Dutch metal: See *Dutch gold.*

Dutch milk: Beer (*American slang*).

Dutch nightingale: A frog. Cf. *Irish nightingale.*

Dutch oil: See *Dutch liquid.*

Dutch oven: The mouth (*pugilists' slang*).

Dutch palate: A coarse taste.

Dutch party: See *Dutch treat.*

Dutch pegs: Legs (*rhyming slang*).

Dutch pen: A quill pen which has been dutched (which see).

Dutch pink: Blood (*boxing slang*).

Dutch pump: A sort of punishment which requires the victim to do considerable pumping so as not to drown (*sailor's slang*).

Dutch reckoning: 1. A lump account generally imposed verbally, without indicating particulars (In German, *Allemal*). [GROSE]. 2. Among sailors "a bad day's work, all in the wrong" [quoted by PARTRIDGE after SMYTH].

Dutch red: A smoked Dutch herring.

Dutch rod: A Luger gun.

Dutch row: A faked quarrel.

Dutch sale: See *Dutch auction.*

Dutch sods: See *Dutch milk*.

Dutch steak: A hamburger.

Dutch straight: An alternate straight, in a game of poker.

Dutch uncle: A paternal sermonizing individual. Hence "to talk to a person like a Dutch uncle" is "to lecture one severely."

Dutch widow: A strumpet.

Dutch wife: A long roundish bolster filled with strips of paper used in beds in the tropics as a rest for the limbs.

Dutcher: A Dutchman.

Dutchie: A German or Dutchman.

dutching plays: 1. Betting on more than one horse in a single race. 2. Crossing the suit at euchre (*gamblers' slang*).

Dutchman: In the United States, the word is mainly applied to a German. On account of the confusion, the Dutch often call themselves *Hollanders*.

Dutchman, as drunk as a: "Drunk as a fiddler."

Dutchman, heavy as a: Massive; ungainly.

Dutchman, I am a: Under no circumstances. Beyond possibility. "I should be outlandish if I could bring myself to do this." "Call me any name, if . . ." e.g., "If I don't come out to California next year, I am a Dutchman."

Dutchman, stolid as a: Unusually impassive and stupid-looking.

Dutchman! well, I'm a: If that isn't the limit! Representative of any attitude expressing amazement.

Dutchman's anchor: A requisite left at home.

Dutchman's-breeches: 1. A delicate herb with finely divided leaves and cream-white flowers. 2. Very wide trousers. "Two streaks of blue in a cloudy sky" (*Sailors' phrase*).

Dutchman's cape: A cloud on the horizon mistaken for land; an illusion of land in the far distance.

Dutchman's drink: An emptied pot.

Dutchman's headache: Drunkenness.

Dutchman's-pipe: A vine with large leaves and flowers blossoming in the early summer. Its tube is suggestive of the bowl of a pipe.

Dutchy: Dowdy, shabby.

E

ebony (a bit of ⌐): A Negro (*American slang*).

Egypt, to go to: To go to the toilet (*slang*).

England's umbrella: Ireland. (Cf. *urinal of the planets*).

English flute: The recorder.

English malady: Chronic discontent or grumbling. In other languages, the English malady is *rickets*.

English manufacture: Ale, beer, or cider.

English melancholy: See *English malady*.

Eskimo: An Indian tribe inhabiting Greenland. The name, as given by the Abenakis, means "eater of raw food." [KLEIN-PAUL].

Esquaw: An Eskimo woman. (A condensation of Eskimo and squaw).

Esquimuff: See *Esquaw*.

Ethiopian heaven: See *nigger heaven*.

Eyeties: Italians (since often mispronounced as *eyetalians*).

F

Fair-gang: Gypsies (*slang*).

Finnglish: Finnish English. Cf. *Yidgin-English* for Yiddish-English (*portmanteau word*).

Fip (or **Flip**): A Filipino (*slang*).

Flamingo: An inhabitant of Flanders. A Fleming. (The bird, according to Weekley, was named after the Flemings).

Flanderkin: A very large man or horse, evidently in an anti-phrastic sense (*colloquialism*).

Flanders fortune: A modest patrimony or amount.

Flanders piece: A picture that looks much better at a distance than close to (*colloquialism*).

Flanders reckoning: A spending of money in a place other than where it was received, and for a different purpose.

Fleming giant: A breed of large grey rabbits.

flemish: To make a quivering movement with the tail and body while searching for the trail, as does a hound.

Flemish account: An unsatisfactory account; a balance sheet showing a deficit; "in the red."

Flemish fake: "A method of coiling a rope that runs freely when let go . . ." (*nautical term*).

Flying Dutchman: 1. A legendary Dutch mariner condemned for his crime to sail the seas until Doomsday. 2. The phantom ship, considered a bad omen when seen.

Frankish fare: Excessive; profuse.

Freddy: A German soldier. Cf. *Fritz*.

French (*verb*): To sham, feign. To go through the motions (as in pretending to photograph); (*noun*) a bolt, a skip, shirking.

French abortion: The oral disposition of the semen incidental to fellation (*slang*).

French article: Brandy.

French cream: Infusion of liquor in coffee (or tea).

French crown: Syphilis.

French curves: A shapely figure.

French disease: Syphilis.

French drain: A rubble drain or sewer.

French elixir: See *French cream*.

Frencher: A Frenchman.

Frenchery: A French wardrobe; French mannerisms (*American slang*).

French, excuse my: A catch-phrase calling attention to one's use of slang or profanity.

French faggot-stick, a blow with a: The loss of the nose through advanced syphilis.

French faith: Unfaithfulness; duplicity. (A phrase occurring frequently in the sixteenth century).

French fake: A rope coiled by running it forward and backward in parallel bends.

French fare: Exaggerated politeness. Cf. *Frankish fare*.

French goods: See *French crown*.

French gout: See *French goods*.

French harp: A harmonica (*American slang*).

French heel: A Frenchman, something of a cad.

Frenchified: Infected with syphilis (*slang*).

French kiss: A tongue kiss; intense and long-drawn out osculation.

French lace: See *French article*.

French leave (take): A hasty departure, generally said of one who absconds or is unwilling to face an embarrassing situation (although originally the phrase was used in a social context, when a guest would leave secretly so as not to break up the party). Cf. *filer à l'anglaise* for the national recrimination. In German, the commercial sense is conveyed by the Yiddish phrase *Pleite machen*.

[33]

French leave-taker: A deserter.

French letter: See *French safe.*

French love: Sensual and generally illicit venery (*amour à la française* is probably an English coinage).

Frenchman, the: 1. Any Latin individual or even only a foreigner (*Sailors' slang*). 2. Syphilis. 3. Liquor.

French pancake: A rectangular academic hat. A beret (*collegiate slang*).

French peasoup: A French Canadian (*slang*).

French pie: Irish stew.

French pig: A syphilitic bubo.

French pigeon: A pheasant shot by mistake (or ostensibly so) during the partridge season.

French prints: Obscene pictures. Thackeray was perhaps the first to use the phrase in English literature.

French safe: A condom. (cf. French recrimination, *capote anglaise*).

French seal: Near seal or dyed rabbit.

French tricks: Various sex paraphilias, e.g. *fellatio.*

Frenchy: A French person. In the Orient, almost any foreigner, especially a girl abducted for harem purposes.

Frenchy (*adj.*): Moody; flighty; capricious; gay.

Fritz: 1. A German (soldier). 2. A simple fellow. Ex nickname of *Friedrich,* a common personal name in Germany, corresponding to Frederick.

Frogeater: A Frenchman (*slang*).

Froggie: See *Frogeater.*

Froglander: A Dutchman (*sailors' slang*).

Froncery: French (also a person of French extraction), ex *français.*

G

Geese, the: Portuguese (troops), (*military slang*).

German bands: The hands. (Probably rhyming slang, also from the association of brawny limbs).

German cockroach: The croton bug.

German conversation water: Beer, especially when strong (*American slang*).

German dogs: Frankfurters (*slang*).

German duck: 1. Half a sheep's head boiled with onions. [Grose]. 2. A bedbug.

German flutes: 1. Thin legs, as in the English saying, "He may well be musical, for he walks upon German flutes." 2. Boots (*rhyming slang*).

German goitre: Beer paunch (*Bierbauch*) (*American slang*).

German gold: Tombac; gold imitation.

German gospel: Braggadocio; a destiny-claim; a superiority attitude.

German measles: A skin eruption of a dusky red color (*rubella*) akin to ordinary measles, but of a milder variety. During the Nazi war, the malady was popularly called "Victory measles" as if the original label were a compliment to the Nazis.

German Michel: The German as a gullible individual, particularly in a political sense.

German pepper: The fruit of the *mezerion,* sometimes used in the adulteration of pepper.

Gers, the: Germans (*military slang*).

Germany, made in: Botched; without value. (This sense of the phrase antedated the first world war by at least a decade).

Gerry: The Germans. In the second World War, particularly the German airmen during the thick and frequent attacks on England during 1940-41.

gibberish: Unintelligible talk, prattle. Originally cant used by the Gypsies and their associates. Possibly a combination of "Gypsy" and "jabber."

Ginzo: An Italian. Probably a variant of Guinea (*American slang*).

Gip, Gippo: A Gypsy.

Gippy: *1.* An Egyptian (*military slang*). *2.* A Gypsy.

Godamland: England (*Ex French slang*).

Godless Country: Russia (thus referred to by fascists, as a rule).

God's image cut in ebony: A Negro (*low usage*).

Go-Ghetto: A Jew. Ex *go-getter* (*vulgarism*).

goo-goo (gugu): A Filipino (Soldier).

Gook: See *goo-goo*.

go Scotch, to: To scrimp, to be miserly.

go turkey, to: To take potluck (possibly because of the fatalism of the average Mohammedan); hence, often to divide the spoils.

Goulash: A Hungarian. *Ex* his national dish (*slang*).

greaser: A Mexican; any one from South America (*low usage*).

Grecian: *1.* A roisterer. *2.* An Irish immigrant; a new arrival (possibly from the jocular contrast between the cultured and the uncouth).

Grecian accent: Irish brogue. (Cf., *pardon my French*).

Greek: *1.* A cheat; a sharper at cards. *2.* A member of a college fraternity or sorority (*collegiate slang*). *3.* (*As language*) unintelligible, unmeaning.

Greekdom: College fraternities and sororities, collectively re-garded (*slang*).

Greek ease: Laziness. (Lotus eaters?).

Greekery: 1. Greek customs or traditions, taken collectively. 2 Cheating, as at cards (*slang*).

Greek gift: A suspicious favor, foreboding treachery; something given with a sinister purpose in view. Ex the Latin *Timeo Danaos et dona ferentes*. See this DICTIONARY, page 76.

Greek hash-house: A lunch stand (*American slang*).

Greek love: Pederasty.

Greek, play the: To drink to excess.

Greek puzzle: See *Chinese puzzle*.

Guinea: An Italian of the laboring class (*low slang*). According to some, the slur goes back to the time when English pennies were circulating in North America, and during a crisis, Italian help would receive them for services. The pennies were called "guineas" in jest. Later, the name was transferred to the recipients, who, it is said, collected these pennies as valuable coins.

Guinea football: See *Italian football*.

Gypsies of Science: The British Association for the Advance-ment of Science (*jocular*). The phrase may refer to the "arts and sciences" (like palmistry) practiced by the Gypsies, or may be an allusion to the distant travels (Canada, Australia) of the members for their annual meetings.

gypsy: There is no good reason why the name of a specific people should not be written with a capital, as is still being done by scholars and literary persons who might know better. Unlike the Negroes, the Gypsies do not air their grievances as a body

H

Haggisland: Scotland. Cf. *Haggis* — a favorite dish in Scotland for centuries.

Hans: A German, occasionally a Dutchman (from a nickname of Johannes, corresponding to John, Jack).

Hans the grenadier: A German infantryman.

have a Chinaman on one's back, to: To crave narcotics.

have an Irish shave, to: To go to the toilet (*American slang, low*).

have an Irishman's dinner, to: To be forced to go without an expected meal (*American slang*).

head over turkey: An Australian.

Hebrew: A Jew. When applied to a Jew in modern times, this honorific has a derogatory aftertaste, in that it implies that to be a Jew, and designated as such, is to have an inferior status.

Hebrew enemy: Pork, pig (*jocular slang*).

Heeb (Hebe): Yiddish, thought by the ignorant to be the same as Hebrew (*slang*).

Heebie: A Jew. Ex *Hebrew* (*American siang*).

Helot: A slave. The inhabitants of Helos were subdued by the Spartans and were put to menial work.

hermit kingdom: Korea (London *Times, Lit. Suppl.* Sept. 15, 1911).

Herring choker: A Newfoundlander (*Canadian slang*).

Hessian: A mercenary; a military hireling. (American slur since Revolutionary days).

Hibernian, la bullie: Cornbeef and cabbage. (Ironically pompous name for the plebeian Irish dish).

Hitlander: A German. (A blend of "Hitler" and "lander").

hog-Latin: See *dog-Latin*.

Hogan-(Mogan): A Dutchman, especially of some standing (ex *hoog mogendheden* i.e., lord high mightinesses).

Holy Land: "Any neighborhood affected by Jews" is one low colloquialism given by Partridge of this phrase.

Holy of Holies: "The Grand Hotel at Brighton: from *ca.* 1890. Because a favorite with Jews." [PARTRIDGE].

hooligan: A rowdy or ruffian. The Russians made the word popular during the Kishineff massacre of the Jews, but the name is that of an Irish family who terrorized their community. The Russians, lacking the *h* in their alphabet, pronounced the name *Khooligan.*

hopscotch: A children's game.

Hottentot (s) An uncivilized and boorish individual. Generally in plural, designating some group collectively.

Hula Land: Hawaii (*American slang*).

Hun: A German, especially a soldier. (Revival of name during first World War).

Hun-hunting: Search for German planes (*military slang*).

Hun-pinching: Rounding up Germans in their trenches in order to secure information (*military slang*).

Hun-pox: Chicken-pox. It is curious that in the first World War, the odious adjective was attached to the illness, while in World War II, German measles was changed popularly, but of course temporarily, to "victory measles."

hungarian: 1. A hungry person (ex *play of words*). 2. A vagabond, a freebooter (*slang*).

hunky: A Hungarian (*American slang*).

Hunkyland: Hungary (*American slang*).

Hunland: The territory occupied by the German military during the World War I.

DICTIONARY OF INTERNATIONAL SLURS

Hunnery, the: The German department in the university (*student's slang applied to Liverpool University*).

Hunnish (ly): In a ruthless, unsportsmanlike manner.

husky: An Eskimo (*American slang*).

I

Ikey: 1. A Jew. 2. A Pawnbroker, ex "Isaac" (*low slang*).

ikey: Wide awake, smart (*Isaac*).

Ikey Mo: See *Ikey*.

India: *Pudendum muliebre* (origin?)

India man, foul as an: Messy, dirty (*sailors' slang*).

Indian devil: The wolverine, because of its craftiness and strength.

Indian file: Single file.

Indian fog: The dwarf houseleek.

Indian gift: Something presented with the intention of asking its return in the future.

Indian giving: The practice or act of asking for the return of something presumably given for good.

Indian up, to get one's: To go on the warpath; to get riled or wrought up.

Indian warrior: The lousewort of western United States.

infidel: A Saracen or Turk.

Injun: An Indian. The phrase *honest injun* is equivalent to "I really mean it."

Injun side: One's right side. *Ex* Indian (*Western slang*).

international banker: Any Jewish banker of some prominence (*a Fascist and anti-Semitic euphemism*).

Irish: Ready to fight; easily angered, as "Do it again, he's Irish."

Irish apricots: Potatoes. "It is a common joke against the Irish vessels to say that they are loaded with fruit and timber, that is potatoes and broomsticks." [GROSE].

Irish arms: Thick legs.

Irish assurance: A bold forward behavior supposedly acquired by being dipped in the Shannon river, which was jestingly said to cure all bashfulness or inhibition in an Irishman.

Irish baby carriage: A wheelbarrow. See *Irish buggy*.

Irish battleship: A barge.

Irish beauty: Two black eyes in a woman. This jocose epithet originated in Ireland [GROSE].

Irish buggy: A wheelbarrow. *Ex* the fact that many of the Irish immigrants were laborers.

Irish bull: A statement, the second part of which annuls the first, *e.g.,* "The British landlords have taken all from their tenants' empty pockets" or "taking a post graduate course in the freshman class."

Irish button: Syphilis. The reference is probably to the bubo that develops in the groins.

Irish car: A light two-wheeled vehicle with seats placed face to face or back to back.

Irish cherries: Carrots. (The metaphor is rather remote).

Irish club-house: A police station (or jail).

Irish confetti: Bricks. See *Irish buggy*.

Irish daisy: The dandelion.

Irish diamond: Rock crystal (*colloquial and jocose*).

Irish dividend: An assessment.

Irish draperies: Cobwebs.

Irish evidence: A false witness [GROSE].

Irish fan: A shovel or spade.

Irish fortune: *"Pudendum muliebre* and pattens" [PARTRIDGE].

Irish horse: Salt beef, especially tough cornbeef *(naval slang).*

Irish hurricane: "A flat calm with drizzling rain" [cited by PARTRIDGE from BOWEN].

Irish legs: Stout legs, sometimes referred to as Irish arms [GROSE].

Irish luck: Good fortune, with the thought that it is undeserved.

Irish mahogany: The common European alder.

Irish man-of-war: See *Irish battleship.*

Irish marathon: A relay race.

Irish mutton: A venereal disease *(cant).* [GROSE].

Irish nightingale: A frog. Cf. *Dutch nightingale.*

Irish pennants: Slovenly trappings or riggings; loose ends of sails, or ropes inefficiently handled *(nautical slang).*

Irish posture: A faint, often a sham.

Irish potato: A potato (as if that were a delicious and rare kind of fruit growing only in Ireland).

Irish promotion: A decrease in pay or status.

Irish rifle: A small comb.

Irish rise: See *Irish promotion.*

Irish root: *Membrum virile.*

Irish theatre: A guardroom *(military slang).*

Irish, to get up one's: To show one's ire (The pun is coincidental).

Irish toothache: 1. A priapism. 2. Pregnancy *(low slang).*

Irish toyles: Thieves pretending to peddle pins, lace, or notions in order to obtain access to houses which they pilfer [GROSE].

Irish turkey: Corned beef.

Irish wedding: The emptying of a cesspool.

Irish wedding, to go to an: To receive a black eye.

Irish wedding, to have danced at an: To display (unintentionally) black eyes.

Irish, weep: To pretend to be sorry or grieved.

Irish welcome: A standing invitation with no restrictions.

Irish whist: Copulation (*low slang*).

Irish, you're: What you are saying is nonsense.

Irishman: Boiled dinner (*underworld slang*).

Irishman's dinner: A fast.

Irishman's fire: A fire that burns only at the top.

Irishman's harvest: The orange season.

Irishman's hurricane: A dead calm.

Irishman's reef: The head of a sail tied up.

Irishman's rest: Ascending a friend's ladder with a hod of bricks.

Irishman's rise: See *Irish promotion*.

Irishman's sidewalk: An avenue. (Because of several walking in line?).

Irishman, the wild: The Irish mail train between London and Holyhead.

I-say: An Englishman. Originally a French epithet for the English.

Ishmael: An outcast, one at odds with society. From the Biblical account of his character.

Italian football: A bomb (*American slang*).

Italian hurricane: Spaghetti with garlic (*American slang*).

Italian manner, in the: *Coitus in ano.* On national differences with regard to sex activities, and their anatomical significance, there are some pertinent observations toward the end of *The Dialogues of Luisa Sigea*. The deprecatory phrase probably originated with the French. Benvenuto Cellini, in his autobiography, speaks of a like charge against him.

Italian perfume: Garlic (*American slang*).

Italian quarrel: "Death, poison, treachery, remorselessness" [PARTRIDGE after WARE].

Italian special: Spaghetti (*American slang*).

Itchland: *1.* Scotland [GROSE]. *2.* Wales [PARTRIDGE].

Itchlander: A Scotchman.

Ities (pronounced *eye-ties*): Italians, during the Nazi war (*nautical slang*).

Ivan: A Russian, especially a soldier (from the very common given name, Ivan, corresponding to John).

ivory, black: Negroes imported from Africa as slaves (*American slang*).

J

Jackeroo: A name applied in Australia to an immigrant from England about to learn sheep or cattle breeding (PARTRIDGE is probably right in suggesting that the word is derived from *Johnny* and the latter part of *Kangaroo*).

Jacko: A Turkish soldier (in vogue during Allenby's 1917 campaign in Palestine).

Jack the Jew: A thief or fence who happens to be a Jew (*low cant*).

Jacques Bonhomme: A French peasant.

Jap: A Japanese (*colloquialism*).

Japan: Bread. Play on *du pain*, in French (*slang*).

japan, to: To ordain as a minister (*slang*). The semantic connection is probably the black "coating" associated with the black varnish called "japan."

Japanese knife trick: The use of one's knife to convey food to the mouth.

Japanese mask, fierce as a: Frightful; hideous.

Japanese, silent as a: Ominously taciturn; watchful.

Japland: Japan (*American slang*).

Jargon: Originally a language mixture without rules or uniform usage, originating from the accidental intercourse of hetero-geneous racial elements, this term (we find in Webster's *New International Dictionary*) when capitalized, applies specifically to Yiddish.

This allusion, based on an attitude toward Yiddish by as-piring intellectuals from the Ghetto half a century ago, is definitely inadmissible, even inexcusable; else a language which normally served, or had at its command, four hundred news-papers and periodicals, and in which Plato's *Dialogues,* Spi-noza's *Ethica,* as well as Darwin's, Spencer's, and Marx's works, not to mention Shakespeare, Goethe, and Schiller, have been translated, and which boasts a literature of many thou-sands of original belletristic books, studied in hundreds of schools — is a jargon, even if with a capital *J.*

S. G. Champion who, in the introduction to his ambitious *Racial Proverbs,* writes "Yiddish, being a jargon . . . .," might also have sought a bit of information on the subject from someone who was conversant with that "jargon." He might then have discovered that a Jew in Australia or South Africa who speaks Yiddish can understand a Yiddish-speak-ing Jew in USSR, Shanghai, or South America far better than an Oxford Englishman can make out the speech of a hillbilly, or even someone from Alabama, or for that matter a yokel from Yorkshire.

jazzbo: An American Negro soldier (*American slang*).

Jazzland: The United States (*American slang*).

Jerusalem letters: See *Jews' letters.*

Jerusalem parrot: A flea (*American slang*).

Jerusalem pony: An ass (*American slang*).

Jerusalem the Golden: Brighton, England (residence of wealthy Jews). *Cf* Grunewald, a suburb of Berlin, called the "golden ghetto."

Jew: 1. A manipulator; trickster, sharper (*low colloquialism*). 2. A tailor (*sailors' slang*).

Jew (*adj.*): Jew used as an adjective is always intended as a pejorative; examples are *Jew banker, Jew writer, Jew manufacturer, Jew man, Jew problem.*

Jew-bail: Insufficient bail; "straw bail."

Jew-balance: A shark with a head like a hammer. *Cf.* "Jewfish" (*sailors' slang*).

jewbarker: A foppishly dressed person—*Ex* the slick appearance of the clothing-stores' "pullers-in."

jewbird: The ani, a bird of the cuckoo family, probably so called because of its arched and laterally compressed bill.

Jew-boy: A Jewish youth. Felix Mendelssohn, in Germany, spoke of a Jew-boy (*Judenbube*) i.e., himself, discovering to the world the greatest musical work of Christendom—Bach's *Passion Music according to St. Matthew.*

jewbush: A tropical American low shrub possessing powerful emetic qualities.

Jewcrow: The chough. Probably, *ex* its rather long bill.

jew down, to: To bargain and haggle until the price is reduced (*low colloquialism*).

Jew-face: An unprepossessing crafty appearance. (The word occurs largely in *Arabian Nights* and other Moslem writings)

jewfish: Any of several groups of fish (*promicrops*). Some of the varieties suggest the physiognomy of some Jews.

Jew flag or **Jewish flag:** A dollar bill; any banknote (*American slang, low*).

Jew food: Ham, bacon. (Ironical, of course).

Jew lizard: A large Australian lizard of the *agamoid* variety.

Jew monkey: A monkey of the *sakis* or *macaques*.

jew nail: A small headless nail of corrugated sheet metal almost as wide as it is long.

Jew Nersey: A perversion of New Jersey (*smart Aleckism*).

jew out of: To use petty means for "doing" someone out of money or property (*low colloquialism*).

Jew Packard: A Ford car.

Jew plum: An otaheite apple which, while its flesh is edible, the rind has the flavor of turpentine.

Jew, rich like a: Very rich. Partly this popular fancy is due to the fact that there is a good deal of exhibitionism displayed among the Jews, particularly their women folk.

jew, to: To cheat, to trick, to drive a hard bargain—often "to jew down." While the usage is low, it frequently is heard in good society. It is not improbable that there is a cumulative effect of the assonant phrase "to do" (one).

Jew trick: An advantage taken that is not strictly dishonest, although hardly in keeping with a business or professional code (*commercial colloquialism*).

jewing: Tailoring (*naval slang*).

jewing-bag: The bag in which sailors keep their sewing material.

Jew-Jack: See *Jack the Jew*.

Jew point: A clothes shop.

Jewish artichoke: A sunflower.

Jewish badge: A yellow patch worn by Jews during the Middle Ages on their clothes to distinguish them from Gentiles— an imposition revived by the Nazis in the fifth decade of the twentieth century.

[47]

Jewish cavalry: The quartermaster corps.

Jewish compliment: A reference to the poor condition or appearance of an acquaintance one meets, *e.g.,* "You know, you are
not looking so well." Translation of a *Yiddisher kompliment,*
which goes to show the Jewish origin of the ironical designation.

Jewish disease: 1. Diabetes (*medical slang*). 2. Amaurotic
idiocy (*psychiatric slang*).

Jewish engineering: Business administration (*American slang*).

Jewish ice cream sundae: An ice cream cone.

Jewish National: Circumcision. The rite makes a Jew out of the
infant.

Jewish nightcap: The prepuce (*low slang*).

Jewish nose: An aquiline nose, which looks like a written 6, with
a slanting stem.

Jewish reply: Answering a question by raising another question.

Jewish time: An hour or so later than an event is called for, as
"8.30 P.M., Jewish time." A wag has said that when a Jewish meeting is called for 8 P.M. sharp, it does not mean 9,
but 10 P.M.

Jews'-apple: The eggplant.

Jew's ear: A tough fungus growing on decaying elder and elm
trees; *Hirneola Auricula Judae.*

It is somewhat strange that the "Jew's ear," in the historical sense, should not have been explained in the dictionaries. It appears to have been a name applied to a piece of
cloth dangling from the special yellow hat which the Jews
were required to wear in many countries, even as late as the
end of the eighteenth century, in order to differentiate them
from the population in general. This special badge formed a

sort of large ear; and the young rowdies in Provençal would single out this feature of the Jew's attire for ridicule.

Jew's eye, worth a: Precious, costly. In the Middle Ages, some of the British Kings (King John) would replenish their private coffers by extorting money from rich Jewish subjects on pain of torture. Each of the visible organs, beginning with the teeth would carry a price, and the gouging out of an eye was the penalty for unwillingness to part with a fortune.

Jews' frankincense: Storax, that is a resin derived from trees of the genus *styrax*.

Jews'-harp: 1. A simple musical device held between the lips or teeth with the sound generating from the vibrations of a metal tongue set in motion by the forefinger. 2. A haircomb with tissue paper attached to one side with which queer music can be made by blowing against the other side of it [PARTRIDGE].

The derivation of this word is mooted. Some think it is connected with the French word *jeu* rather than with *Jew*.

Jews' houses: Remains of ancient tin-smelting furnaces and miners' houses in Cornwall and Devon, England.

Jews' letters: Tattooing (*naval slang*).

The reference is puzzling, since in general Jews look upon tattooing with disgust—the relic of a taboo from Biblical days. Probably strange-looking symbols were identified with Hebrew.

Jews' lime: Asphalt.

Jew's mallow: A tiliaceous plant used in the East as a potherb; (*Corchorus Capsularis*).

Jews' myrtle: 1. The butcher's-broom. 2. The common myrtle

Jews on a payday, as thick as two: A cockney simile describing intimacy, inseparableness (*low slang*).

Jews' pitch: Asphalt; bitumen of Judea.

Jews' poker: One who kindles or puts out the fire in Jewish homes on Saturday. In Yiddish, he is called *der shabbes-goy* (fem. *shabbes-goye*).

Jews' slime: See *Jews' lime* (as if lime were not offensive enough).

Jews' stone or **Jewstone:** 1. A clavate spine of a sea urchin. 2. A hard rock of uneven fracture with reference especially to certain basalts, and limestones. 3. The mineral *marcasite*.

Jews' tin: Slabs of tin, in the vicinity of the Jews' houses (*which see*).

jew's-trump: See *jew's-harp*.

Jews' thorn: *Paliurus Spinacristi,* or Christ's thorn.

Jew wattle: A wattle or colored skin projection on the base of the carrier pigeon's bill.

Jewy: After the fashion of a Jew (*used in a derogatory sense*).

Jew York: New York (*smart Aleckism, low*).

jigaboo: A Negro.

Jim Crow: A Negro (*generalized*).

Jimmy Round: A Frenchman (*naval slang*).
　　Derived by Ware from *je me rends,* i.e., I give up, which is ingenious but not probable — almost like Chamberlain from *j'aime Berlin.*

Joan Bull: An English woman (in general).

John Bull: The English nation (collectively and personified).

John Crapose: A Frenchman (ex *crapaud,* a toad — a frequent insulting interjection among the uncultured French).

John Tuck: A Chinese mandarin. *Ex* hands tucked in sleeves? (*naval slang*).

Johnnie or **Johnny:** 1. A Greek (*naval slang*). 2. A Turk (*military slang*).

Johnny cake: A French Canadian. (A children's doggerel in Montreal protestant schools around 1900 contained the following lines:

French peasoup and Johnny cake
Make your father a bellyache).

Johnny squarehead: A German soldier (*military slang*).

Judaic superbac(e)y: A "Jew in all the glory of his best clothes." [WARE, quoted by PARTRIDGE]. (*London theatrical slang*).

Judas: A betrayer: a traitor.

Judische compliment: "A large penis but no money" [PARTRIDGE]. Why the inaccurately Germanized version of "Jewish"?

K

Kaffir's lightener: A heavy meal.

Kanaka: A South Sea Islander. One of the Malayan or Polynesian race.

kangaroo: An individual of European stock, born in Australia.

kelt or **keltch:** A quadroon or octoroon, who could pass for white.

kike: An uncouth Jew (*low slang*).

Kiltie(y): A Scotchman. *Ex* the garb.

kosher cutie: A trim Jewish girl (*American slang*).

L

laconic: Very brief, brusque, and often drastic. Ex *Laconia*, another name for Sparta.

Land of Regrets: India (*American slang*).

Land of the Rag-head: India. The turban gives rise to this epithet (*American slang*).

Land of the Setting Sun: Japan.

lapland: *Pudendum muliebre.* The pun is obvious.

Lapland day, interminable as a: Tediously long.

Latin from Manhattan, a: A New-Yorker, born of Central or South American parents, or posing as a genuine South American. *Ex* the title of a popular song (*American catch-phrase*).

lesbian: A woman sexually interested in one of her own sex. The women of Lesbos were regarded as the chief offenders in this respect.

Levi Nathan: The boat *Leviathan.* The assonance and the patronage of Jews explain this expression bordering on cant (*nautical slang*).

Lewis Baboon: The French people, collectively, of which the peasant is representative (*English slang*).

lily-white: A Negro (*ironically*).

lime-juicer: An Englishman (*American slang*).

Limey: An Englishman, particularly a "tar" because of the lime juice the British sailors were ordered to be given at one time.

Limeyland: England.

Lombard fever: The disease of laziness; a spree of idleness. Although the word *Lombard* is probably a corruption of *lumber,* the popular association with a supposed Italian trait is the deciding factor.

loose French, to: To indulge in a torrent of Billingsgate (*London lower colloquialism*).

Louseland: Scotland [GROSE].

M

macaroni: An Italian. (In several languages the favorite dish represents the collective eaters).

Mack: A Scotchman. *Ex* the prefix *Mac* in Scotch surnames.

Madamoizook: A French woman, of a flirtatious bent (*slang*).

Manaland: Mexico, *i.e.,* the "land of *tomorrow*" (postponing to *Mañana,* being a Latin-American characteristic).

Maori kiss: A greeting consisting of rubbing noses.

Marianne: The French nation, personified.

Market-Jew: Cornwall, England. "In your own light, like the Mayor of Market-Jew," whose pew was so placed that he was in his own light.

Mexican bag: A paper bag containing a sailor's few chattels (*slang*).

Mexican dish: A Mexican girl (*American slang*).

Mexican iron: Rawhide.

Mexican it, to: To get a Mexican divorce (*American slang*).

Mexican liniment: Petroleum (*American slang*).

Mexican navy: Beans. Generally in the phrase "A bowl of fire and Mexican navy"; a bowl of fire standing for a plate of chili (*slang*).

Mexican strawberries: Mexican beans, of a reddish color (*slang*).

Mick, Mick(e)y: An Irishman. Cf. *Mike* (*low colloquialism*).

Mickyland: Ireland.

Mike: An Irishman of no breeding.

Mockie: A young Jew (*American slang, low*).

Mohican: "A very heavy man that rides for a long way in an omnibus for sixpence" [PARTRIDGE].

Mohock, Mohawk: "An aristocratic ruffian night-infesting London" [PARTRIDGE].

Moke: A Negro.

mongolian: A type of idiot to which has been given that name by Langdon Down, because it was believed that Mongolian features always characterized this particular form of amentia (*technical term*).

Moon-man: A Gypsy.

Morocco man: A promotion of bogus lottery insurance (in England).

mosey, to: To move briskly with a purpose. (Probably ex *Mosey,* diminutive of *Moses*).

mosey along, to: To plod along; to come through; muddle through.

mosey off, to: Slink away; depart for fear of being questioned.

Mouchey: A Jew. (From *Moishe* i.e. *Moses. Cf.* German *mau-scheln* — gesticulating, intoning words, or talking Yiddish (*low slang*).

Mounseer: A Frenchman (i.e. *Monsieur*).

Munster plums: Potatoes (*Irish slang*). [GROSE].

murderin' Irish: An expletive expressing startled feelings at the outcome.

Murph(y): A potato. The Irish for generations survived on potatoes.

Murphy's countenance: A pig's head (*low slang*).

Murphy's face: See *Murphy's countenance.*

mustard: A Chinese (*underworld slang*).

N

Naziland: Germany.

Nazi-scrammer: A Jew of the acting guild who left Germany and the occupied countries to continue stage activities in a free country. See *Hitler-Jew* (*actors' slang*).

negro: Whenever the word is not capitalized, it reveals the contemptuous attitude of the writer. This discriminatory practice was more in vogue ten or fifteen years ago, provoking the Negroes to voice their protest.

Negro-nosed: Having a flat nose.

Negro, to wash a: To do the impossible (like *catching the wind in a net, draining the ocean,* or *changing the spots of a leopard*).

Negro's head: A loaf of brown bread (*sailors' slang*).

Netherlands, the: The sex organs (either male or female). The origin is of course a low play of words (*colloquialism*).

Newfie: Newfoundland (*Canadian slang*).

nigger: A Negro (*low colloquialism*).

niggers!: An oath.

nigger brand: A saddle sore on a horse.

nigger driver: A hard taskmaster.

nigger flea: A broomstraw covered with a tallow coating.

nigger gin: Inferior synthetic liquor.

nigger-heeled: The front toes (of a horse) pointing outward.

nigger killer: A whip scorpion.

nigger local: A freight train requiring heavy labor.

nigger luck: A piece of good fortune.

nigger night: Saturday night.

nigger-rich: Having barely enough to live on. (The standards have changed since).

nigger roll: A roll of single dollar bills.

nigger-shooter: A sling shot.

nigger special: A watermelon.

nigger-spit: Lumps in cane sugar.

nigger steak: Liver.

nigger tip: A slight tip or gratuity.

nigger tone: A low buzz produced by the throat muscles on a wind instrument.

nigger-wool: The kinky hair of a Negro.

niggers in a snow-storm: Stewed prunes and rice.

nigger in the woodpile, to see a: To sense or perceive the root of the mischief — something suspicious lurking in a project.

nigger on the fence: See *nigger in the woodpile.*

niggered log: A log that had been burnt at the end.

niggerhead: 1. A black boulder. 2. The main dome at the head of a boiler.

nigger heaven: 1. The top gallery in a theatre (*actors' slang*). 2. The roof of a freight car (*tramp slang*).

nigger, white: An opprobrious epithet used by colored people against Whites and light-skinned Negroes.

niggerly: Niggardly (*American slang*).

niggertoes: Brazil nuts.

Niggertown: The section in any town which is compactly inhabited by Negroes.

No rats: A catch-phrase equivalent to "He (or she) is Scotch." As Ware explains it, the rats make themselves scarce when they are subjected to bagpipe music.

Norsker: A Norwegian (*nautical slang*).

Norway neckcloth: "The pillory, usually made of Norway fir" [GROSE].

O

Olaf: A Swede, in general. From the frequent given name in Sweden.

Old sweat: A veteran soldier. Weekley thinks it a derivative from the German *alter Schwede* (old Swede) used in the same sense during the Thirty Years' War, and spread in England through Dalgetty and his friends.

ou-la-la girl: A French girl.

P

Paddy: An Irishman. The abbreviation is a diminutive of Patrick — favorite Irish name [GROSE]. Cf. *Pat.*

paddy: A tantrum. Ex *Patrick* and the choleric reputation of the Irish.

Paddyland: Ireland.

Paddylander: An Irishman.

Paddyw(h)ack: A strapping Irishman [PARTRIDGE].

parleyvoo, (to): French language; to speak French (*jocular colloquialism*).

Parthian shaft: A shot while retreating; figuratively, in having the last word, although ceding the point.

Parthian war: A retreat. The Parthians were reputed to have done some skillful shooting while retreating.

Pat: A nickname for any Irishman — from *Patrick.* Cf. *Paddy.*

patent Frenchman: An Irishman. An allusion to *Pat* and *patent* or showy (*tailors' slang*).

Patess: An Irishwoman. (Cf. *Pat*).

Patland: Ireland.

Patlander: An Irishman.

Paulite: A Boer. (Paul Kruger was the beloved president of Transvaal during the Boer War).

Pauly: A Boer.

Pawnee Indian: A rough petter (*American slang*).

Pax Britannica: British peace; an imposed settlement. The phrase is sometimes employed sarcastically as signifying a peaceful domination after a cruel subjugation.

peddler's French: 1. Underworld slang [GROSE]. 2. Gibberish in general. Cf. American "excuse my French" when using slang or vulgarism.

Peruvian Jews: Jews, who having been unable to cope with colonization conditions in South America come to settle in South Africa (*Transvaal colloquialism*).

pharisee: A bigot or overliteral devotee. The Pharisees were the dominant Jewish sect when Christianity was founded.

philistine: A humdrum middle-class person unalterably opposed to culture; a babbit.

pig-tail: A Chinese (*slang*).

Pigtailiana: China (*slang*).

pikey: A Gypsy; a tramp (*slang*).

pinch-penny: A Scotchman. The reference is to his reputed thriftiness (*colloquialism*).

pinkie: A light-skinned colored girl (*slang*).

piou-piou: A French soldier (*slang*).

plica Polonica: See *Polish disease*.

pock-pudding, poke-pudding: An Englishman. From poke i.e. bag, bag-pudding, hence a gourmand (*Scotch colloquialism*).

Polack: A Pole, usually of the slow and ungainly type, but in low or jocular parlance applied to any Polish immigrant or even one of that origin (*colloquialism*).

Pollack: A species of vicious-looking fish. Although the etymology of this term is obscure, it is quite possible that the appearance of the fish is associated with the physiognomy of the under-world Pole. Compare *Gadus Pollachius*.

Polander: A Pole. Unlike the name *Hollander*, which serves to avoid confusion between Dutchman and German, "Polander" carries a somewhat jocose sense.

Poland China: An American breed of large solid pig.

Polish disease: A disease of the scalp (*plica*), endemic in Eastern Europe, which results in the matting of the hair.

Polish plait: See *Polish disease.*

Pommy: A British immigrant (*Australian slang*).

porch-geese: Portuguese. The pun is obvious.

Pork and Beans: Portuguese. From the food they would eat during the first World War (*military slang*).

porker: A Jew (*antiphrastically*).

porky: A Jew (*a teasing epithet*).

Portuguese man-of-war: A siphonophore of the genus *Physalia* with long tentacles and the power of stinging very severely.

Portuguese parliament: A session with many speaking at once, and hardly anyone to listen (*sailors' slang*).

Portuguese pig-knot, in a: "Confused not knowing where to begin a yarn" [BOWEN].

Portuguese pumping: A phrase of uncertain but unquestionably questionable meaning, in the opinion of both Ware and Partridge.

Portugoose: A Portuguese (*military slang*).

Portuguee: A Portuguese (*careless colloquialism*).

Prussian junker: An arrogant scion of a so-called noble family, one whose surname is introduced by "von," and who sees in militarism his goal.

Q

quashee (ie): A Negro (seaman).

Quisling: A traitor. *Ex* the name of the man who betrayed his country (Norway) to Germany in 1940. The slur does not apply to the country, however, nor to its people.

R

rabbi: One who aids in securing special favors (*post office slang*).

rag-head: A Hindu (*underworld slang*).

Rastus: A nickname for any Negro.

Redland: Russia (since the establishment of Bolshevist rule).

refujews: Refugee Jews from Germany and occupied countries during the Nazi war (*sophisticated slang*).

Roman holiday: An entertainment provided by the ancient Romans in which the entertainers (prisoners of war) were the victims.

Russian: An animal difficult to handle (*Australian slang*).

Russian bear: Russia, collectively, as a military force especially under the Czarist regime (*journalese*).

Russian boots: Leg chains.

Russian law: "A hundred blowes on his bare shins" [John Day (1641) cited by Partridge].

Russian socks: Rags covering the feet of Russian soldiers prior to the Soviet outfitting of the army.

S

Sambo: A nickname for a Negro in general.

Sandy: A Scotsman. The abbreviation is of Alexander—perhaps the most common given name in Scotland [GROSE]. Cf. *Alexander*, also *Sawney*.

Sawney: A Scot. Cognate with Sandy.

Sawny: See *Sandy* [GROSE].

Scandihoovian: Scandinavian (*sailors' slang*).

Scandiwegian: See *Scandihoovian*.

Scot: An irascible individual.

scot: A temper. "What a scot he was in!"

Scot, false as a: Insincere, hypocritical.

Scotch: Stingy, petty, mean.

Scotch attorney: Any plant of the genus *Clusia*, which has the property of squeezing the life out of the tree enveloped by them.

Scotch bait: The practise of peddlers to halt and rest on a stick [GROSE]. Letting a horse stop for a rest at the top of a hill.

Scotch blessing: A vehement scolding.

Scotch bonnet: The fairy-ring mushroom.

Scotch boot: An instrument of torture by which the legs were crushed.

Scotch bum: A bustle worn during the seventeenth century (*colloquialism*).

Scotch casement: A pillory.

Scotch chocolate: Brimstone and milk [GROSE].

Scotch coffee: Hot water flavored with burnt biscuit.

Scotch cousin: A distant relative. Contrast with *cousin-german*.

Scotch fashion, to answer: Replying to a question by asking another. See *Jewish reply*. The Yankees are also supposed to have the same tendency.

Scotch fiddle: The itch [GROSE].

Scotch greys: Lice.

Scotch greys, headquarters of the: A head teeming with lice.

Scotch hobby: A scrubby diminutive Scotch horse.

Scotch marriage: A common-law marriage.

Scotch mist: A drizzling rain. "A Scotch mist will wet an Eng-lishman to the skin" [GROSE].

Scotch navy: The clan steamers (*naval slang*).

Scotch ordinary: A latrine.

Scotch organ, to play the: To put money in a cash register.

Scotch peg: A leg (*rhyming slang*).

Scotch pint: A two-quart bottle. (Evidently the opposite of what one would expect).

Scotch prize: A capture by fluke (*nautical slang*).

Scotch seamanship: Naval prowess marked by sheer force rather than intelligence.

Scotch sixpence: Threepence (*colloquialism*).

Scotch tape: A thin and transparent mending tape, particularly for torn pages.

Scotch verdict: A verdict of "not proven," colloquially referring to anything inconclusive.

Scotch (Scottish) warming pan: *1.* A wench [GROSE]. *2.* Flatus [PARTRIDGE].

scotchies: The figures in a hopscotch.

Scotchman: A piece of metal or wood, usually a ring placed on rigging for the purpose of preventing chafing (*nautical term*).

Scotchman: A florin (*South African slang*).
According to the story, a Scotsman was passing florins as half-crowns among the natives.

Scotchman hugging a Creole: A sort of creeper (*Clusia*) in West Indies.

Scotchmen: Lice (*low slang*).

Scotchy: A Scotsman. Having the characteristics of the Scots; generally used in a pejorative or jocose sense.

Scotland, the curse of: The nine of diamonds.

Scots convoy: Escorting a guest to the door or over the threshold but no further.

Scots grey: The yellow-fever mosquito.

Scotsman's cinema, the: Piccadilly Circus, because this London counterpart of Times Square can be enjoyed without admission charge (*English slang*).

Scotty: 1. A Scot. 2. Irritable, exasperated.

Scowegian: A Scandinavian, especially a Norwegian (*Canadian slang*).

Scowoogia: Scandinavia (*American slang*).

Scythian: A coarse barbarian, often ruthless and dogged. Ex *Scythia.*

Seedy: A Negro (*American slang*).

sepian, or **sepe:** A Mulatto (*American slang*).

set the swede down, to: To take a nap (*soldiers' slang*).

shade: A Negro (*American slang*).

Sheba, proud as the Queen of: Inordinately haughty.

Sheeny: A Jew (*low usage*).

shoneen: An Irish upstart.

shonnocker (shonnicker): A Jew (*underworld slang*).

Sicilian Vespers: The name given to the massacre of the French (by no means unprovoked) in Palermo, on March 30, 1282. It is said to have begun at the first stroke of the Vespers bell.

Sick Man of Europe, the: Turkey, around the time of Gladstone, and up to the establishment of the Republic (*journalese*).

skibby: A Japanese (*American naval slang*).

Originally the word meant a Japanese courtesan, but the sense was extended, after its dilution, alike, to loose and chaste, man and woman.

[63]

skinflint: A Scotchman. The reference is probably to his alleged inexorableness.

Slave: "A bond servant; one who is wholly subject to the will and power of another; one who has lost the power of resistance; a mean abject person; a drudge."

These meanings taken from the dictionary only serve to accentuate how a name, originally *Slava,* signifying "glory" in the Slavic languages, can be perverted and degraded at the will of the conquerors, as was the case with the Slavonic tribes subjugated by the Germanic hordes in the tenth century.

slawmineyeux: A Dutchman (*nautical slang*). A corruption of *ja mijnheer* (yes, sir) [PARTRIDGE].

Smous — (**Schmouss,** pronounced **Shmoos**): Originally a Jew from Germany, but later any Jew. Grose restricts it to the former. The word is evidently from the Yiddish, *shmuess,* i.e. chat, from Hebrew, *shmuah* — news.

Smoke: A Negro.

snide and shine (or **S and S**): "A Jew especially of East London." Partridge, citing Ware, says, it is East London Gentiles' slang. Possibly the combination stems from a vaudeville team (like Snitkin and Snotkin), or from some phrase current among Jewish salespeople like *'skleid is shein* — "it's a smart dress." Of course, there is the slang word, *snide,* meaning a crook, a cutthroat.

snooser: A Scandinavian (*American slang*).

sodomy: Pederasty. From the Biblical story about the Sodomites seeking the angels in Lot's house.

Spaniard, a bold: An over-ardent lover. The phrase is largely an Irish importation. To the Irish, the Spaniards were a symbol of passion.

Spanish: *1.* Money in ready coin. *2.* Earth or clay unfit for brickmaking.

Spanish athlete: A braggart; a pompous or conceited talker, i.e., one who "throws the bull."

Spanish bayonet: A stiff short-trunked plant (*Yucca Aloifolia*).

Spanish beard: Long moss; an epiphytic plant. A long-beard.

Spanish boot: An instrument of torture. See *Scotch boot.*

Spanish castles: Castles-in-the-air; day-dreaming. *Ex* the imaginative literature of Spain.

Spanish coin: Fair words, compliments, flattery [GROSE].

Spanish dagger: A plant (*Yucca Gloriosa*), very much like the Spanish bayonet but shorter.

Spanish faggot: The sun [GROSE].

Spanish flag: 1...A California rockfish. 2. A West Indian fish of the *Serranidae* family.

Spanish flesh: A yellowish color (putty).

Spanish fly: Cantharides.

Spanish Fury: The three days' massacre of Antwerp, by the Spaniards, in 1576.

Spanish gout: The pox; syphilis.

Spanish influenza: The grippe, on an epidemic scale.

Spanish lady: The ladyfish, or Spanish hogfish.

Spanish mare, to ride the: "To sit astride a beam, guys loosed, sea rough as a punishment." [Partridge, after Farmer and Henley's *Slang and its Analogues*].

Spanish measles: Black measles.

Spanish money: Fine words that cost little; flattery; "soft soap" smooth talk; "blarney."

Spanish padlock: A species of chastity girdle.

Spanish pike: A needle.

Spanish plague: A building [PARTRIDGE, after RAY].

Spanish pox: Syphilis.

Spanish soldier: A spear grass of New Zealand.

Spanish spoon: A long-handled dipper or narrow shovel.

Spanish toothpick: The bishop's-weed *Ammi Viznaga.*

Spanish topaz: A yellow kind of rock crystal.

Spanish trot: An easy trot (of a horse).

Spanish (or **King of Spain's**) **trumpeteer:** An ass when bray-
ing [GROSE]. Partridge connects it with the pun *Don key.*

Spanish walk: See *walk Spanish.*

Spanish waves: Large and formidable billows. (Probably *ex*
Armada days).

Spanish windlass: A straitjacket (*American slang*).

Spanish worm: A nail, so called by carpenters when they strike
one while sawing [GROSE].

Spanisher: A Spaniard (*American slang*).

Spaghettiland: Italy (*American slang*).

Spick: A Mexican or any dark-complexioned person of Southern
European stock. *Ex* pronunciation of "speak." Cf. *Greaser*
(*American slang*).

Spinach: A Spaniard (*American slang*).

spiggoty: A Latin-American. Ex *spick,* which in its turn is derived from the phrase "No spick Ingles." See Mencken's *The
American Dictionary,* fourth edition, page 296, footnote.

steppe-sister: A Russian woman.

Stiff-necked people: The Jews, as referred to in the Bible by
Moses when his patience became overtaxed.

St. Patrick: Whiskey of the finest quality (*slang*).

street Arabs: Urchins of the slums; city youngsters of the poorer
class.

Suisse or **Swiss:** A porter, lackey, doorman.

suisses, to have the: To be in a state of delirium tremens or great excitement (*American slang*). Doormen at night clubs are said to imbibe a good deal of liquor.

sun-burned Irishman: A Negro (*American slang*).

Swearing Nation: The English. "Nay have we not been called in the vulgar dialect of foreign countries 'The Swearing Nation'?" [DEFOE].

big Swede: A large clumsy person (*American colloquialism*).

Swede fiddle: A cross-cut saw (*American slang*).

Swensky: Swedish, from *svensk*—Swedish (*American slang*).

Swiss admiral: A man who gives himself out to be a naval officer, although without foundation. The ironical expression is due to the inland frontiers of Switzerland. Cf. *amiral suisse.*

Swiss guard, grim as a: Stern-looking and immobile.

Swiss navy: A fictitious department; a class of which no members exist.

T

tadpole: A French youngster. Cf. *Froggie.*

Taffy: A nickname for any Welshman. Diminutive of David (St. David) the tutelar saint of Wales, hence the frequency of David as a given name in that country.

tamale: A Mexican girl (*American slang*).

tan: A Mulatto (*American slang*).

Tartar: An old hand at . . .; a sharper or vagrant; a difficult or cruel person to deal with. Cf. the phrase "He caught a Tartar" i.e., he holds someone who is more than a match for the captor.

tartan, tearing the: Speaking Gaelic.

Thirteener: A shilling in Ireland, where it was considered to be worth thirteen pence. *Cf.* "Scotch sixpence."

Tommy: An English soldier.

Tony: A Portuguese soldier; (the abbreviation of *Antonio*).

Trojan horse: A ruse bordering on treachery, dating from the Homeric version of the Trojan war. During the Nazi war, the phrase was often applied to the German "tourists" traveling to neutral countries, who afterwards turned out to be spies, Gestapo officers, or men on military missions.

Turk: 1. A bully, a hardhearted person [GROSE]. 2. Frequently, the name of a dog.

Turk, the unspeakable: A phrase oft recurring in the press and periodical literature of English and the United States during the '90's, and later, to show the temper of the Anglo-Saxon peoples over the atrocities of the Turks perpetrated on the inhabitants of their enslaved vassal states. One of the celebrated statesmen to employ the phrase was Gladstone.

Turk, to turn: To change completely for the worst. "If the rest of my fortunes turn Turk with me." SHAKESPEARE: *Hamlet*, III, *sc.* 2.

turkey, to talk: To speak frankly; to get down to the point. Although the phrase is associated rather with the fowl, which seems to make important pronouncements, rather than the country which was supposed to have been its original habitat, there may also be a political slant to the locution. In connection with a visit to Stalin by one of the American emissaries in 1942, we are told by a columnist that the Russian war chief, or rather the interpreter, misunderstood the American when he said "Now, let's talk turkey," and thought that they were to discuss the Turkish situation in relation to the Nazi war, which he was disinclined to do.

Turkish medal: A button (undone) showing on the fly.

Turkish treatment: "Barbarous usage" [GROSE].

Turk's head: A round broom with a long handle.

U

urinal of the planets: Ireland (so named because of the fre-quent rains in that country).

unbleached American: A Negro, native of America (*American colloquialism*).

Uncle Shylock: The Americans, collectively, because they ex-pected the debts of the first World War to be paid back.

V

vandal: One who wantonly destroys property — especially of cul-tural significance. *Ex* The German tribe which destroyed the precious treasures of Italy in the fifth century.

Vulgaria: Bulgaria (*American slang*).

W

walk Spanish, to: To make a hasty departure, to take French leave; to be taken by the scruff of the neck or the seat of the pants and walked off; to desert (*nautical slang*).

wear the leek, to: To be Welsh (*colloquialism*).

weep Irish, to: To shed crocodile tears (Ex the opposite of wail-ings at a wake?).

Welsh: Something unintelligible. Cf. *double Dutch*.

welsh: mawkish; flat; insipid from *wallowish* (*dialectal English*).

Welsh ambassador: The cuckoo or owl, *i.e.*, a pseudo-wise person.

[69]

Welsh bait: Allowing a horse to catch his breath at the top of a hill. See *Scotch bait.*

Welsh comb: "The thumb and four fingers." [GROSE].

Welsh fiddle: The itch. *Cf.* Scotch fiddle.

Welsh mile, like a: Tedious and drawn out.

Welsh parsley: A hempen halter (*slang*).

welsh, to: To evade payment of obligations.

welsher: One who fails to carry out an agreement; a defaulter.

Welshman's button: An artificial fly, in angling, so constructed as to resemble a beetle.

Welshman's hose: Something that is wrested awry.

Welshman's hug: See *Welsh fiddle.*

Whigland: Scotland.

white nigger: See *nigger, white.*

wild Arabian: A problem child; *enfant terrible.*

wild Indian: See *wild Arabian.*

Wolfland: Ireland (*slang*).

wooden shoes: German, also Dutch, fighters [WESEEN].

woolly head: A Negro (*slang*).

wop: An Italian. Although there seems to be some mystery about its origin, I am told by my barber that he has heard it often in his town, Palazza, between Bari and Calabria, where *uap* means a fop, a swell, a show-off (*American slang*).

wophouse: An Italian restaurant (*American slang*).

Wopland: Italy.

wop special: 1. Macaroni. 2. Spaghetti.

wopstick: A clarinet.

Y

yah-for-yes folk: Germans and Dutch. Ex German *ja* (*naval slang*).

Yankee doodle: "A booby or country lout, a name given to the New England men in North America" [GROSE].

Yankeedom: United States (*slang*).

Yankee heaven: Paris (*slang*).

Yankee paradise: Paris. The American tourists are responsible for this phrase.

Yankee trick: A petty act or practice.

Yankees of the South: The Argentinians, regarded by the other Latin states as aggressive.

Yellow: Cowardly; underhanded; ex *yellow* race i.e., Japanese and Chinese, possibly *via* mystery novels of last generation. The attack on Pearl Harbor, while diplomatic negotiations were in process, was not calculated to make this connotation of the word obsolete.

yellow-belly: A Chinese (*American slang*).

Yellow peril: The Chinese and Japanese military awakening. The phrase was much heard in the early part of this century, with far greater fear of China than of Japan.

Yid: A Jew of the Ghetto. Among low-class Gentiles, anyone of Jewish descent (*American slang*).

Yiddisher: A Jew (*low colloquialism*).

Yiddish cologne: Gasoline (*American slang*).

Yiddisher piano: See *Jewish piano*. (According to Partridge, *Cockney slang*).

Yiddle: A Jew (*low slang*) According to Partridge, the word is applied especially to a Jewish boxer, in pugilistic circles. If so this is a perversion; for the contemptuous *Yiddle,* in Yiddish, means a physically slight and otherwise insignificant Jew — a "little Jew." Furthermore, to say that it is an elaboration of *Yid* is as much as to make out that *Johnny* is an elaboration of *John*.

Yidgin-English: Yiddish-English dialect (*colloquialism*).

Yodelania (or **Yodel Land**): Switzerland (*American slang*).

young Turk: A problem child; *enfant terrible* (*colloquialism in England*).

Z

zigaboo: A Negro.

Zulu: A car conveying immigrants and their chattels (*railroad slang*).

Zulu-ticket: A credit slip given to a Negro for his part in a spectacle (*circus slang*).

PART TWO

FOREIGN ETHNOPHAULISMS

COLLECTIVE SLURS IN ANCIENT LANGUAGES

(Greek words containing letters having no counterpart in our alphabet appear in the original. Words in other non-Latin alphabets have been transliterated)

akum *(Hebrew)*: The initials of *oved kokh'vim umazolot,* i.e., worshipper of the stars and zodiacal signs, in reality all Gen-tiles at the time were included. (The O and A sounds are often interchangeable in composites).

Anglicus, sudor *(Latin)*: "English sweat." Sweating sickness *(medical term).*

arel *(Hebrew)*: See *Orel.*

Barbaros *(Greek)*: Foreign, strange, rude, from a root which means to stammer; applied to anyone who was not Greek, hence barbarian.

b'laaz *(Hebrew)*: "In the stammering (or jabbering) language." In any language other than Hebrew or Aramaic.* It happens that the word *laaz* contains the initials of *loshon avodah zorah,* i.e., the language of strange worship, and has been so inter-preted, and accepted, but I think erroneously.

Boeothios sus *(Greek)*: "Boeotian pig." A Boeotian, a "hog."

Borussia, miseria in *(Latin)*: Misery in Prussia.

Cappadocians, inarticulate as the: *(Greek).*

---

*RASHI, the foremost of Biblical and Talmudic commentators, employs the word *b'laaz,* when he has occasion to mention French, his vernacular, in the French glosses of his famous commentary.

Corinthians: See Κορινθία.

Cretans, the weapons of the (*Greek*) : Lies and deception. See also Κρητίζειν.

Danaos, timeo ꜛ et dona ferentes (*Latin*) : I fear the Greeks, though bearing gifts. [VIRGIL].

Ethiopian, can the ꜛ change his skin and the leopard his spots? (*Hebrew*). [JEREMIAH].

Ethiopian, I am trying to wash the ꜛ white (*Greek*). [LUCIAN].

Ethiops non dealbavit (*Latin*) : The Ethiopian cannot be washed white.

gadarogámai (*Greek*): "Ass-kissers". Jews. The Jews were accused of worshipping the ass even by celebrated Greek and Roman historians.

Gallicus, morbus, (*Latin*): "French disease". Venereal infection. (A comparatively modern medical phrase).

Germanica, latta, (*Latin*): "German insect". A cockroach.

goy (*Hebrew*): A Gentile, non-Jew. (Originally meaning a nation).

Graeca fide mercari (*Latin*) : "To buy on Greek credit". To pay cash.

Graeca sunt, non leguntur (*Latin*) : "Greek; not to be read." In the Middle Ages, classical Greek was so unfamiliar even to outstanding scholars that often Arabic had to be invoked as an intermediary between Greek and the then universal language of the educated — Latin. Whenever Greek was cited in a book, it was done with the apologetic note that it was not to be read.

Greek, never trust a (*Greek*). [EURIPIDES].

Helotes (*Greek*): Bondsman. The supposed derivation is from the city of Helos in Greece.

Hunnicus, equus (*Latin*): "A Hungarian horse". A gelded horse.

What suits the Jews does not suit the Syrians. (*Danish*).

Ilium, Corinthiis non indignatur (*Latin*): Troy should not take it out on the Corinthians.

Ilium, fuit (*Latin*): Troy is a matter of the past. [VIRGIL].

Israelita, brachyurus (*Latin*): A variety of the common crab, characterized by a short abdomen.

Judae, auricularia auriculae (*Latin*): A common though edible fungus, growing on decayed wood.

Judaeus, curtius (*Latin*): "The curtailed Jew". *Ex* the loss of the prepuce.

Kaffir (*Arab*): "God-denying". *1*. Kaffir (in Africa). *2*. Kafir (inhabitant of Kafiristan, in Asia).

Κορινθία κόρη (*Greek*): "Corinthian wench." A prostitute.

Κορινθιαστής (*Greek*): A whoremonger.

Κορίνθιον κακόν (*Greek*): "Corinthian ill." Venereal trouble.

Κρητίζειν (*Greek*): "To Cretanize." To tell tall stories.

Lithuanicus, pons ↳ et Polonicus nihil valet (*Latin*). Lithuanian and Polish bridges are worth nothing.

loäz (*Syriac*): "To speak barbarously, to stammer". To speak Egyptian [GESENIUS].

Locrian lewdness (*Greek*).

Megarian tears (*Greek*): Crocodile tears.

Milesians, once the ↳ were powerful (*Greek*).

Orel (*Hebrew*): "Uncircumcized". A Gentile.

Phryges, sero sapiunt (*Latin*): The Trojans became wise too late. This refers to the release of Helen, after the Trojan War had begun.

Pollachius, gadus (*Latin*): A species of fish — the pollack.

Polonica, plica (*Latin*): "Polish plait." A disease of the scalp, in which the hair becomes matted.

Polonicus: See *Lithuanicus, pons* ⌐ *et Polonicus.*

Polonicus, coccus (*Latin*): "Polish microbe". An insect of the louse family.

Polonicus, margarodes (*Latin*): Polish shield-louse; plant-bug

Punica fides (*Latin*): "Punic faith", i.e., treachery, first applied by SALLUST.

Saxonum, stultitia (*Latin*): Saxon stupidity.

Sclavus saltans (*Latin*): The prancing Slav.

Secta nefaria (*Latin*): "The nefarious sect." The Jews as designated in the royal decrees during the Middle Ages.

Soloikos (*Greek*): Speaking or writing ungrammatically or incorrectly, using *solecisms*. Ex *Soloi*, in Cilicia, where the colonists spoke a corrupt form of the Attic dialect.

Suevorum, libido (*Latin*): Swabian lust.

Teutonici sunt nati, venerunt de culo Pilati (*Latin*): "The Teutons were born, coming out of the fundament of Pilate".

Teutonicus, furor (*Latin*): Teuton fury, in dealing with the subdued.

CROATIAN SLURS
See under SERBO-CROATIAN ETHNOPHAULISMS

CZECH ETHNOPHAULISMS

anglisovati: "To English." To nick the tail of a horse.

čina: "China." 1. A pattern. 2. Rough weather.

čech neplech (*Moravian* vs. *Czechs*) : The lazy Czech.

flámamovati: "To live Flemish fashion." To roam about with no work in mind. To bum one's way.

flamendr: "A Fleming." A vagabond. *Vesti flámovský život* is to lead the life of a tramp. In the sixteenth and seventeenth centuries, the Flemish deserters overran Bohemia and became vagrants.

flamendrovati: See *flámamovati*.

francouze: "Frenchmen." Venereal disease (*slang*).

francouzštiti: "To affect French mannerisms; to glorify any-thing French.

holundr, pije jako: He drinks like a Dutchman.

irská samolibost: Irish assurance.

maďar: "A Hungarian." A boil.

maďarik: "A Hungarian," (in a somewhat jocular sense). A gou-lash (*colloquialism*).

maďaron: A Magyar chauvinist; a 101% Hungarian.

maďarošílenec: A Magyaromaniac.

moravec nemravec (*Czech* vs *Moravians*) : The uncouth (ill-mannered) Moravian.

němčeata: "German stuff." Potatoes, to which the Czechs at first did not take kindly.

němčour: "A 'Cherman'." A German who would have no truck with other nationalities.

němec: "A German." Fritz.

němec potměšilec: "German sneak." *Parietaria glabra* — a seem-ingly smooth sort of nettle.

německa myš: "German mouse." A rat.

německa růžička: "German rose." A thistle.

německopitomý: The stupid German.

německů, sny: Germanomania.

německy rak: "German crab." A frog.

polách: A Polish hog (*provincialism*).

polák: "A Pole" (when capitalized). 1. A Polish horse. 2. A Polish hog. 3. Polish sausage. 4. Polish wind, *i.e.*, the Northwest wind. 5. A Polish shilling.

polákavati: 1. To consume; to gorge. 2. To lure.

polácký: " 'Polackish'." Polish, in a pejorative sense, the proper word being *polský*.

polsko: "Poland" (when capitalized). Flatland.

ruska: "A Ruthenian (rarely, a Russian) woman" (when capitalized). 1. A pale yellow cow. 2. A sardine.

španělka: "A Spanish woman" (when capitalized). 1. A cane, a rod. 2. A Merino. 3. A red onion.

španělský (a): Spanish. *To jest mu španělská ves (nice)*. That's all strange to him. He can't make anything out of that. (Evidently a transfer from the German.)

švejcar: "A Swiss" (when capitalized). A kreuzer or other small coin (*provincialism*).

švejda: "A Swede" (when capitalized). A crude, awkward fellow (*provincialism*).

švýcar: "A Swiss" (when capitalized). 1. A shepherd. 2. A dairyman.

uher: "A Hungarian" (when capitalized). A pimple; a boil; a ringworm.

uherčina: 1. Hungarian language or manner. 2. Hungarian wine. 3. Fever (the Hungarian disease). See HERZER'S *Böhmisch-deutsches Wörterbuch*.

žid: "A Jew." *1.* "One of the boys," a Jacobin, a kike. *2.* A bitter-tasting mushroom. *3.* A vein in a rock. *4.* A spotted bean.

židačisko: An ugly or hideous-looking Jew. (Also in the meta-phorical sense.)

židátko: "A Jewish youngster." A crested lark.

židek: "A Jew-boy." Greedy guts; a glutton.

Note: The derivation is no doubt different for these homo-phones, yet the fact that the word in both cases is spelled the same would connote assimilation or adaptation, through the association of ideas.

židisko: See *židačisko.*

židlati: To play badly.

židovec: *1.* A Jew. *2.* A Jewish votary. *3.* *Myricaria,* a common plant with a balsamic bitter bark, formerly used as an astringent.

židovina: *1.* Jewish manners and customs. *2.* Jewish stench. *3.* Jewish clique. *4.* Jewry. *5.* A Jew. *6.* A Jewess. *7.* Whiskey. *8.* Confusion; disorder.

židovka: "A Jewess." *1.* A tam o'shanter. *2.* A lady-bird. *3.* A kind of plum. *4.* Whiskey.

židovská škola: "Jewish School." Bedlam; pandemonium.

židovsku, jednati po: To talk or gesticulate like a kike.

DANO-NORWEGIAN ETHNOPHAULISMS

(Exclusively Danish phrases are indicated as such)

engelsken: A Britisher; John Bull.

engelskjord: "English earth." Rottenstone — used in polishing, cleaning, etc.

engelsk læder: "English leather." Sateen.

finne, sint som en: Mad as a Finn.

franske, den ↪ **Syge** (*Danish* vs. *French*): "French disease." Syphilis.

fransk, tage ↪ **Afsked** (*Danish* vs. *French*): To take French leave.

Franzoser (*Danish* vs. *French*): "Frenchmen." French pox.

græsk Bøjning (*Danish* vs. *Greek*): "Greek inflection." An ex-aggerated bustle in a dress.

hollænder, tjukk som en: Fat as a Dutchman.

irlænder, dum som en: Stupid as an Irishman.

islandske løver: "Iceland lions." Dutch mountains; snakes in Ireland.

jødepris: "Jewish price." Exorbitant rate.

jødesmaus: Sheeny; kike.

jødetamp: Mockie. A nasty Jew.

jødetræk: "Jew trick." Fool's mate (in chess).

Kineseri (*Danish* vs. *Chinese*): "Chinese stuff." Official red tape.

kineserengelsk: "Chinese English." Pigeon-English.

Krabat, en vilter (*Danish* or *Norwegian* vs. *Croats*): "A wild Croat." An untractable fellow.

Nederlandene, fra ham: (To wrench) the Netherlands from his grasp. [BRYNILDSEN].

norsknorsk (*Danish* vs. *Norwegians*): "Norwegian Norwegian." Ultra-Norwegian [LARSEN].

polsk ekteskap: "Polish marriage." Concubinage.

polsk, en ↪ **Forstrækkelse** (*Danish* vs. *Poles*): "In a Polish strain." A mortal funk [LARSEN].

polsk, en ↝ rigsdag: "Polish parliament." Dover Court; bed-lam.

polsk forbandt: "Polish bond." Flemish bond; fleeting attach-ment.

polsk, leve paa: "To live (together) in Polish style." To live tally; to have relations under a common law understanding.

Prøjser, være en riktig (*Danish* vs. *Prussians*): "To be a real Prussian." To be a bully.

Prøjseri (*Danish* vs. *Prussians*): "Prussianism." Iron-clad bureau-cracy; pedantry; small-mindedness.

Schakterjøde (*Danish* vs. *Jews*): "Jew-hawker." A Jewish street vendor.

Schweizer (*Danish* vs. *Swiss*): "A Swiss." A doorman; a lackey.

skotte, dum som en: Stupid as a Scotchman.

skotte, gjerrig som en: Greedy as a Scotchman.

spansk, det kommer mig noget ↝ for (*Danish* vs. *Spanish*): That strikes me as rather odd.

storsvensker: "Big Swede." Equivalent to "You think you're everything, don't you?"; an ultra-patriotic Swede.

svenske, gjöre ↝ av sig: "Make a Swede of yourself." Be sure not to appear on time, "stand one up." An ironical reminder of what the Norwegians consider in the Swedes a characteristic failing, viz., not to keep appointments. The Swedes, of course, take it as a projection of a Norwegian practice. Other meanings are: wriggle out of obligations, such as hotel rent, military service, etc., in other words, "give the slip."

Svensker, full som (*Danish* vs. *Swedes*): Drunk as a Swede.

svensk kaffe (*Norwegian* vs. *Swedes*): "Swedish coffee." Insipid or poorly made coffee.

tydska (*Norwegian* vs. *Germans*) : "To German." To speak in-coherently or unintelligibly.

tydska (*Norwegian* vs. *Germans*) : "German." Gibberish.

tyrk, bande som en: "To curse like a Turk." To swear like a trooper.

Tyrkertro (*Danish* vs. *Turks*) : Turkish fatalism; fanaticism.

tyrk, sint som en (*Norwegian* vs. *Turks*) : Mad as a Turk.

tyrk, vred som en: "Crazy like a Turk." Mad as a hatter.

tyske: "To speak German." To jabber, to gabble.

Tysker (*Danish* vs. *Germans*) : "A German." A sot, pighead. [K].

DUTCH AND FLEMISH ETHNOPHAULISMS

Arabier: "Arab." A joke, a card, a comical fellow.

arabier, per: "By an Arab." Through an irony of fate; by a fluke (*student slang*).

Chinees: "A Chinese." A queer person; an eccentric, especially in the phrase *rare Chinees*.

Chineesche kerk: "Chinese church." A rumor; a questionable piece of news.

chineezerij: " 'chinesery'." A stupid prank.

Croaet: "A Croat." A queer or peculiar fellow; an eccentric

Deen, lompe: The awkard Dane.

Deen, norsche: The sullen Dane.

dronkelap: See *Lap, dronken*.

Engelsch, het is ⌐ gaar: "It is done the English way." It is underdone; half raw, very rare.

Engelsch draven: "To trot English." To trot briskly.

Engelsch? Spreekt hij: "Does he speak English?" "Does he have money?"

Engelsch zweet: "English sweat." The sweating sickness.

Engelsche ziekte: "English disease." Rachitis; rickets.

Engelschen, een ⌐ brief schrijven: "To write an English letter." To take a short nap.

Engelschen schroevendraaier gedaan, dat is met den: "That was done with an English screwdriver." That received rough treatment (with a hammer).

Feling (*East Frisianism*): "A Westphalian." A vulgarian, a "roughneck."

Flamingo: 1. A Fleming (when capitalized). 2. A flamingo.

Fransch, een ⌐ kompliment maken: "To pay a French com-pliment." To take French leave. [CALISCH] To flatter [VAN DALE].

Fransch met haar op: "French with the hair up." Pidgin-French; French badly spoken.

Fransch praten: "To talk French." To put on a swagger; to "talk big."

Fransche: "French." Brandy. (Cf. *Scotch*, in English).

Fransche colère schieten, in eene: "To burst into a French rage." To flare up; to fly off the handle.

Fransche eed: A French oath. A light promise which one does not expect to fulfill.

Fransche gedachten: "French thoughts." Idle sentiments; pious wishes; superficial ideas.

Fransche verschooning: "A French laundering." Turning soiled wearing articles inside out.

Fransche wasch doen, zijn hemd in de: "To put his shirt into the French wash." To wear a soiled shirt on the wrong side.

Franschelaar: A Francophile; one for whom nothing exists but French and the French.

Franschen, loop naar de: "Run to the French." Go to the deuce.

Franschen slag, met den: "In the French manner." Superficially, perfunctorily; just to "get by."

Franschje: 1. A little Frenchman. 2. A flat bread without crust. 3. A kind of cheese.

Franschmans: "A Frenchman." A braggart. One who "talks big."

Fransoos (Franzoos): A Frenchman, in a pejorative sense.

fransquillon: A non-French Francophile; one who toadies to the French and exalts their culture (*Belgian-French colloquialism*).

Fries, koppige: The pigheaded Frisian.

Hollandsche kaaskop: "Dutch cheese-head." The obdurate Dutchman.

Hollander, botte: The blunt Dutchman.

Ier, de wilde: "The wild Irishman." *Wilde ieren* is used as metaphor for boisterous or mischievous children. The doings of the Irish troops during the British invasion in the seventeenth century gave rise to this epithet.

Joden: "To Jew" (someone). To do someone; to engage in petty dealing.

Jodenhandel: See *Jodenkoop*.

Jodenkerk: "Jewish church." A boisterous assembly.

Jodenkoop: "Jew-trading." Petty manipulation.

Jodenstreek: A Jew-trick.

Jodentoer: "Jew-job." 1. Something requiring ingenuity or skill. 2. A mean trick. 3. A night shift in a factory.

Kroaet: See *Croaet*.

Lap, dronken: The drunken Laplander.

lombaerden: "To 'Lombard.'" To practise usury. *Daer gaet men in den Lombaerd* — there prices are sky-high *(Flemish)*.

mof (or **moffen**): *1.* A muff. *2.* A greenfinch. *3.* A Westphalian; A German. *4.* One who sulks or frowns, as the Germans were wont to do.

mof, hij is zoo lomp als een: He is rough like a German.

mof, zitten als een: "To sit like a German." To take a stiff pose.

mof, zwijgen als een: "To be mute like a German." To be glum.

moffelaer: A sharper, chiseler, trickster. Ex *Moff*, a German. It may be also due to the fact that a sharper at cards makes use of his muff to hide something.

moffenzon: "A German sun." A deceptive sun, which shines and hides an impending cloudburst.

mofferij: German manner of speech, German behavior or policy (censoriously considered).

Moffrika: Germany (A blend of *mof* and *Afrika*).

Moffrikaan: A German.

poepenzon: See *moffenzon*.

Polak, drinken gelijk een: Drink like a Polack *(Flemish)*.

Pool: "Pole." A person of dubious descent, usually rough and uncivilized.

Poolsche landdag: "Polish parliament." Bedlam.

Pruisen: "Prussians." A variety of potatoes growing in South Holland.

Pruisisch: "Prussian." Excitable, wrought up. *Het ging er Pruisisch toe*—things were pretty rough; there was enough unpleasantness.

Pruisisch, het zal ↰ zijn: "It will be Prussian." No good will come of it.

rotte Wale: A rotten Walloon (*Flemish*).

Rus: "Russian." A "cop" in civilian clothes. An ordinary police-man. Ex *rechercheur.* Cf. *Dick* and *detective* (slang).

Rus, de ⌐ gezien hebben: "To have seen the Russian." To be dead drunk.

Rus, slapen als een: "To sleep like a Russian." To be dead to the world; to sleep like a log.

***schots (or schotsen):** An icicle; (*as adverb*) roughly, boor-ishly.

Schotsch: "Scotch." Dishonest; uncivil, rude, callous, awkward, cowardly, stupid.

***schotsch en scheef:** "Scotch and askew." Topsy-turvy; at sixes and sevens; messy.

Schotschrift: "A Scotch writing." A libel; a lampoon.

Smous (or Smousen): 1. A low Jew. 2. An Arab skinflint. 3. A profiteer.

Smousentael: 1. Gibberish. 2. Yiddish.

Spaansche pokken: "Spanish pox." Syphilis.

Spanje, gezien hebben: "To have seen Spain." To have under-gone a good deal of punishment; to have been infected with a venereal disease.

Spanjool: "Little Spaniard" (in a pejorative sense).

steertman: "Tail-man." An Englishman. The Dutch, according to REINSBERG-DÜRINGSFELD, believed that the English, be-cause of the murder of Thomas à Becket, were punished by being born with tails after 1170. It seems too infantile a story to believe.

Turk, rooken als een: To smoke like a Turk.

---

*There is a probability that these words are not cognate with the national name, yet the homonymity has a psychological bearing in this connection.

Walenbeest: "A Walloon beast." A Walloon (*Flemish*).

FRENCH ETHNOPHAULISMS

agraco, avoir une chose d': "To have something from a Greek." To get a windfall; to have unexpected luck. See *grec, etc.*

alboche: A German. *Boche* is an abbreviated form which, probably on that account, became more current.

Allemand, jouer de la fluste de l': "To play the German flute." To overcharge. Cf. *Dutch reckoning.* The "German flute" here represents the tall and narrow German glasses in the tavern.

allemand, le bonheur: "German happiness." As Johanna Schopenhauer explained it, a German who broke his leg feels fortunate that it was not his neck which was broken.

Allemand, le lourd: The clumsy German.

allemand, peigne d': "A German comb." The four fingers (which Germans use to groom their hair).

allemand, querelle d': "A German quarrel." Much ado about nothing; a feud over trivialities.

Allemand, rou(x) comme un: Red like a German.

allemand, saut de l': "A German leap." Jumping from bed to the covered table, and back to bed [Leroux]. See also *haut allemand.*

Allemand, une saignée d': "A German bleeding." Loosening the clothes after a hearty meal.

Alphonse: A common French name. A pimp, procurer. (This representative name is adopted in most European languages).

Alsatia: The underworld (*slang*). A good many of the felons in France probably came from Alsace.

[89]

américain, (e): "American." Alert, shrewd. *Avoir l'oeil américain*—to take in a practical situation at a glance. *Oeillade américaine*—ogling, leering, "goo-goo eyes" (*slang*).

anglais: "An Englishman;" when capitalized. A creditor. *J'ai un tas d'anglais à mes trousses* may be freely rendered as "I have a bunch of creditors at my coat tails." These creditors are never supposed to be paid; for the Englishman is reputed to be rich and trusting. Another sense of *anglais* is a man who keeps a mistress. To cabbies, *anglais* represents a tight-wad.

anglais: Menses. *Elle a ses anglais*—She "has come around" (*slang*). The English, more than any other people, are periodic visitors to France (even during 1943).

Anglais, damné comme un: Damned like an Englishman.

Anglais, grossier comme un: Coarse like an Englishman (*Belgian analogy*).

Anglais, jurer comme un: to swear like an Englishman.

Anglais, méchant comme un: Ill-natured like an Englishman.

anglaise, capote: See *capote anglaise*.

anglaise, dents à l': "English teeth." Buck teeth.

anglaise, faire une: "To do it in English style." To chip in and send for drinks, each of the club afterwards receiving his share; to pay one's own way.

anglaise, faire un lit à l': "To make the bed the English way." Not to take the trouble to remove the covering.

anglaise, marriage à l': "An English marriage arrangement," i. e., by which, soon after the wedding, the husband and wife live in separate domiciles. It is employed also to designate cohabitation after a casual meeting, as at a dance.

anglaise, s'en aller à l': To slip away; to take French leave.

anglaiser: 1. To nick (a horse's tail). 2. To hog (a horse's mane).

angliche: Pejorative of *Anglais*—the English. *Les angliches*—the English people (*slang*).

anglois, (anglais), soûl comme un: "Drunk as an Englishman." The saying, dating from the Hundred Years' War, as the archaic form *Anglois* indicates, relates to the excessive drinking of the invading British troops, who gorged themselves with unknown wines they found in the cellars.

angulas, anglice: A goose, bird, derived from *anglais*, whose preoccupation with the sea and birds has been remarked as far back as Charles V, when he is alleged to have said that with birds he spoke English (*slang*).

apache: A ruffian, strong-arm man. *Ex* The North American Indian tribe. *Ruses d'apache*—savage cunning.

arabe (*noun*): Besides Arabian, the word, in a secondary sense, means colloquially a *usurer*, also a *screw;* the semantic kinship is obvious.

arabe (*adj.*): Mixed-up. *Fourbi arabe*—a sorry mess.

arbico(t): An Arab (*slang*).

Athénien (ne): "An Athenian." An elegant but sometimes frivolous intellectual.

aztèque: "An Aztec." A puny or stunted individual.

bamboula: A negro (*slang*).

Basque, courir comme un: "To run like a Basque." The Basques were famous for their speed and were employed by the French nobility as couriers.

basque espagnol: "Spanish Basque," *Parler français comme un basque espagnol*—to murder the French language.

basquerie: "A Basque act." A mean trick.

basques, ne pas quitter les ⤳ de quelqu'un: "Not to leave someone's Basques" (i.e., a sort of skirt). To be following

one around continually. *Il est toujours pendu à mes basques*—
he is at my heels (is hanging around me) all the time.

Belge, comme une oie: As silly as a goose.

Belgique, filer en: To abscond, to bolt. Cf. *filer à l'anglaise.*

Béotien (ne): "Boeotian." Churlish, rustic, ungainly.

Bavière, aller en: "To go to Bavaria." To be treated for syphilis.
Baver means to drivel. A popular syphilis cure was sweating,
hence the play of words.

Berlin, il y a des juges à: "There are judges in Berlin." The
reply is said to have been made by a miller of Sans-Souci
to Frederick the Great when the latter threatened to appropriate his mill, if he did not agree to sell it. The French
seized on this courageous answer in the face of arbitrary
authority.

Birmingham, être de: "To be from Birmingham." To be bored
to death. Birmingham is famous for its razors; and *rasoir* in
French is both a razor and a bore, although only heaven
knows why.

bisness: Trade or business, in a pejorative sense, as *faire son bisness,* to ply one's trade, with reference to street-walking
(*slang*).

boche: A German, viewed from a war angle.

bocherie: German atrocity.

bochie: Germany.

bochisant: Collaborationist, Germanophile.

bochiser: To spy.

bochisme: *Kultur* of the military or Nazi brand.

bohême (la): "A Bohemian." A Gypsy; a vagabond; (the loaf-
ing fraternity; irregular living; Gypsydom; Greenwich Village life).

bohémien: "A Gypsy." An unconventional, erratic, and not too responsible fellow, with artistic pretensions.

bohémien, foi de: "Gypsy faith." Honor among thieves or crooks.

bohémienne: "A Gypsy woman." An adventuress.

bretonner: To stammer; to speak unintelligibly (ex *Breton*).

bulgare: "Bulgarian." Huge, enormous. Probably from a play of words on *Bulgare* and *bougre* (buggerish, devilish, brutish).

camarade, faire: To give oneself up. From the cry *Kamerad,* when a German was caught up with.

capote anglaise: "English hood." A condom.

castille: "Castile." A quarrel, bickering. *Chercher castille à quelqu'un*—to pick a quarrel with someone. *Être en castille* —to be at loggerheads.

chausettes russes: Rags wound around (Russian) soldiers' feet. *Porter des chausettes russes* is just another way of saying "wearing no socks."

chine: "China." A loan of an article, usually not to be returned; a cadge (*slang*).

chiner: "To China." 1. To toil and moil. 2. To rip up, to chaff; to poke fun at. 3. To carry a load (on the back). 4. To palm off (something). 5. To cadge (cigarettes, a drink, etc.).

chineur (se): "A Chink." 1. One who criticizes malevolently on a cultural level. 2. A hard-worked laborer. 3. A worker who peddles his own wares. The sense, colloquial, is probably derived from the coolie. *chineur de la haute*—"classy Chink." A "has-been" who, in straits, capitalizes on his former connections, in selling his wares (*colloquialism* or *slang*).

chinois: "The Chinese." Cafeteria (*colloquialism*).

chinoiser: "To Chinee." To jabber, talk gibberish, cant or slang, double talk (*underworld slang*).

chinoiserie: *1.* A Chinese knick-knack or curio. *2.* A mean trick (*colloquialism*).

chinoiserie de bureau: Red tape.

choucroutemane: A German, literally a *Sauerkrauter*.

cosaque, monter comme un: "To mount like a Cossack." To make a skillful rider. In an ironical sense, to mount a horse awkwardly.

cosaque, poste à la: "Cossack-post" in the army. An insignificant and irregular job.

cosaquerie: "Cossackry." A sudden intrusion of rowdies, resulting in pillage.

Cracovie, venir de: Also *avoir ses lettres de Cracovie.* "To come from Cracow." "To have letters patent from Cracow." To play the braggart. The fact that *craquer* means to bluff, and Cracow was the old capital of pompous Poland accounts for the idiom.

dasticotter: To use German. From "das dich Gott," The favorite unfinished imprecation in Germany.

débauche grecque: "A Greek orgy." Pederasty.

écossais, fier comme un: Haughty as a Scotchman.

écossais, être en: "To be in a Scotch plight." To be down at the heel, to be reduced to the point of starvation. See also *hospitalité écossaise.*

Égypte, affaires d': "Egyptian" or "Gypsy affairs." Smuggling, thieving. [MÉRIMÉE in *Carmen*].

Égyptien: "An Egyptian." A Gypsy; a vagabond.

Espagne, châteaux en: "Castles in Spain." All sorts of fantastic schemes; castles in the air.

espagnol: "A Spaniard." When uncapitalized it popularly refers to a louse.

espagnole, parler français comme une vache: "To speak French like a Spanish cow." To speak so as to butcher the language. Gottschalk, in his *Die sprichwörtliche Redensarten der französischen Sprache* (page 63) believes *vache*, in this case, to be a corruption of *vacce*, through *vasco*—Basque, changed to *vacco*. The original proverb, then, would mean "He speaks French like a Spanish Basque." This sounds plausible enough, in view of the linguistic remoteness of Basque from both French and Spanish.

espagnol, ventre à l': "Spanish belly" *i.e.* swelling from starvation.

espagnole: Uncapitalized the word, which should mean a Spanish woman or girl, is colloquially intended to designate a flea.

faire Flandre: "To make Flanders." To become a bankrupt.

faire suisse: "To do it the Swiss way." To drink by oneself or in seclusion.

feu persan: "Persian fire." Erysipelas.

flamingue, espèce de: "Flemish kind." 1. An insincere person. 2. One who speaks French badly.

flaminguer: "To 'Flemish'." To speak without sincerity.

Flandre, aller en ⌐ sans couteau: "To go to Flanders without a knife." To go somewhere or undertake anything without the necessary preparations. The saying stems from the fact that guests at the inns in Flanders were expected to bring their own knives.

Flandre, être en: "To be in Flanders." To be a goner; to "go gaga" on someone.
See also *faire Flandre.*

Flandrin: "An inhabitant of Flanders." A sluggard, and often, a simpleton as in the phrase *"grand flandrin."*

flandrin: "A Fleming." A lummox, a large flabby man without energy or "pep."

frise: "Curley-pated." A Jew (*slang*).

fransquillon: A non-French Francophile; one who toadies to the French and exalts their culture (*Belgian-French colloquialism*).

gabaï: (*Gascon* vs. *Northern French*). A glutton.

gascon, faire la lessive du: "To do the soaping of a Gascon." To turn one's soiled shirt inside out, before wearing it again. The Gascons were regarded as a different national element by the Northern Frenchmen, and they were. Cf. Renan's statement (in his *Souvenirs d'enfance et de jeunesse*) that he was partly a Gascon, and partly a Breton.

gasconnade: Bravado; braggadochio; bluff.

germanie, aller en. To alter, repair remodel, adapt, fix up, "doctor." The play of words *je r'manie* and *je remanie* (I re-shape) is at the bottom of this slang locution.

grec: "A Greek." A sharper at cards, a "chiseler," a crook. The word had a similar connotation in England during the seven-teenth and eighteenth centuries. "Grec" denotes also an in-dividual who would not tip for services. Cf. *anglais*.

grec, c'est du: It's all Greek to me.

grec, être ↰ en: "To be a Greek at . . ." To be a shark at . . . In Corneille we find the line, *l'amour, j'y suis grec*.

Grèce: Besides signifying Greece, it also means, in slang, the *world* of *racketeers*, the underworld.

grecquerie: Greediness.

grecque, vivre à la: To live in grand style.

grecque, vol à la: "Greek theft," *i.e.*, a confidence game. See also *agraco* and *débauche grecque*.

guinol: A Jew. Probably from the Italian slang *guino*, q. v. (*slang*).

hâbler: To speak in Spanish style (from Spanish *hablar*—to speak) *i.e.* to swagger, to "talk big."

hacher de la paille: "To chop straw." To talk German; to jabber.

haut allemand.: "High German." *C'est du haut allemand pour moi* means I can't make head or tail of it.

hébreu, c'est de l' ⌐ pour moi: "This is Hebrew to me." It's all Greek to me.

Hollande, râpé comme la: Shabby like Holland.

hongrer: "To 'Hungary'." To geld a horse.

hospitalité écossaise: Scotch hospitality. To some it denotes a niggardliness, but the French usually are impressed with the cordiality of a Scotch reception, and use the phrase in a positive sense.

indien, faire l'échange de l': "To make an Indian exchange." To give something practically worthless in lieu of something valuable.

indienne: "Indian." Clothes (*underworld slang*).

irlandaise, banquette: "Irish banquette." A snag in a horse-race (*colloquialism*).

irlandaise, prendre des ris à l': "To take in a reef after the Irish fashion." To handle the sails recklessly, often slashing them.

Iroquois: "An Iroquois." A perverse individual, whose actions make no sense.

Iroquois, parler français comme un: To talk an atrocious French.

Italien: "An Italian." A jealous person.

italique, avoir pincé son: To have one's Italian (leg) caught. Not to be able to walk straight, from drinking (*slang*).

italiques, avoir les jambes: "To have Italian legs." To be bandy-legged. The slant of the italic type may have something to do with this slur.

judaïser: "To do a Judas act." To betray (*slang*).

judasserie: "A Judas trick." An overwhelming demonstration (*slang*).

Judée, la petite: The prefecture of police in Paris about a century ago, probably because it happened to be situated on Rue de Jérusalem (*slang*).

juif: "Jew." 1. A money-lender. 2. A hammer-head shark. 3. A swift (*ornithology*).

juif, c'est un ↰ errant: "That's a wandering Jew." That fellow can never settle down. He has the *Wanderlust*.

juif, le petit: "The little Jew," i. e. the funny bone (*slang*).

juiverie: "Jewish quarter," "Jewry," "Jewish stunt," usury. *Il m'a fait une juiverie.* He has played me a dirty trick.

jus de réglisse: "Liquorice juice." A Negro.

Lapon: "A Lapp," "Laplander." A dwarfish person.

Latin: "Latin." Slang (*slang*). Cf. *Peddlar's Greek; excuse my French.*

lifrelofe: A Swiss, because his speech seems to consist of such sounds (*slang*).

Lombard: "An Italian from Lombardy," extended to all Italians. A usurer; a coward.

Lombard, boucon du: "A Lombard's mouthful." Poison.

Macaroni: An Italian.

macédoine: "A 'Macedony'." A literary miscellany, often a hodge-podge.

mal florentin: "Florentine disease." Syphilis, or any venereal disease.

maroquin: "A Moroccan." A fierce sot.

maroquin: "Morocco" leather. The face. *On lui donnera sur le maroquin*—He'll get his fizz knocked in.

More, être pris comme le: "To be taken in like the Moor." To be outwitted when least expecting it.

nègre (négresse): "A Negro (Negress)." *1.* A drudge, facto-tum, ghost-writer, hack, 'do-all'. *Il me faut un nègre—I* need someone to do the donkey-work. *2.* A fish of the mackerel variety. *3.* A satyr butterfly. *4.* A monkey.

nègre, c'est le: That's a knockout, a wow, a pippin, *the* thing. *Nègre* seems to be a corruption of *nec* from *nec plus ultra* (*student slang*).

nègre, parler petit: "To speak a bit of niggerish."

négresse: "A Negro woman." *1.* A flea; a bug. *2.* A bottle of red wine. *Une négresse morte* is not a dead Negro woman, but an empty bottle (*slang*).

négrier: *1.* A slave-trader. *2.* A slave-ship.

négrerie: "Negro quarters." A barracoon; a slave compound or enclosure.

négrillon: "Pickaninny." A swarthy youngster; a child with a soiled face.

normand: A sly fox. When capitalized, "a Norman."

normand, réponse de: An evasive answer.

norois: "Norwegian." High-handed, overbearing (*Old French*).

onguent napolitain: "Neapolitan ointment." A salve, the active ingredient of which is mercury, used in the treatment of syphilis, which the French and the Spanish call "the Naples disease."

Ostrogoth: An uncouth or crude individual of either sex.

ours du nord: "The Northern bear." The German. (KÜFFNER, who cites Kriegk, thinks it is a reference to German industry).

Panama: A financial bubble; a stock fizzle, a shady deal on a large scale. *Ex* the Panama scandal.

pays-bas: "Netherlands." The genital organs (*slang*).

Pékin: "Peking." *1.* A civilian, through the eyes of a warrior. *2.* A bourgeois. *Etre en pékin*—to be in civies or mufti.

Perse, des rideaux de: "Persian curtains." Curtains with holes acquired from wear. The play of words between *percé* (pierced) and *Perse* is quite clear (*slang*).

Picard, ressembler le: "To be like the Picard." (*i. e.,* from Picardy). To keep out of danger; to be on the safe side.

picart: "A Picard." A rogue; a man who lives by his wits.

polonais: "A Pole." A bouncer in a disorderly house.

polonais, soûl comme un: "Full as a Polack." Disgustingly drunk.

portugal: A poor horseman, in the phrase *une entrée de portugal* (*colloquialism*).

Prusse, je m'en moque comme du roi de: "I care about it as much as about the King of Prussia." I don't give a hang about it.

Prusse, faire une: "To do a Prussia." To be dead drunk.

Prusse, travailler pour le roi de: "To work for the King of Prussia." To slave without getting anything for it.

prussien: "Prussian." The seat of the pants. Thus, *exhiber son prussien* denotes to scamper off in headlong flight.

prussiens: "The Prussians." Syphilis (in retaliation for the word, *Franzosen*, which means the same thing in German).

rabougris: *"re-Bulgarized"* (ex *bulgare*). Of arrested growth; stunted.

rastaquouère: A South American parvenu making himself obnoxious by squandering his money ostentatiously.

rosbif: An Englishman. The origin is obviously from *roastbeef* Cf. *macaroni*.

romain, e: "A Roman." A hired applauder in a theatre.

romaine: "A roman *object*." A "lecture," a rebuke.

Rome, aller à: to get a lacing.

Russe: "A Russian." One who poses as a nobleman.

Scythe: "A Scythian." A coarse and ruthless person from beyond civilization.

secours vénitien: "Venetian aid." Help that has come too late. Sometimes the adjective is *lombardien*.

sénégalais, il est: "He is a Senegalese." He is dead drunk (*slang of the poilu*).

Siamois, les: "The Siamese (twins)." The testicles. The semantics is obvious.

siamoise: "Siamese." A sort of bug.

stockfish: An Englishman (*slang*).

Suède, aller en: "To go to Sweden." To take the sweating cure for syphilis. The play of words between *Suède* (Sweden) and *suer* (to sweat) is responsible for the playful euphemism in literary quarters.

suisse, fumer comme un: To smoke like a chimney.

suisse, n'entendre plus raison qu'un: See under *Proverbs and Sayings* (Swiss section).

suisse, penser à la: "To think in Swiss fashion." To be daydreaming; to be plunged in a brown study.

suisse, rêver à la: "To dream in Swiss fashion," *i. e.* with gaping mouth and bulging eyes

suisse, un amiral: "A Swiss admiral." A naval officer who has never been to sea. The English have adopted this phrase.

suisse, ventre: "A Swiss belly." A large paunch (because the porter just drinks, eats, and smokes).

suisserie: "Switzery." The hotel porter's lodge.

tartare: "A Tartar." A military chamberlain, because of the looting done while his master, the king, is away fighting.

tête-de-Turc: The butt or "niggerhead" at fairs and amusement parks; dodger. Whipping boy.

Thébaïde: "Thebaid," an Egyptian retreat of early Christian monks. Deep solitude; mentally desolate state.

Tombouctou: "Timbuctoo." Some God-forsaken spot at the other end of the world.

Turc: "A Turk." 1. A jeweller's tool. 2. A tinker's iron. 3. A Touranian (*underworld slang*).

turc, (que): "Turk-like." Harsh, predatory, unyielding. *Traiter quelqu'un de Turc à Maure* is to abuse one frightfully; literally "to treat one as a Turk would a Moor."

turc, face du grand-: The posterior (*antiphrastically*).

turque, installation à la: A toilet without a seat (*slang*). See also *tête-de-Turc*.

Venise, secours de: Assistance that has come too late.

youdi: A Jew (*slang*).

youpin,(e): A Jew (*slang*).

youtre: A Jew (*slang*).

GERMAN ETHNOPHAULISMS
(Including Austrian and Swiss Dialects)

Amerikanismus: A materialistic, utilitarian, or commercial point of view.

aegyptische Finsternis: "Egyptian darkness." One of the plagues related in the Bible.

altfränkisch: "Old Frankish." Outmoded, ancient, (*figuratively*).

balkanische Zustände: "Balkan conditions." Continual disorder.

Bemsche (*provincial*): "Czech." A scalawag, scamp (*jocose*).

Biemschen (*Sudeten dialect*): "Czechs," in a derogatory sense.

blesch Arbet (*Carpathian Saxon dialect*): "Wallachian (Rumanian) work." A botched job.

Böhm (*Austrian vs. Czechs*): "A Bohemian." A tartar, as in "*O, du Böhm!*"

böhmakeln: To speak with a Czech accent or intonation (*slang*).

böhmische Dörfer: "Bohemian villages," whose names sound so unpronounceable to a German. Impossible or strange things.

Böhmsche (*dialect*): "A Czech woman." A gaudily dressed woman.

Chineser: "Chinaman." An impractical, inefficient, or daydreaming fellow; a schlemihl (*colloquialism*).

deutscher (teutscher) Baccalaureus: "A German graduate." An ignoramus and boor.

Engländer: "An Englishman." A creditor.

englisch, sich ↰ empfehlen: To take French leave.

englische Krankheit: Rickets.

Fidschiinsulaner: "Fiji Islander." The wild man of Borneo.

flandrische Liebe: "Flanders love." Fickle affection; a short-lived bond.

Franzose, fluchen wie ein: To swear ("like a Frenchman")—like a trooper.

Franzos: "Frenchman." Monkey wrench.

Franzosen: "Frenchmen." Cockroaches. (A bit of revenge on the part of the Germans for the almost universal Prussianizing of the kitchen pest.)

Französelei: "Frenchification." Aping French manners.

französischen Abschied nehmen: To take French leave.

französische Krankheit: *Morbus Gallicus;* syphilis.

Franzosenwurm: "French worm." A skin disease in horses.

Froschesser: "Frog-eater." A Frenchman.

Griechenland? Wie steht's um: "How about Greece?" How's your girl-friend? Have you a girl-friend? (*Student slang*).

Gudde or **Guddas:** A Pole, Lithuanian, or Russian, as in the proverb "When the Prussian speaks, it is for the Gudde to be silent." It is evidently a nickname for an Eastern (Northern) Slav.

Holland, in ⌐ sein. "To be in Holland." To be in debtor's jail. Another expression is *"nach Holland reisen."* In Stettin, the jail happened to stand on the site of a Dutch windmill, but the French *faire un tour en Belgique,"* i.e., to become bankrupt, is similar only by coincidence.

Holland, nun ist ⌐ in Not: "And now the Dutch are in distress." Well, we certainly are in a pickle, "in dutch"; we are "in for it." (The imminent breaking down of the dykes and dams to avert invasion is the basis for this phrase.)

Holland und Brabant versprechen: To make golden promises; to deceive oneself.

Holländer, wie ein ⌐ auskratzen (or **laufen,** or **durchgehen**): "To scurry away like a Dutchman." To run as fast as one's legs will carry one.

Holländerei: 1. Dairy-farming. 2. A high bosom. *Sie hat eine tüchtige Holländerei* — she has a fine bookrest (*slang*).

holländern: To manage, or rather mismanage, foolishly. The word *ausgeholländert* means to become ruined financially through poor management.

Indianerarbeit: "Indian work." A childishly slow or botched job. The slur is of Peruvian origin.

Indianergeheul: "Indian cries." Infernal howling, pandemonium.

Jargonsprache: "Jargon language." Yiddish [LÜCK: *Der Mythos*, etc., page 105].

Jauk (*Austrian dialect* vs. *Slovenes*): Wind coming from the South of Kärnthen. The word is intended as an insult to the Slovenes. Ex *Jauche* (suds or ditch-water)?

Jud: Jew (*common slang*).

Judaskuss: "Kiss of Judas." A betraying kiss.

Jude, ewiger: "Eternal Jew." A wandering Jew. "*Er ist schon ein ewiger Jude*" — "he can't stay put."

Jüdelei: Jewish ways, practices, or idiom; "chiseling."

jüdeln: 1. To live like a Jew. 2. To bargain, to jew. 3. To talk like a Jew.

Juden: "Jews." The jitters; fright (*student slang*).

Juden, einen ⌐ anhängen: "To fasten a Jew on someone." To give one the lie; to show someone up.

Judenangst: "Jew anxiety." The phrase "*Judenangst ausstande haben*" i.e., to endure that specific Jewish anguish, we read in a compilation of 1870, dates from the time of Jewish perse-cution (?!)

Judenapfel: "Jew apple." Adam's apple.

Judenbart: "Jewish beard" (goat's beard). *Wandering Jew* or sailor-plant.

Juden, einen ⌐ begraben: "To bury a Jew." To make ink-blots.

Judenbengel: Jewish youth, mockie, smouch, Ikey.

Judenbeifuss: Judean wormwood.

Judenbeinchen: "Jewbone." The funny bone.

Judenblatt: "Jewish paper." Any newspaper favoring or sympathizing with Jews.

Judenbude: "Jew-hut"; "Jew-den." A name applied familiarly by the Nazis to the huge crate or box in which the Jews, permitted to emigrate, during the early part of the Hitler Walpurgis night, would pack all their chattels, including massive furniture, in readiness for transportation to friendlier countries. The proper word for this container is *Lift* (probably from the English for "elevator").

Judenbusch: Jew-bush.

Juden Christtag, auf den: "Jewish Christmas." Never.

Judendeutsch: "Jew-German." Yiddish (which Goethe called "baroque"), gibberish.

Judendorn: "Jew-thorn." Jujube.

Judenfenster: "Jew-window." Four (in dice).

Judengesicht : Jewish physiognomy. The slur is in the formation of the word, analogous to the English "Jew physiognomy."

Judengesind(el): "Jew rabble." A pack of Jews.

Jundenglanz: "Jew-shine." The gloss of old clothes.

Judenhaar: "Jew-hair." The down babies show at birth. This appears to be an Austrian word.

Judenhänger: "Jew-hanger." The Wiltau inhabitants in the Ziller valley would be called thus because of a charming custom they had of raising a red flag on the mast of the church steeple, but when a flag was not available, a Jew would take its place.

Judenharz: "Jew-resin." Bitumen.

Judenheller: "A Jew-farthing." A worthless coin as in the saying "he is not worth a Jewish farthing."

Judenkirsche: "Jew-cherry." Winter-cherry, alkekengi.

Judenleim: Jew's-lime.

Judenmünze: "Jew-coin." *Pecunia accisa;* a special tax for the crime of being born a Jew.

Judenpack: "Pack of Jews;" Jewish rabble.

Judenpech: "Jew-pitch." See *Judenharz.*

Judenpfeffer: "Jew-pepper." Jamaica pepper.

Judenschule, ein Lärm wie in der: "A commotion like in a synagogue, *i. e.,* a regular hubbub or uproar, bedlam, hell broken loose.

Judenschwamm: Jewish fungus.

Judenspiess: "Jew-lance." Usury. A very common word in some of the older anti-Semitic literature.

Judentücke: A Jew trick.

Judenwitz: "A Jew joke." Biting sarcasm.

Judenwürfel: "Jewish die." *Er ist ein Judenwürfel*—he is pointed on all sides. This lead top is a toy for both young and old on the Feast of Lights.

judenzen: "To Judaize." To act like a Jew.

Judenzopf: "Jew-braid." Polish plait; *Plica Polonica.*

Juderei. Jewish manners; speech; usury.

Judhanf: Jute-yarn. The linguistic principle seemed to be. "If in doubt, dump it on the Jew."

jüdische Hast: "Jewish hurry." Unnecessary haste. The phrase "*Nur keine jüdische Hast,*" may be translated "Where's the fire? What's the rush?"

kaiserliche (*Swiss* vs. *Austrians*): "The Imperial." Austrian.

The slur is on the doting admirers of the Austrian emperor, whose imperial "this" and imperial "that" were always symbols in the minds of the Austrians.

Kasblooch (*Carpathian Saxon* vs. *Rumanians*) : "Cheese Wallachian." A cheap Rumanian.

kaschubsch (*dialect*) : "Kashubish." Not functioning; a poor fit. *Ex* the West Slavic tribe, Kashubes, living in Pomerania.

Katzelmacher: An Italian. After the first World War, the Italians, because of their about-turn in joining the Allies, were very unpopular in both Austria and Germany. A macaronic doggerel, circulating widely then, expresses this contempt in allusion to the organ-grinder's trade.

> *Italiano,*
> *Nix in la mano,*
> *Caccelimacca,*
> *Drecco in sacca.*

Kauderwelsch: "Corrupt Welsh." An outlandish jargon or cant. Our own *Welsh* originally too, meant "alien" or "foreign" in Anglo-Saxon. The Welsh call themselves *Cymry*. Welsh, in the sense of alien, however, was a name given centuries ago to Italians and other Latin peoples.

Krowot (*Austrian* vs. *Croats*) : "Croat." A reckless adventurer; a ne'er-do-well (*slang*).

Lause-Wenzel: "Louse Wenceslaus." *1.* A tatterdemalion; a knave. *2.* Foul tobacco. The slur is against the Czechs, because Wenceslaus is their patron saint. The last syllable of the name possibly suggested the offensive application.

lampartisch Tükki: Lombardian knavery.

Litauer: "Lithuanian." A jackdaw (because of the *kr* sounds in the Lithuanian language).

Magyarsky: Hungarian (*jocose*).

mauscheln: To speak with a Jewish accent or intonation; or in Yiddish.

Mohren: "Moors." Anxiety, terror—"*Er hat Mohren*"—he has the jitters (*student slang*).

Miklos: A Hungarian. *Ex* the commonness of this given name in Hungary.

Módjorbitschko (*Carpathian German dialect*): "Hungarian knifer." An impetuous or fly-off-the-handle person.

nordische List (*Austrian* vs. *Prussian*): Nordic cunning.

Normann: "A Norman." A crafty fellow; a fox.

oesterreichische Wirtschaft: "Austrian management." Carelessness, inefficiency.

palätschen (*Saxon dialect*): To jabber Polish.

palatschkern (*Silesian dialect*): See *palätschen.*

pallebratsch reden: To speak too familiarly, as the Poles are supposed to do. Ex Polish *panie bracie* ("sir brother").

Piefke (*Austrian* vs. *German*): A German (*slang*). The formation sounds like that in a number of Prussian names ending in a cacophonous syllable

poalsch (*dialect*): "Polish." Clumsy; clownish.

Polack: 1. A "Polack." 2. A polish horse. 3. A kind of potato. 4. A flogging on the posterior. 5. Dregs in a glass or in a pipe. 6. A carved fowl. 7. A vagabond (*police slang*). 8. A kind of fish (*Pollack?*).

Polack, er schlägt: He beats his chest crosswise, as when chilled.

Polacke, pralichter: The swaggering Polack (*archaism,* 17-18th century).

Polackei: "Polanderland." Poledom. "Ein Pole aus Polackei"— "a dyed-in-the-wool Pole" will be found in HEINE.

Pole, falsch wie ein: Insincere like a Pole.

polisch, das kommt mir ⌐ vor (*Bavarianism*) : That looks goofy to me.

polnisch, auf ⌐ beenden: "To finish in Polish manner." To leave something in the air; to leave loose ends.

polnisch aussehen: "To look Polish." To be dressed in gay attire.

polnische Brücke: "Polish bridge." A treacherous contraption hanging on a thread.

polnische Höflichkeit: "Polish politeness." Ceremonialism; unctuousness.

polnischen Bogen, im ⌐ (berechnen): "To compute on the Polish sheet." To make a superficial calculation.

polnischen, einen ⌐ machen: "To do a Polish." To blow one's nose into the hand.

polnische Nudel: "A Polish ball of fat." A slovenly woman.

polnischen Urlaub nehmen: "To take Polish leave." To absent oneself from work.

polnischer Abschied: "Polish leave." Equivalent to "French leave" in the English phrase. *Den polnischen Abschied nehmen* or *mit polnischem Abschied weggehen* means "to slip away on the quiet."

polnischer Bock: "Polish billygoat." A bagpipe.

polnischer Reichstag: "Polish Parliament." Reign of confusion; bedlam.

polnischer Wechsel: "Polish note." A monthly note for a trifling sum among poor students.

polnisches Geschnatter: "Polish cackling." Polish as spoken.

polnische Wirtschaft: "Polish management." A disorderly household; inefficiency.

polsch Botter (*East Prussianism*) : "Polish butter." Salt on bread.

Polsche (*dialect*) : "A Polish woman." A slut.

polsche Hering (*dialect*): Diluted vinegar and onions with imaginary herring.

polschen Bock, in den ⌐ spannen (*dialect*): "To stretch into the Polish goat" *i. e.*, bagpipe. To drive someone against the wall.

poolsches Mosta, e (*Silesianism*): "A Polish pattern." A loud design.

preussisch: "Prussian." Aloof; not on speaking terms after a tiff; rude, irascible.

preussische Zustände: "Prussian conditions." Roughshod treatment; rigorous rules.

Pulke (*dialect*): "A 'Polackess'." A slattern.

pulsche Hacke: (*dialect*): Polish heel, applied often to the Water-Pole (bordering on the Baltic).

Quatschkowski: A Polish chatterbox (*slang*).

Ratt-und-Mäusefaller: "Rat and mouse trappers." Slovaks, because in North Germany they peddled these appliances.

Rotwelsch: See *Kauderwelsch*.

Russe: 1. Russian. 2. The black beetle. 3. A cockroach (in return for the Russians calling cockroaches "*Prussaki*"). 4. A glutton for punishment. *Der ist ein Russe* may be rendered as "That man will stand anything" or is "as tough as they make 'em."

russischen Adler machen, den: "To do the Russian eagle." To turn one's back (upon someone). The imperial eagle was a two-headed creature.

Scheissfranzose: Muck Frenchman; a little sh- of a Frenchman.

schwabeln: "To talk like the Swabians." To engage in silly chatter and talk fast (*colloquial*).

Schwabenalter: "Swabian age." The age of forty, before which according to the other Germans, a Swabian has no sense.

Schwabensprung: "A Swabian jump." A short distance, as it were.

Schweize (*Swiss dialect*): "A spiced butter-sauce." *Eine lange Schweize* (or *Schweizi*)—a long-winded explanation, a rigmarole, often without rhyme or reason. In the provincial Swiss dialect, *mache Schwai(t)zi* means "to lay it on thick," "to give taffy."

Schweizerbart: "A Swiss beard." A profuse growth of hair on the chin; "alfalfa," a flowing beard.

Schweizerblut: "Swiss blood." A sort of wine.

Schweizerdegen: "A Swiss sword"—a weapon half way between a sword and a knife, used in combat at close quarters. A pressman who is also a compositor; a twicer, one who "doubles in brass."

Schweizerhieb: "A Swiss stroke." A hefty blow.

Schweizerkrankheit: "Swiss malady." Home-sickness; nostalgia.

schweizer Meile: "A Swiss mile." A short mile.

Schwaben: (*Austrian* vs. *Swabian*) Cockroaches. The Prussians have sometimes adopted that nickname too. Probably the similarity between *Schaben* (*Küchenschaben,* i. e., kitchen roaches) and *Schwaben* has led to this slur.

Schwabenstreich: "Swabian trick." A stupid prank.

Schwedenkopf: "The head of a Swede." Closely cropped hair.

Schwedentrunk (trank): "Swedish drink." An allusion to the story that the Swedes during the Thirty Years' War would pour ditch water down the throat of their German prisoners and would then tread on their bellies.

schwedische Gardinen: "Swedish curtains (blinds)." Prison bars made of Swedish iron.

Schwelemer: A Gypsy (*cant*).

spanische Dörfer: "Spanish villages." Queer places.

spanische Krankheit: "Spanish disease." Syphilis.

spanische Nudeln: "Spanish noodles." A sound flogging; a round trouncing.

spanischer Ernst: "Spanish seriousness." Exaggerated gravity of mien.

spanischer Kragen: "A Spanish collar." *1.* Strangulation of the *glans penis.* *2.* The complete wrapping up of a patient in wet blankets (*hydrotherapy*).

spanischer Reiter: "Spanish rider." *Cheval-de-frise;* in fortification, a heavy bar traversed by stakes, often surrounded by barbed wire, serving as a barricade or used to close a breach. The shape of the contrivance suggests a horse and rider.

spanischer Ritt: "Spanish ride." See *spanische Nudeln.*

spanischer Stiefel: The Spanish boot. (A torture instrument).

spanisches Gesicht machen: "To make a Spanish face." To affect an over-dignified air; to show indifference or aloofness.

spanisches Kreuz: "Spanish cross." In lovemaking, a style of kissing. *Spanische Kreuze drücken* means to describe a cross by kissing a woman on the forehead, on the two cheeks, and on the mouth.

Spanischfliegenpflaster: "Spanish-fly plaster." A blister.

spanisch vor, das kommt mir: "This sounds Spanish to me." This is all Greek to me; I can't fathom that.

St. Simon Jüd: "St. Simon the Jew"—October 28—supposed to be a cold and dreary day, as the proverb "St. Simon the Jew brings the winter before it's due" (*St. Simon Jüd bringt den Winter unter die Lüt*) [i.e., *Leute*] would indicate. Also the day is regarded as an ominous one.

Stinkjude: "A stinking Jew." According to Lück, this expression is current in all Germany. With sardonic cynicism, Lück (page 154 of his *Der deutsche Mythos,* etc.) adds that "as soon as he embraces Christianity, he naturally ceases to stink."

Suppenschwabe: "A soup-Swabian." Anyone who is very fond of soup.

Switzer: A personal guard. *Ex* the fact that many monarchs retained Swiss mercenaries for this purpose.

Szkeber, Szkieber: A Pole, in a derogatory sense.

Tatarennachricht: "A Tartar (or really Gypsy) report." A canard. This word received its vogue at the time of the Crimean War, when the Gypsies spread the unfounded news, in 1854, that the fortress of Malakoff was taken by the Allies.

Tschechuzen (*Sudeten dialect*): Czechs, always pejoratively.

Türkenwein: "Turkish wine." Sour wine. In 1529, when the Turks were besieging Vienna, the winter was almost unbear-ably cold, the suffering was great, and not only the wine but even the vegetation seemed to turn sour and the word was thus applied to everything that was disappointing.

Türkenkopf: "Turk's head." The face on a pipe.

wallachen: "To Wallach." To geld. (Gelding beasts was com-mon in Rumania).

welsche Treue: "Italian faith." Treachery.

welsches Süpplein: "Italian broth." Poison.

(Modern) GREEK DEROGATIVES
(Except for those words which contain letters without equivalents in the Latin alphabet, the Greek terms have been transliterated).

Βλάχος: "A Rumanian." A herdsman.

Βουλγάρος: "Bulgarian." Crude, cruel.

βρωμόβλαχος: "Stench-Wallachian." A Rumanian, particularly

one from the province, who uses a dialect and cannot understand the literary language.

γαλλίζω: To affect French manners.

gállos: "A turkey." A generic slur-word including Frenchmen
(because of the resemblance in sound of the names?) and
Americans, also Canadians.

Gouroúni: "Pig." A Turk.

'ebraíico pazári: "Jewish bazaar." A haggling-place.

'Ebraîos: "A Jew," "Jewish." Stingy.

Ἑβραῖος, φωνάζει 'σαν: "He cries out like a Jew." He howls before he is hurt. [KYRIAKIDES].

Kinézos: "A Chinaman." A 'queer duck'; an erratic or unpre-
dictable fellow.

Κουτσόβλαχος: "Lame Wallachian." A Rumanian, especially
one who speaks the dialect only.

makaronàs: "Macaroni." An Italian.

philárgyros: "money-lover." A Jew.

tokoglýphos: "Usurer." A Jew.

τσίφούτης: "miser," "skinflint." A Jew.

τσιγγούνης: "A Jew." The origin of this ethnophaulism, used
mainly in Salonica, seems to be the Turkish word, *chifut*—
a greedy person [Kl]. The classical Greek word for Jew
is 'Ιουδαῖος.

tsiphoutià: 1. Jewishness. 2. Mean trickery. 3. Greed.

tsiphoútia (*pl.*): Poppets, *i.e.,* timber props in a boat. [KYRIA-
KIDES].

Tourkogýftos: "A Turk-Gypsy." An Armenian.

Toúrkos: "Turkish." Impudent; rough, fierce.

zoúrnas: 1. A primitive musical instrument, the bottom of which
resembles the mouth and snout of a pig. 2. A Turk.

HUNGARIAN ETHNOPHAULISMS

amerikázni: "To American." To loaf on the job while pre-tending to work hard (*slang*).

angolkór: "English malady." Rickets.

angolosan távozni: To leave the English way. To take French leave.

bakszász: "The buck Saxon." A German.

büdös oláh: "A stinking Wallach." A foul Rumanian.

buta tót: The stupid Slovak.

cigányhal: "gypsyfish." Tench (a species of fish known for its tenacity of life).

cigánykereket hányni: "Throwing Gypsy-wheels." Turning somersaults sideways.

cigánykodni: "to act the Gypsy." To haggle; to cheat.

cigányság (cigánykodás): "Gypsydom (Gypsery)." Petty trickery; deceit.

cigánytégla: "Gypsy-brick." Brick burnt in a clamp.

cigányútra téved: "To err onto the Gypsy way." To get food or drink into the windpipe.

csehül áll: "He stands in a Czech way." He is in a bad way, going "to the dogs."

csehül van: "He is in a Czech way." He is going from bad to worse.

drotos tótok: "A wire Slav." A tinker.

franc (*short for "francia"*): "French." Syphilis (*slang*).

hunczut mint a német: He is as crafty as a German. (Usually said of a swindler).

kínabor: "China wine." Quinine wine.

kína-ezüst: "China silver." Silver-plated metal.

kínai, ez nekem: "That's Chinese to me." That's Greek to me.

kutyafejü tatár: "Dogheaded Tartar." An uncouth barbarian.

német-has: "German bowel." Diarrhea.

német rák: "German crab." A toad.

órült spanyol: "Mad Spaniard." A "Tartar;" an unruly person (colloquialism).

russzni: "Russian." 1. A small spiced fish. 2. A bug (colloquialism).

spanyol nátha: "Spanish cold." Influenza epidemic, especially after the first World War.

sváb (sváb-bogár): "Swabian (Swabian beetle)" A cockroach; a black beetle.

szegény tatár: "Poor Tartar." The poor devil.

törökot fogtam: "I caught a Turk." An achievement of doubtful value.

törökülés: "Turkish seat." Sitting crosslegged on the floor.

vigyen el a tatár: "The Tartar take you!" The devil take you!

ICELANDIC SLUR-LOCUTIONS

danskan, eiga ekki ↪ túskilding: "Not to have even a Danish two-shilling." Not to have a red copper; to be broke.

djöflaþýzka: "The devil's German." Gabble; any foreign speech; a language badly spoken.

finnabrækur: "Finnish pants." A dead man's breeches.

finnagaldur: Finnish witchery.

fransós: "French disease," Syphilis.

gyðingur: "Jew." A shrewd dealer; a profiteer.

hundtyrki: "Dog-Turk." A scoundrel.

spánska veikin: "Spanish disease," Influenza.

ITALIAN SLUR-LOCUTIONS

americanacci: Italians who have lived in America.

americanata: "An American stunt." A play for publicity; an advertising scheme (slang).

carpio: A Spaniard (slang).

ebreaccio: See Ebreuzzo.

ebreuzzo: A Jew, in the pejorative sense (slang).

fede greca: "Greek faith." Unfaithfulness; disloyalty.

francese, mal: "French disease." Syphilis.

francese, partirsi alla: To take French leave. Thus the Italians show their neutrality toward the French and the English by playing off each other's taunt against both.

franceseria: An aping of French mannerisms or customs.

francesume: Frenchism, rather than Gallicism (used pejora-tively).

francisinu: A swell, a fop (Sicilian colloquialism).

germanismo, affetti di: Imbued with the German doctrine.

germanismo, portare il ↢ in Polonia: To bring the despotic rule to Poland. [PETRÒCCHI].

giudaicamente: "In Jewish manner." Rigorously; cruelly; cling-ing to the letter of the law. (ZINGARELLI's Vocabolario della lingua Italiana). Pagare giudaicamente—"To pay in Jewish fashion" i. e., to be very close; to consider every penny.

Guidea, noto in: "Well-known in Judea." Notorious.

giudeaccio: A Jew; a kike (*slang*).

giudeo: "Jew." A usurer. A hard-hearted person; an obstinate or incredulous individual. *Trattar peggio d'un giudeo:* "To treat one worse than a Jew." To deal ruthlessly.

giudesco: Jewish (in pejorative sense); kikish.

greca: See *Fede Greca*.

grecastro: A person born in Greece, although not of Greek descent.

grechesco (grecesco): Greek (*jocose*).

guino: A Jew. Compare *guinol* in French (*slang*).

indiano, far l': "To 'throw a Hindu'." To simulate ignorance. Compare *far l'inglese*.

inglese: "An Englishman" (derivatively *American* too). An easymark, prosperous and ready to spend, as a good many American and English tourists have been considered to be by predatory continentals. When an Italian will try to take advantage of another, he might be checked by the question, *"mi prende per inglese?"* ("What do you take me for— an Englishman")?

inglese, andarsene all': "To walk off in English fashion" which means "to depart stealthily." See also the same slur in a French setting.

inglese, far l': "To do the English stunt." To feign ignorance or the inability to understand. *Cf.* the Spanish similar phrase in regard to the Swedes.

l'inglese: "The English." Water-closet. The original was a compliment, meaning, (when extended) the English lavatory, *i. e.,* of the sanitary type.

Spagna, grande di: "A Spanish grandee." One who takes himself very seriously, or puts on airs.

spagnola: "The Spanish." Influenza.

spagnolata: "A Spanish article." A whopper; a bluff (*slang*).

spagnolismo: "Spanish mannerism." Haughtiness.

spagnoleggiare: "To 'throw' the Spanish." To swagger; "to put on the ritz."

svizzero: A Swiss, (pejoratively considered); a coxcomb, a conceited simpleton.

tedesca, ridere alla: "To laugh the German way." To be smiling unnaturally, in a grimace; to show a forced smile.

tedescheggiare: To affect German mannerisms.

tedeschi magnasego: German tallow-eaters.

tedeschi patatucchi: German potato-swallowers (*slang*).

tedeschi, ridere come piangono i: "To laugh as the Germans cry." To laugh the other way.

tedesco: "Teuton." A pig-headed, stubborn man. Formerly, the Austrians were called *tedeschi* in disparagement.

tedesco, parlare: "To speak German." To speak gibberish. To the Latins, naturally the Teutonic languages would be unintelligible.

tedesco, porco: "German swine."

turco, aver preso il ↰ pei baffi: "To have seized the Turk by his whiskers." To have had special luck in some venture.

turco, bestemmiare come un: "To blaspheme like a Turk." To swear like a trooper.

turco, fumare come un: To smoke like a Turk.

turco, parlare: "To speak Turkish." To say something that makes no sense.

NORWEGIAN SLURS

See under DANO-NORWEGIAN ETHNOPHAULISMS

POLISH ETHNOPHAULISMS

Angielska, wygląda jak ↷ śmierć: "As pale as an English death scene." Colorless, insipid, uninteresting.

angielsku, wynieść się po: "To slip away in English style." To take French leave.

Anglik(a) or Anglelczyk: "An Englishman." A phlegmatic person; a coldblooded or indifferent person. *Nic go nie zajmuje to Anglik!*—Nothing excites him. He's an Englishman.

barani język: "Wether language." German, because to the Poles it sounds like a bleating. The Germans reciprocate by calling Polish the "quack language," from *tak, tak.*

bismark: 1. A dirty brown. 2. A privy. The Poles apparentlv never shared Premier Winston Churchill's admiration of the Chancellor of "iron and blood" (*localism*).

chachoł: "Clown," "lout." An Ukrainian. The great Russians use the same contemptuous nickname.

chałaciarz: "Begabardined." A Jew, because of the robe-like kaftan he generally wore.

cygan: "Gypsy." A crook; a swindler.

cyganek: "Little Gypsy." A peasant; a wooden jack-knife.

cyganka: "Gypsy woman." An adventuress.

czerkieski: "Circassian." Frivolous; superficial; inaccurate. *Czerkieska odpowiedź*—a rude answer. *Po czerkiesku co zbyć*—to dismiss one in short order; to deal summarily with one.

Dajczmanek: "Little Dutchman." A German.

derdydasy: Germans, a parody on *der, die, das*—"the."

fadry-mutri: Germans, ex *Vater* (father) and *Mutter* (mother).

farfluk: "Damned" (from the German *verflucht*). A German. Cf. the French nickname for the English, *Godam.*

franca: "The French" (disease). Venereal disease.

francik: a smooth fellow; a sophisticate; a young rogue.

francuz: "Frenchman." A cockroach, of the smaller variety.

fryc: "Fritz." A gullible fellow.

frycować: "To 'befritz' " (from *Fritz*). To dupe.

głuchoniemcy: "Deaf Germans." A nickname for the German colonists in Galicia.

Greta: "Gretchen." A frivolous girl of easy virtue. Other forms of the original Margarete, are *Gretka, Grytusia,* often employed, according to Lück, in Polish poetry of the sixteenth and seventeenth centuries.

Hanysek: "Heinie." A German.

hadiuga: "A snake." An Ukrainian peasant in Eastern Galicia (a Ruthenian).

Hajdamak: "One of a certain Cossack tribe." A looter, a blood-thirsty trooper.

Holender: "A Dutchman." A farmer or free peasant.

Holendernia: "Dutchery." A farm.

holynder, psiakrew: "Dog-blood of a Dutchman." A g—— d—— German.

Icek: "Ikey." A Jew, in general.

jamroty: "To jabber." 1. A German. 2. A Jew.

judzić: 1. To lure; to give bad counsel. 2. To importune.

judzki: Jewish, in a derogatory sense.

kartoflannik: "Potato glutton." A German.

kartoflarz: "A potato eater." A German.

kasztan: "A Chestnut." A German, because of the color of his hair.

kulturnik: "Culturist." A German immigrant or colonist [LÜCK].

kulturtregier: "Bearer of culture." A German settler, in parody [LÜCK].

kusielec (or **kusal**): "Short-coated." A German, because of the sack coat (with swallow tail) the Germans began to wear earlier than their neighbors.

lichwiarz: "A usurer." A Jew.

litewska, napaść: "A Lithuanian attack." A stab in the back.

Litwin, skryty jak: "Secretive like a Lithuanian." Insincere, scheming.

Mosiek: Mosey; a general name for any Jew.

Moskal: A Russian. Cf. *Muscovite,* in English (*pejorative*).

Moskwicin: A Russian, in a contemptuous sense. The use of both of these terms was interdicted at one time in Poland.

Moch: A Muscovite, perhaps a rejoinder to the Russian "Lyakh."

niedowiarek: "An infidel." A German.

Niemczura: " 'Germooch'." A lout.

niemczyk: "The German fellow." The devil.

niemiec: "A German." With the accent on the c (niemieć) the word means "To become speechless," "to turn mute."

Niemiec, twardy: The harsh German.

Niemiec, zabity: The touchy German.

niemiecka grubość: German bulkiness.

niemiecka, kawa: "German coffee." Chickory.

niemiecki, abszyd: "A German farewell." An ejection, a showing of the door.

niemiecku, szwargotać po: To jabber in German.

[123]

niemkini: The Germans, in a derogatory sense [LINDE].

niemra: An ungainly ugly German woman.

obrzezaniec: "A circumcised one." A Tartar. The Tartars take this nickname as a special insult.

obrzynek: "A circumcized one." A Jew.

oszwabić: "To 'beswab'." To cheat.

oszwabka: "A Swabian article." Something inferior; a substitute.

pejsak (pejsaty) Żyd : "Earlocks." A Jew, because of the religious custom, among the ultra-orthodox, of wearing ear-locks.

Pepik, Pepiczek: A Czech, in a derisive sense. Ex a diminutive form of Joseph, a common given name in Czechoslovakia.

Persak: "A Persian." A cockroach of the oriental variety.

pludry: "Pantaloons." Germans.

pludrak: "Pantalooner." A German, because of his wide breeches.

prosiak: "A sucking pig." A Prussian, as a parody on Prusak.

prusak: "Prussian." A cockroach.

pruska, mina: "A Prussian air." An arrogant expression or attitude.

pruski dar: "Prussian gift." Indian giving.

psiakrew Niemiec: "Dog-blood of a German." A g—— d—— German.

raichy: "A 'Reicher'," from the German Reich. A German.

Rusak: "A Ruthenian" i. e. an Ukrainian in Galicia. A kitchen knife.

Ruski miesiąc, poleżysz mi z: "I'll see to it that you are laid up a Russian month." (Twelve days behind the Julian month, it appears a wearisome period to the Poles). A Russian month is thus a long-drawn out and tedious affair.

Ryfka: "Rebecca." A Jewess in general.

suka: "Bitch." A Jewess (thus spoken of in Mazovia, central Poland).

szachrajstwo: "Petty dealing" from the German *Schacher*, and Aramaic-Hebrew *sakhar* (gain, profit). Jewish manipulation; unethical or unsubstantial trading [MRONGOVIUS].

Szwabi, głupi: The stupid Swabians. Swabians were regarded as the worst type of Germans, hence the word *Szwab* became the generic term for all Germans.

Szwabić: "To 'Swab'." To steal (*archaism*).

Szwed: "A Swede." An unpresentable or filthy person.

Szwed, czarny jak: "Black as a Swede." Unprepossessing, ill-natured. (The adjective describes a disposition or attitude rather than a physical fact).

Turek: "A Turk." The name of a dog.

Węgier: "A Hungarian." An abscess in animals.

węgiersku, kiepski po: Foul as a Hungarian.

Wencliczki: "Wenceslaus." Any Czech, nicknamed after the Bohemian patron saint.

Żyd: 1. "A Jew." 2. An ink-blot. 3. A boil. 4. A certain toy.

Żyd, parchaty: "Mangy Jew;" "scurvy Jew." Another adjectival form is *parszywy*. The substantive alone is frequently used to designate a Jew by the Poles of anti-Semitic tendencies, namely *parch* ("scab") and its various pejorative or augmentative forms like *parchacz, parchol, parchula,* and *parszywiec.*

Żyd śmierdzi: "The Jew stinks." In certain Polish circles, the same fairy tale is current as about Negroes among American whites. Apparently, the same statement was made about Ukrainians by German settlers in Poland. (See LÜCK, page 154), where, with cutting sarcasm, he remarks that evidently after a sprinkling of baptismal water, "the Jew ceases to stink."

Żydek: "Little Jew." *1.* A Jew-boy, an insignificant Jew. *2.* A cheap jack-knife in wooden frame.

żydogłowy: "Jew-headed." Having the head of a Jew.

Żydówica: "A Jew-woman." The non-derogatory word for a Jewess is the same minus the *i*.

Żydowska niemoc: "Jewish disease." Hemorrhoids.

żydowską piosnkę komu śpiewać: "To give one the Jewish 'spiel'." To sound out as to bribes.

Żydowstwo: *1.* Jewry. *2.* Jewish neighborhood. *3.* Jewish practices.

Żydziak: "Jew-boy." A mockie; a little kike.

Żydzisko: A wretched Jew.

It is only fair to draw attention to the fact that there are two melioratives bearing upon the Jews in the Polish language, and also in some of the other Slavic tongues, viz., **Żydoweczka**—a darling Jewess, and **Żydowin**—a scholarly or venerable Jew.

PORTUGUESE ETHNOPHAULISMS

See under SPANISH-PORTUGUESE SLUR-LOCUTIONS

Note on Provençal ethnophaulisms

In Provençal, there are numerous epithets and proverbs by no means flattering to the Jews; and the Comtat-Venaissin (which included Carpentras and Avignon) has been called the Jewish paradise (*paradis di Jusiòu*) by Frenchmen. Because of its general affiliation with French, it was my intention to omit the section on Provençal ethnophaulisms among which, in addition to general slurs, there are many degrading expressions with reference to the

Jews, who, toward the beginning of the nineteenth century, were still wearing their yellow cap to distinguish them from non-Jews. Yellow was a symbol of Jewry; and "Jew" and "yellow" became synonyms. In one of the Provençal dictionaries, we read that from time to time the church articles were examined to see whether they became yellowed as a result of Jewish influence.

The term "Jew's ear," because of the yellow bow-like patch which hung down from the cap, was heard in the streets at every turn, and "Jew" became a euphemism for "serpent" in some of the incantations. Jews who did not wear a yellow cap were molested by the young rowdies. Even the Christians in Carpentras were called Jews, due to the large proportion (nearly 15%) of Jews in that city, during the eighteenth century.

The lack of uniformity in spelling (*aleman, alemand; judiéu, judiou, jusiòu*) is due to the fact that the language has scarcely been regularized. Also the phrases date from different periods.

PROVENÇAL SLUR EXPRESSIONS

alemand, auturious coumo un: "Haughty as a German" is one of the Provençal's estimates of his Nordic neighbor. Another simile of the Southern French is *coulerous coume un Alemand*, i. e., "huffy as a German."

alemand, desboutounat coumo un beure à ventre: Loosening up like a German beer-belly.

alemand, beure coumo un alemand: To drink like a German.

alemand, flabuta coumo un alemand: To be "fluted" like a German. To be "soused." See *jouer de la fluste de l'Allemand* under French ethnophaulisms.

alemans, moucade dous: "German nose-blowing"—*i. e.*, in the hand.

aleman, pinta coumo un alemand: Drunk like a German.

alemand, sadou coumo un: Drunk like a German.

anglés: "An Englishman." A raging creditor.

braiman: "A Brabanter." A freebooter.

bretonejar: "To 'Breton'." To gabble, to stammer, to talk barbarously.

franchimand: A Northern Frenchman.

franchimandeja: To speak with, or affect, a Northern accent.

espagnola, aver lou ventre de l': "To have a Spanish stomach. To stint oneself in food and drink.

espagnòu, buffa (boufa) coume un: Puffed up like a Spaniard.

espagnòu, faire l': "To act the Spaniard." To put on airs.

espagnoulado: "Spanish stunt." Swagger, bravado.

judiéu, gros coume lou bras d'un: "As big as a Jew's arm." "Jew's" is a euphemism for "serpent's," in the child's description, so as not to be hurt by the snake.

judiou: 1. A Jew. 2. A profiteer; a usurer.

judiouva: 1. A Jewess. 2. The color yellow, because of a decree by Louis, in 1227, that the Jews wear a circular yellow patch on their chest. 3. A species of mollusc *Helix Algira*, common in Southern France, and the least edible of that genus.

jusiòu, li ⌐ de Carpentras: "The Jews of Carpentras." The inhabitants of C.

Prussien, encoulèrit coumo un: Wrathful like a Prussian.

RUSSIAN ETHNOPHAULISMS

angliyskaya boliezn: "English disease." Rachitis; rickets.

armyanskiy anekdot: "An Armenian anecdote." A dialect

story, a "dumbbell" tale, where the Armenian is generally the butt.

burlak (*Ukrainian* vs. *Russian*): "Churl, boor, lummox." A Russian.

frantsuzik: "A little Frenchman." The word occurs in Russian literature as belittling the spirit of the Frenchman.

frantsuzkaya boliezn: "French disease." Syphilis.

frantsuzkoye zoloto: "French gold." A species of gold of the worst grade.

gollandskiya: See *selyedki gollandskiya*.

grecheskaya kukhmisterskaya: "A Greek restaurant." A slop-house.

ispanka: "The Spaniardess." Influenza.

kartoshka: "A potato swallower." A German. *Cf.* similar Italian nickname.

katsap (*Ukrainian* vs. *Great Russian*): A Russian, in a pejorative sense. The picture suggests a burly and crude bearded rustic.

khokhol (*Russian* vs. *Ukrainian*): "The crest of a cock," hence a bushy forelock. An Ukrainian; a boor.

kitaĭ podimayetsya: "China is rising." Something is brewing; something is up.

kitaĭskaya, eto dlia menya ↳ azbuka: "This is the Chinese alphabet to me." It's all Greek to me.

kitaĭskaya gramota: "Chinese writing." Anything unintelligible.

kitaĭskaya stena: "Chinese wall." An inaccessible sphere; an insuperable barrier.

kolbassnik: "Sausage-glutton." A German.

latinskaya kukhnya: "A Latin kitchen." A pharmacy

latysh: A Lett; Latvian. *Ni odnovo slova* . . . . . *ne poĭmesh, slovno latysh kakoy*—I can't understand a word (he says) as if he were a Lett.

likhoimets: "A usurer; profiteer." A Jew.

lyakh: "A Polack." There is a slight contempt in the term.

makaki: "monkeys." The Japanese. See the supplementary essay in this volume, "Aspects of Ethnic Prejudices," section on Orientals.

nemak (*Ukrainian* vs. *Germans*): A German boor.

nimota (*Ukrainian* vs. *German*): "Germandom." All dubious blessings coming from Germany, in the form of technical or cultural novelties.

nyemchura: " 'Germanry'." A bunch of Germans, usually keeping to themselves. In 1914, the Germans were designated by the name *germantsy,* which, before then, was applied to the ancient Germans.

nyemets (*ye* as in *yes*): A German. Originally the word meant one who cannot make himself understood.

pan: "Sir." A Pole. (A sarcastic reference to the pride of the Polish squire).

prussak: "A Prussian." A cockroach.

rostovshtshik: "A usurer." A Jew.

ruminskiy orkestr: "A Rumanian orchestra." Inferior restaurant music.

russak: A Russian, in a pejorative sense.

samoyed: "Self-eater" *i. e.* without the aid of utensils or the facilities of fire, like the eskimo. A Samoyed (a backward tribe of Tartaric origin, inhabiting the province of Tomsk in Siberia). [KL.]

selyedki gollandskiya: "Dutch Herrings." Articles of food peddled and scarcely edible.

sharamýzhnik: "Dear friend" (from *cher ami*) with reference to any Frenchman, then, in a transferred sense, to a confidence-man, who·often would be French.

shvabanok (*Ukrainian* vs. *Germans*): "Big 'Swab'." A hulking German.

shval: "A horse," *ex* (French) *cheval.* A fourflusher, a confidence-man, having a sleek manner about him, reminiscent of the French. See *sharamýzhnik.*

shveytsar: A doorman, porter, swiss. This word does not mean an inhabitant of Switzerland, as the analogy with other languages might lead us to suspect; for "a Swiss" is rendered *shveytsarets.*

tatarskiy rebyenok: "A Tartar child." An imbecile; a moron.

tshud: See *tshukhonets.*

tshukhonets: A Finn. There is also a more dignified name, *finn,* but the common word has sprung from the root *tshud,* connoting peculiarity, a strange phenomenon, prodigy, foreign, etc.

tsigan: A Gypsy; a cheat; an underworld character.

tsiganit: "'To Gypsy'." 1. To scoff at; make a monkey of. 2. To engage in shady deals. 3. To importune, beg.

tsiganstvo: "Gypsying." "Monkey shines;" "gypping."

zhid: A Jew, usually in derogatory sense (the proper appellation being *yevrey*); a miser; a greedy person.

zhidishka: A contemptible little Jew.

zhidedyonek: A nasty little Jew.

zhidomor: "Jew-skinner." A skinflint, a miser.

zhidovat': "To Jew." To haggle; to behave in Jewish fashion; to gesticulate or speak with a Jewish accent.

zhidovatyi: Jew-like.

zhidovin(na): A d--d Jew; "sheeny."

zhidovskaya morda: "Jewish snout." Jewish 'mug' (usually in vocative).

zhidyonok: A Jew, in a pejorative sense.

zhidyuk: A mean Jew.

SERBO-CROATIAN ETHNOPHAULISMS

(Owing to typographical difficulties, the Serbian words have been transliterated).

avra (*Croatian* vs. *Jews*): A Jewish assembly; a synagogue.

čifutaria (*Croatian* vs. *Jews*): "Jewish practice." Usury.

čifutariti (*Croatian* vs. *Jews*): "To 'Jew'." To act or speak in the Jewish manner; to engage in petty trading.

čifutče (*Croatian* vs. *Jews*): 1. A Jewish child. 2. A crab with a small abdomen.

čifutin (*Croatian* vs. *Jews*): Jewry; ghetto.

ciganiti (*Croatian* vs. *Gypsies*): "To 'Gypsy'." To cheat.

čudan (*Croatian* vs. *Spanish*): "Odd." Spanish (*jocose*).

lekh: (*Serbian* vs. *Poles*): A Pole. Compare the Russian pejorative *lyakh*.

sirov (*Serbian* vs. *Hungarians*): "Crude;" "raw." Hungarian.

šišo (*Croatian* vs. *Swedes*): "Cropped." A haircut, Swedish style.

tsigansky posao (*Serbian* vs. *Gypsies*): A Gypsy trick.

tsudan (*Serbian* vs. *Spanish*) : "Peculiar." Spanish.

vrancljiv or francuzljiv (*Croatian* vs. *French*) : Syphilitic.

židovo uško (*Croatian* vs. *Jews*) : "Jew's ear." A species of marine gastropod.

SPANISH-PORTUGUESE SLUR-LOCUTIONS

(*Unless stated otherwise, the ethnophaulisms are Spanish*).

aleman de mierda: "Muck-German." (*Chileanism*).

al(l)emão batata (*Portuguese* vs. *Germans*) : "Potato German." (*Brazilianism*).

algarabía: "Arabic." Jargon, gabble.

breimante: "A Brabanter." A bugbear, a bloody-bones.

cabeza cuadrada (*Latin-American* vs. *German*) : "Square head." A German.

canisa: The offspring of a mestizo or half-caste father and an Indian mother (*Mexicanism*). [REINSBERG].

Castilla, mal de (*Portuguese* vs. *Spanish*) : "Castilian disease." Syphilis.

China (*Portuguese* vs. *Chinese*) : 1. China. 2. Money.

chinos: See ¿somos chinos?

chistes alemanes: "German jokes." Flat or dubious humor.

chuetas: The descendants of converted Jews in the Majorca Islands. Whether the word is derived from *chuya* ("pork" "a pig" or "pork-eater," in irony) or from *chuco*, (a call-sound to a dog, in Spain), or from *jueto* (the Catalan for "little Jew"), the sobriquet by which these centuries-old Christians are still called exclusively is not a compliment. See *Marrano*.

flamenco de Roma: "A Roman(y) Fleming." A Gypsy. Mérimée, in his *Carmen*, tells us that the "first Gypsies seen in Spain probably came from the Low Countries, hence their name of Flemings." *Roma* here is a corruption of *romi*— "married folk," as the Gypsies call themselves.

francesa, despedirse á la: To take French leave.

francesear (*Portuguese* vs. *French*): To speak a poor French.

francesismo (*Portuguese* vs. *French*): "A Gallicism." Affected or insincere amiability.

francez, mal (*Portuguese* vs. *French*): Syphilis.

franchute: "A Frencher." A Frenchman, in a pejorative sense. (*slang*).

gabachos: "Curs." The French.

gálico: "French." Syphilis.

galicoso: "Frenchfield." Infected with syphilis.

gallico, o (*Portuguese* vs. *French*): "The French (disease)." Syphilis.

germanía: Gypsy cant. Kleinpaul thinks that the word has no connection with Germany, but rather with the word for kinship, fraternity (cousin-german); but, on the other hand, German was as much cant to the Spaniards as Spanish was to the Germans.

griego, hablar en: "To speak Greek." To say something unintelligible.

gringo: A foreigner, especially an American (Yankee) or Englishman, much suspected in Latin-America; possibly from *griego*, Greek, i. e., strange, unfamiliar.

indiano: A nabob; one who returns from America rich.

indiano de hilo: "A thread Indian." A miser, skinflint.

indios: See *¿somos indios?*

inglesidad: An English mob (*Argentinism*).

inglezada: An English crowd (*Brazilianism*).

inglezia (*Portuguese* vs. *English*): Words mispronounced, gib-berish, anything unintelligible, as in the English phrase, "That's Greek to me."

judaria: See *judiaria.*

judear: "To act the Jew." To be tricky or scornful (*Argentinism*).

judearía: "A Judas act." Deviltry, treachery (*Argentinism*).

judeu (*Portuguese* vs. *Jews*): 1. A Jew. 2. A usurer. 3. A disagreeable person. 4. The jewfish.

judeu, cara de (*Portuguese* vs. *Jews*): "Jew-face." An ill-looking fellow.

judia (*Portuguese* vs. *Jews*): "A Jewess." A jeering or sneer-ing woman.

judía: 1. A string bean. 2. A Jewess.

judiada: An inhuman act (*Mexicanism*).

judía de careta: A small spotted French bean.

judiar (*Portuguese* vs. *Jews*): "To Judaize." To mock, laugh at, scorn.

judiaria (*Portuguese* vs. *Jews*): 1. Jewry, ghetto. 2. Jewish peculiarity or mannerism. 3. Jewish trick, derision, insult. 4. Cowardice.

judihuelo: 1. A small French bean. 2. A small Jewish boy or girl.

judío: "A Jew." A word of contempt used by angry persons. [VELAZQUEZ].

judio, dia: 1. Usurious. 2. A Jew.

judión: 1. A large variety of kidney bean. 2. A kidney bean.

marrano: (*Noun*) "A pig." (*Adj.*) "filthy." A baptized Jew who secretly observes the Jewish religion. See *chuetas.*

mestizo: "Mongrel;" "half-breed." The offspring of a white father and Indian mother, or vice versa.

morlaco: "A man playing the simpleton." A Dalmatian.

moros, hay ⤳ en la costa: "There are Moors on the coast," i. e. "you had better be on the alert."

Napoles, mal de (*Portuguese* vs. *Italian*): Venereal disease.

negrada: A collection of Negroes.

negros, boda de: "A Negro wedding." A boisterous party.

parlar: "To speak," (French *parler*). To prattle, "chew the rag." A friendly reprisal for the *hâbler* slur in French.

polacca: "A Polish woman." A prostitute; because the white slave traffic, at one time, drew on Poland for its recruits (*Argentinism*).

portuguesada: "In the Portuguese vein." The Spaniards mean by that *a vain boast.* See *gasconnade* in the French section, and *spagnolata* in the Italian section.

preto (*Portuguese* vs. *Negro*): "Black." A Negro, a "darkie" (*Brazilianism*).

¿Somos chinos? "Are we Chinamen?" The popular reaction in Spain to long-winded explanations of simple matters.

¿Somos indios? "Are we Indians?" Do you take us for saps?

sueco, hacer el: "To play the Swede," i. e., to act as if one did not understand.

suiza: "A Swiss woman." Commotion and "hell broke loose."

suizo: A lackey; anyone who takes orders implicitly.

vasconcear (*Portuguese* vs. *Basques*): "To Basque." To speak an unintelligible language.

vascuence: "Basque language." Gibberish, any outlandish talk.

zangano: A drone; an idler, a sponger. The word is cognate with *zingara*, a Gypsy (*colloquialism*).

SWEDISH ETHNOPHAULISMS

äppeltysk: "An Apple German." The lower middle-class person; one of the *petite bourgeoisie,* possibly because of the rosy and round checks.

dansk, törstig som en: "Thirsty as a Dane." Danish (or Dutch) with thirst; aching for a long drink; dipsomanic.

danskar, skrämma: "To frighten the Danes." A certain children's game.

danskt hjärta: "Danish heart." An insincere or untrustworthy streak.

engelsk spleen: English glumness.

engelska sjukan: "English disease." Rickets.

engelska svetten: "English sweats." Sudatory fever.

finna-student: "Finnish student." A dunce. The proper phrase is *"Finsk student."*

finne, arg som en: Surly as a Finn.

finnhuvud: "Finnhead." A pighead; a stubborn fellow.

finntamp: A lumbering Finn; a chump of a Finn.

fransysk visit: "A French call." A flying visit, one too brief.

jutar skrämma: "To frighten the Jutes." A kind of game played by children.

kinesa: "To 'Chinese'." To stay over night.

kosacker: "A Cossack." A mounted policeman (*slang*).

kroat, en vild: A wild Croat.

norsk norrmann från Norge: "A Norwegian Northman from Norway." This jest is heard in Norway also, though originally Swedish, but in another form. The Norwegian, too, is somewhat amused at the rugged patriotic individualism of the provincial who supposes that the farther North, the more sublime the virtue. The Norwegian phrase is *Norsk nordmand fra Norge.*

ockrare: "A usurer; a profiteer." A Jew.

polsk riksdag: "Polish Parliament." Utter confusion, a hullabaloo. The phrase was taken over from the German, as a slur on the filibustering in the Polish Sejm. The same phrase in Norwegian is *polsk rigsdag.*

rotvälska: "Red Italian." Cant, underworld slang. Red Italians were supposed to be particularly ingenious crooks.

ruotsi: "Inarticulate; jabberers." Finns.

rysk: "Russian." Mad, crazy. *Är du rysk, pojke?* Are you crazy, boy?

ryss, leva som en: "To live like a Russian." To be a roisterer; to make whoopee.

skotte, snål som en: Stingy as a Scotchman.

spanska sjukan: "Spanish disease." The influenza.

svensk avundsjuka: Swedish envy. (Shortened from the phrase which means "Royal Swedish envy").

turken, akta dig för: Look out for the Turks.

YIDDISH ETHNOPHAULISMS

altfrenkish: "Old-Frankish" *i. e.,* antiquated, pre-Victorian.

amolek: The Rumanians, who, since obtaining their independence as a nation, had consistently been plaguing the Jews, were regarded by the latter as their inveterate foe, the analogue of the Biblical *Amalek.*

beytzimer (beytz): An Irish person. From the Hebrew *beytzim*, eggs, in Yiddish *eyer*. The pun explains the rest. There is a remote association of the *testes*, in Yiddish—*eyer*.

bovel skhoireh: "Babylon (or Babel) goods." Undesirable or stale goods.

deitshuk: A German. The terminal formation is pejorative, as in American slang, *Canuck*. Chinook, the language, seems also to suggest a pejorative sense.

englishe sazhe: English soot or chimney smoke, in the phrase *Blut un milkh, un englishe sazhe*, said of a cherub-like boy with a peaches-and-cream, but soiled complexion. ("Blood and milk and English soot").

farfrantzevet: Infected with syphilis. See *frantzn*.

fonye ganev(f): "Vanya, the thief." Foxy Ivan.

frantzimerke: A girl cuddling herself *à la française*. The word is a pun composed of *froëntzimmer* (woman) and *frantzoiz* (French). The word occurs in Peretz's "Meshupeh," but it apparently has made its way into Yiddish through the Polish avenue.

frantzoiz, fun dem altn: "Dating from the old Frenchman." Out-of-date, antiquated, very old fashioned. The reference is probably to the Napoleonic invasion of Russia.

frantzn: Syphilis. The *France* element in the word is quite evident.

galitzianer: "Galician (Jew)." A fawning, cringing individual (from the point of view of the Lithuanian and Russian Jew).

goy: "Gentile." An illiterate, coarse, or lowbrow person.

goyishe kop: "Gentile head." A dunce, bonehead. It may be noted that the Gentiles referred to here were peasants, but the Jewish folk mind denies far-sighted, sensitive intelligence, understanding, and brilliance even to highly trained and distinguished non-Jews. Thus *A goy bleibt a goy* ("A Gentile remains a Gentile") is usually said in disappointment or mild digust at the intransigent.

goy, fressn vi a: To gourmandize "like a Gentile."

goyisher mazzl: "Gentile luck." Said of someone whose good fortune is undeserved. Cf. *Irish luck*.

kirre deitsh: A German (or Austrian) "sap."

kozak hanigzl: "The robbed Cossack." This phrase, in its Hebrew setting, to make the situation appear more ludicrous, pictures the wild and unruly Cossack of old vociferating that he was robbed (while preparing to undo his victim).

litvack: "Lithuanian." A herring—a favorite taunt among the Polish and Ukrainian Jews because the Lithuanian Jews were often *necessarily* fond of this sort of fish.

loksh: "Noodle," (the nearest equivalent in the Jewish *cuisine* to macaroni) hence, an Italian.

mameligge: "Maize pudding." A Rumanian (Jew), because the dish is the staple of the peasant class in Rumania.

moldevan: "A Moldavian." A boor or lout, yokel.

moldevaner getsh: "A Moldavian icon." A dummy; a lumbering blockhead.

oisgeputzt vi an italiener um zuntik: "Dressed up like an Italian on Sunday," *i.e.,* in loud gaudy colors. Of course the simile takes into consideration the laborer; for Italian taste is not to be ridiculed by any people.

opfritzeven: To dupe. Ex *Fritz*. See *befritz,* in English section.

poilishe dripke: Polish slattern. The epithet is applied to Jewish-Polish housewives by their Lithuanian or Russian sisters.

preissn: "Prussians." Cockroaches. The Prussian origin was the general belief in Russia.

russisher mi-shebeyrakh: "A Russian blessing" *i.e.*, the usual obscene reference to the victim's mother.

shokher: A Negro. The word is derived from the Hebrew, meaning "black."

sheyggets: 1. A non-Jewish boy. 2. An impudent fellow. Derived from the Hebrew *sheḳets*, disgusting (because uncircumcized).

targum-loshn: "Translation-language." Unintelligible, gibberish; Greek; double dutch. The translation of the Bible into the polysyllabic and diffuse *Aramaic* served as a source of many colloquialisms in Yiddish.

terkish: "Turkish." Something unintelligible.

terkish hartz: "A Turkish heart." A callous or truculent streak.

terkish, opton oif: To play a trick on; steal a march on; literally, to *requite after the Turkish fashion*. Dates probably from the Russo-Turkish war.

timkhe: "Thou shalt obliterate." This Hebrew word in the Bible, with reference to Amalek, the hereditary foe of the Israelites, curiously enough, is employed by the Jews in Galicia (*Poland*), as a nickname for the Armenians, whom, for some reason, they look upon as the descendants of that eternally detested people.

totter: "A Tartar." A queer bird, an outlandish fellow; a Gypsy.

tzeylem-kop: "Cross-head." A Lithuanian or White Russian Jew, according to the other East-European Jews. The origin is obscure but it is possibly from the alleged susceptibility of Lithuanian Jews to embrace Christianity in order to make a literary or professional career, or at any rate, to delve into secular learning, forbidden though it was to the pious.

tzigeinershe shtik: "Gypsy stuff," *i.e.,* blandishments, wiles.

yahudim: "Jews." The prosperous, assimilated element, mainly of German-Jewish stock, regarded as patronizing and uplifting by the Jews of East-European origin. The name, in derision of the super-dignified attitude and articulation of the German Jews and the rich East European Jews who join their temples and social organizations, is equivalent to Israelites, as "distinct" from Yiddn (Jews).

yekke: A German, with reference to his simpleton attitude.

yovn: "A Greek." According to the Hebrew, but in Yiddish the word signifies a *Russian trooper,* a roughneck. *Er is areinge-falln vi a yovn in sukke*—"like a trooper he broke into the tabernacle," is equivalent to "He noisily invaded the peaceful abode."

yiddishe bizness: Any misunderstanding with a Jew, particularly due to the failure to adhere strictly to the agreement; misrepresentation in any degree.

zaks-amolek: "Saxon Amalek." Saxon Jew-baiter. The Saxons at one time were particularly anti-Semitic, as compared with other Germans.

MISCELLANEOUS SLUR-EXPRESSIONS

alaman (*Bosnian* vs. *Germans*): "A German." A crafty fellow. [R]

bulgăros (*Rumanian* vs. *Bulgarians*): Chunky, massive, lumpy.

dilszi (*Macedonian Turkish* vs. *Slavic Mahommedans*): "Tongue-less." Slavic Mussulmans.

fan kuai (*Chinese* vs. *Whites*): "Foreign devil." Any one of European stock.

giaur (*Turkish* vs. *non-Mahommedans*) : "Blasphemous." A non-Mahommedan; a European.

grecoteu (*Rumanian* vs. *Greeks*) : A Greek, in a pejorative sense.

gweitz (*Chinese* vs. *Japanese*) : "Devil." A Japanese.

havra (*Rumanian* vs. *Jews*) : A synagogue, a Jewish school (ironically) probably *ex* the Hebrew-Yiddish *Khevreh*—a society.

jidan (*Rumanian* vs. *Jews*) : A Jew (somewhat contemptuously).

jidov (*Rumanian* vs. *Jews*) : "A Jew." A giant.

jidoviĭ, de când cu ⌐ sau cu tatariĭ (*Rumanian* vs. *Jews, Tartars*) : Since the days of the Jews or the Tartars.

jidovină (*Rumanian* vs. *Jews*) : "Jewess." A ravine, a hollow road.

kafir (*Arabic* vs. *Kaffirs*) : "Atheist," "infidel." Kaffir.

kafiristani (*Persian* vs. *Kafiristani*) : Inhabitants of Kafiristan (Hindu-Kush). See *kafir*.

lacmanska vira (*Dalmatian* vs. *Italians*) : "Italian honor." Untrustworthiness.

Muskof (*Albanian* vs. *Russians*) : "Muscovite." A Russian.

mustaleinan (*Finnish* vs. *Gypsies*) : "Blackies." Gypsies.

rumân (*Rumanian* vs. *Rumanians*) : "Rumanian." A serf.

Saksa (*Estonian* vs. *Germans*) : "Saxon" (any German). A schemer.

teh (*Chinese* vs. *Europeans*) : "Rascal" (?). Any European. [KL].

vacieja (*Lithuanian* vs. *Germans*) : "Unintelligible ones." Germans.

vociete (*Lettish* vs. *Germans*) : "Dumb people." Germans.

yang kuei tse (*Northern Chinese* vs. *Occidentals*) : "Foreign devil." A Westerner.

yang weitz (*Chinese* vs. *European*) : "Foreign devil." Any European.

PART THREE

NATIONAL SLURS IN PROVERBS

A NOTE ON PROVERBS

Foreword: Those who are acquainted with the difficulty of tracing cultural origins will scarcely need reminding that the national designation after a saying is in some cases debatable. Often an immigrant will be astonished to learn that a proverb which he considered indigenous to his native land is thought to have had its source in his adopted country.

There is nothing in national cultures which travels so rapidly as proverbs. Some of them are translated literally; others are somewhat adapted to suit a foreign trait or milieu. Undoubtedly a few sayings are of such a universal nature that they may well have sprung up spontaneously in different countries.

In general, it may be considred that a proverb which berates a certain people will not have originally come out of its midst, but there are exceptions here too; and in the case of the Jews, it seems to be the rule. Here, however, it must be made clear that occasionally the use of the word Jew (*yid*) in Yiddish means simply *man*. The constant comparison between Jew and Gentile in Yiddish proverbs is proof positive of the Jew's consciousness of the environment. The Jew is like a pattern against a Gentile ground.

Another caution that is apt to escape the general reader is that the Gentile (*goy*) who is repeatedly mentioned in Yiddish proverbs is always the Russian or Polish peasant.

In other connections, a more specific appellation is used, e.g., *poritz*, that is, the baron or squire. The Jews in the small Russian or Polish town would hardly ever come in contact with Russian or Polish writers, artists, professional men, or executives. The petty officials that they would meet could not induce them to think highly of the "goy."

It is astounding how differently a proverb will be interpreted by investigators in accordance with their particular bias. "The wish is father to the thought" applies here perhaps more than elsewhere. Thus Friedrich Seiler, in his *Deutsche Sprichwörterkunde* (page 295), unhesitatingly tells us that in the saying, "What will the German not do for money?" (*Was macht der Deutsche nicht für Geld?*) his efficiency and industry are singled out, and, further, that when the Englishman says: "The German's wit is in his fingers," he is recognizing the superior skill of the Germans, whereas in reality, the observation is a left-handed compliment which requires no subtlety to perceive.

To what lengths a German apologist will go to turn a vice into a virtue may be seen from the fact that Reinsberg cites the proverb, "Should his bride die on Good Friday, the Swabian will still marry before Easter" as evidence of the German's resourcefulness in that "he knows how to quickly save himself in a momentary great embarrassment" (*Internationale Titulaturen*, volume I, page 69). And Küffner, in his *Die Deutschen im Sprichwort* (page 7) cites the nickname "German bears," which, according to Kriegk, is a North American epithet, as a symbol of "ceaseless industry." The same author gives us to understand that in French Switzerland, the phrase "*valser comme une Allemande*" is a compliment to the German woman "whose dancing art is so highly regarded" there. A Scotchman would say at this, "I hae my douts." On the same principle, one who is a Spanish apologist might inform us that the Gallic phrase which is equivalent to "He speaks French like a Spanish cow" is intended to show that in Spain even the cows are articulate. At any rate, it is clear that German paroemiographers entertain no paranoid ideas.

In translating the hundreds of proverbs, I have endeavored to give a literal rendering in most cases. Occasionally, however, where the point of the proverb lay more in the rhyme than in the message, an attempt was made to preserve the rhyme, provided the idea embodied could be left intact.

Not all the quotations are, strictly speaking, proverbs or maxims. Some are superstitions, expressions of the rabble, folk rhymes, and jingles; but for our purpose, since they voice a popular attitude derogatory of a certain nationality, they are pertinent to the collection and have therefore been included.

In separating the Ukrainian and Ruthenian proverbs, no political judgment is implied on the question of whether the two groups are distinct in their culture. Most likely they are both Ukrainians, but the term Ruthenian is useful in localizing the Ukrainians in Galicia.

In general, the groups included stand for separate nationalities or cultures, even though a fusion may have taken place since. In some instances, the specific allusion to a Prussian, Swabian, Saxon, or Westphalian, is a slur upon the Germans as a nation, as typified by the particular group with which the libellers (Poles, Russians, Estonians,

Rumanians, Hungarians, Dutch) came in direct contact. In such instances, the name "Prussian" or "Swabian" *e.g.*, becomes a generic term, and such slurs appear under the head of "German." Where, however, the Germans themselves singled out the Prussians, Saxons or Swabians for special (unfavorable) traits, the latter were regarded as separate units.

NATIONAL SLURS IN PROVERBS

AFGHANS

Trust a Brahman before a snake, and a snake before a harlot, and a harlot before an Afghan. (*Hindu*).

AMERICANS

A Jew will dispose of three Christians, and a Yankee will outwit three Jews. (*German*).

Help me to betray the Indians, and I'll give you half. (*German*). Supposed to have been the attitude of the pioneer settlers in North America.

In America the hour has forty minutes. (*German*). Everything is done in haste, as if the hour were shorter.

ARABS

The Yemen is the cradle of the Arab race; the Iraq is its grave. (*Iraq*).

All is soap to Bedouins. (*Arab*).

Not all the Arabs are in the desert. (*Provençal*). In other words, there are quite a few "brutes" in our midst.

An Arab seeks the bath in vain; he will become no whiter. (*Turkish*).

Judicious as an Arab. (*Turkish Simile*). Of course the comparison is in a negative sense.

The serpent who seduced Eve spoke Arabic; Adam and Eve entertained each other in Persian, and the angel who drove them out of Paradise spoke Turkish to them. (*Persian*).

I do not wish for camel's milk nor the sight of an Arab. (*Turkish*).

An Arab with an Arab, your face is like a black tooth. (*Osmanli*). The meaning is "you will be crushed."

That you may know that the jealousy of an Arab is jealousy itself. (*Persian*).

Arab diligence, Persian genius, Greek intelligence. (*Osmanli*).

The oppression of Turks rather than the justice of Arabs. (*Arab*).

ARMENIANS

One Jew can cheat ten Greeks; one Greek ten Jews; and one Armenian ten Greeks. (*German*).

Trust a snake before a Jew, a Jew before a Greek, but never trust an Armenian. (*French*).

God made serpents and rabbits and Armenians. (*Turkish*).

It takes three Jews to cheat a Greek, three Greeks to cheat a Syrian, and three Syrians to cheat an Armenian. (*Levantine*).

He waddles like an Armenian bride. (*Osmanli*).

The prince with the Armenian is not distinguishable. (*Osmanli*). The meaning is "If you associate with the low, you are regarded as one of them."

If you can make a good bargain with an Armenian, you can make a good bargain with the devil. (*Persian*).

AUSTRIANS

Austrian, Austrian, four cats he bit to death; on the fifth he choked to death. (*Czech*).

BAVARIANS

God is no Bavarian; He doesn't allow himself to be made fun of. (*German*).

The Bavarian will not budge before you actually walk on him. (*German*).

BELGIANS

The Belgians are belligerent. (*German*). In original, *Die Belger sind Balger.*

THE CHINESE

China uses paper boats and iron oars. (*German*).

This fellow has had Chinese luck. (*Spanish*).

He is a Chinaman. (*Modern Greek*). He is an eccentric person; quite a character.

He has much China. (*Portuguese*). He has plenty of money.

Nothing is thrown away in China. (*German*). It can always be used by the half a billion people in that country.

China has more tutors than scholars and more physicians than patients. (*Chinese*).

Beat a Chinaman enough and he will speak Tibetan. (*Tibetan*).

A Chinaman is ill only once in his life, and that is when he is dying. (*Turkish*).

The Chinese must go, and a rat a day. (*American*). This slogan attributed to Dennis Kearney, an Irish labor agitator, circulated widely on the West coast of the United States, leading eventually to a law, in 1882, suspending Chinese immigration for a period of twenty years, and finally to the Chinese Exclusion Act, in 1892. More than 50 years later, in 1943, Congress, thanks to President Roosevelt's move, has now repealed this discriminatory law.

There are only two kinds of Chinese—those who give bribes and those who take them. (*Russian*)

All Chinamen look alike. (*American*).

Yellow as a Chinaman. (*American simile*).

It is Chinese grammar to us. (*Russian*).

CYPRIANS

In Cyprus, three things are cheap when bought wholesale, but dear when bought retail: salt, sugar, and whores.

CZECHS

"What a stupid lot those Germans are," says the Bohemian, "I have been here ten years, and they still can't understand me. (*German*).

It stinks like Bohemian cheese. (*German*).

He sets out like the sparrows in Bohemia. (*German*). Without zest or zeal.

The Bohemians are smacking. It's going to rain. (*Austrian*) When they see Czechs kissing on both cheeks, as is their custom.

DANES

Denmark is a prison. [SHAKESPEARE].

Something is rotten in Denmark. [SHAKESPEARE].

It would kill the Danes. (*English*). This may hark back to the days when another saying — a fervent plea — was current in England, namely: **From the fury of the Danes, O Lord deliver us!**

THE DUTCH

I don't have to go to Holland; my fortune is made. (*German*). Said in sarcasm to a high-pressure promoter.

The Dutch hold the cow; the Chinese and Arabs milk it. (*Dutch East Indian*).

Holland is a country where the earth is better than the air; where profit is sought more than honor; where there is more sense than *esprit*, more goodwill than good humor, more prosperity than pleasure and where a visit is preferable to a stay for life. (*German*).

How can we secure some food when the Dutchman spoils what is good? (*German*).

The English eat most, the Germans drink most, while the Fleming eats and drinks most of all. (*German*).

The Dutchman comes into the world with a nightcap. (*German*). Criticizing the Dutch habit of wearing a cap all the time, even while in bed.

A dark German, a fair Italian, and a red Spaniard seldom bode good, as does a Dutchman of any color. (*German*).

See also FLEMINGS.

CRETANS

All Cretans are liars. (*Greek*).

EGYPTIANS

The riches of Egypt are for the foreigners therein. (*Arab*). The Egyptians are unable to manage their own resources, and have been ruled by others for centuries.

Twisted like an Egyptian cripple. (*American simile*).

THE ENGLISH

The English have one hundred religions, but only one sauce. (*French*).

Only Englishmen and dogs walk in the sun. (*Italian*).

A demon took a monkey to wife — the result, by the grace of God, was the English. (*Hindu*).

England will fight to the last American. (*American*). This

catch-phrase was heard a good deal in the United States in isolationist circles prior to the attack on Pearl Harbor by the Japanese, but dates back to the last part of the first world war.

The English are the apes of the French. (*English*). This bit of self-incrimination was calculated to raise the English spirit of independence in the seventeenth century.

Don't trust an Englishman who speaks French with a correct accent. (*French*).

The Englishman is a drunkard. (*Spanish*).

England is every dog's spiritual home. (*Probably an English saying*).

A right Englishman knows not when a thing is well. (*English*).

England is the paradise of women. (*English*).

England is the paradise of women, the purgatory of men, and the hell of horses. (*Italian — Old Tuscan*).

Beware of a white Spaniard and a black Englishman. (*Dutch*).

Lang beards heartless, painted hoods witless, gay coats graceless, mak' England thriftless. (*Scotch*).

The English rule, salary at an appointed time. (*Marathi*). An Indian opinion of British domination.

The Englishman weeps, the Irishman sleeps, but the Scotsman gangs till he gets it. (*Scotch*).

It is like the Dutchman's anchor; he has got it at home. (*English*).

The High Dutch pilgrims, when they beg, do sing; the Frenchmen whine and cry; the Spaniards curse, swear, and blaspheme; the Irish and English steal. (*Spanish*).

This is an English oath. (*Dutch*). As good as none.

From England, neither fair wind, nor good war comes. (*French*).

An **English summer, three hot days and a thunderstorm.** (*English*).

An Englishman loves a lord. (*English*). The trait referred to is snobbishness.

The English are a nation of shopkeepers. Probably the French were the first to designate them as such. The English do not deny it.

The English are the swearing nation. Defoe speaks of this epithet of the English in continental Europe.

The English never know when they are beaten. This saying has been attributed to Napoleon.

The Englishman Italianate is a devil incarnate. (*Italian*).

It is an Englishman's privilege to grumble. (*English*).

One Englishman can beat three Frenchmen. (*English*).

The heart of an Englishman toward a Welshman (Probably *Welsh* in origin). The concealed hatred of the one for the other is more than hinted at here.

The peerage is the English Bible. (*English*). An allusion to English snobbery.

The way to an Englishman's heart is through his stomach. (?).

Do you speak English? (*Spanish*). The basis for this is "Money talks." See the comeback by the English under the Spanish rubric, in this section.

England a good land and a bad people. (*French*).

England were but a fling
Save for the crooked stick and the grey-goose wing. (*Probably Scotch in origin*). If it were not for the art of archery, England would not have amounted to anything. The Scotch admired English archers.

The Englishman is never happy but when he's miserable. (*Irish*).

Gluttony is the sin of England. (FULLER, in 1640).

War with all the world and peace with England. (*Spanish saying, as a result of the Spanish Armada experience*).

The best thing that could happen to England would be for Ireland to be submerged in the Atlantic for twenty-four hours. (*Irish*).

The only time England can use an Irishman is when he emigrates to America and votes for Free Trade. (*Irish*).

England is a prison for men, a paradise for women, a purgatory for servants, a hell for horses. (*Italian*).

The Englishman is never content but when he is grumbling. (*Scotch*).

Among three Italians will be found two clergymen; among three Spaniards two braggarts; among three Germans, two soldiers; among three Frenchmen, two chefs; and among three Englishmen two whoremongers. (*German*).

England lives on coal, tea, and plum pudding. (*German*).

This place is enough for an Englishman to forget England. (*German*).

The Englishman leaves his morals in Cape of Good Hope, but when he returns, he becomes pious again. (*German*).

The English whip the whole world, but the Americans whip the English. (*American*).

The Englishman has his understanding at his fingertips; the Frenchman on the tip of his tongue. (*Russian*).

To speak English and with intentions devilish. (*German*).

The German originates it, the Frenchman imitates it, and the Englishman exploits it. (*German*).

NATIONAL SLURS IN PROVERBS

ETHIOPIANS — See NEGROES

FINNS

Finland is the devil's country. (*Russian*). Unfertile, rocky.

FLEMINGS

That isn't a man [or a dog]; that's a Fleming. (*Walloon*).

THE FRENCH

The English love, the French make love. (*English*).

The Frenchman sings well when his throat is moistened. (*Portuguese*).

The Frenchman's legs are thin, his soul little; he's fickle as the wind. (*Russian*).

One Englishman can beat three Frenchmen. (*English*).

A fighting Frenchman runs away from even a she-goat. (*Russian*). With this compare the Frenchman's own estimate of himself: "Were the devil to come from hell to fight, there would forthwith be a Frenchman to accept the challenge." (*French*).

The Emperor of Germany is the King of Kings; the King of Spain, King of Men; the King of France, King of Asses; the King of England, King of Devils. (*Current during the reign of Emperor Charles V, and was attributed to the French*).

Have the Frenchman for thy friend; not for thy neighbor. (*French, but applied to the Dutch who were too close to France for their own good. In Mencken's New Dictionary of Quotations, the maxim is attributed to Nicephorus I, Byzantine Emperor, c. 805*).

When the Frenchman sleeps, the devil rocks him. (*French*).

The Italians are wise before the act, the Germans in the act, the French after the act. (*Italian, English*).

[159]

Proud as a Gascon. (*English simile*).

I have a good jacket in France. (*Spanish*). There is a mild scorn here of French travellers who claim to have left their good things behind.

He is like the Gascon; he has but one vice; he is too brave. (*French*). The Gascons are regarded as braggarts.

Attila, the scourge of God; the French, his brothers. (*Italian*).

When Venice was in power, there were noon and evening meals, but when the splendid Frenchmen came [to rule San Marco] there were only noon meals. (*Italian*).

The French don't say what they mean; don't read as they write, and don't sing according to the notes. (*Italian*).

For the slain French, a large hell is waiting. (*German*).

When the Frenchman comes to Petrovskoy palace, his first word is "Napoleon." (*Russian*). Napoleon is said to have stayed there for some days before his rout.

To speak French means not to have any sense. (*French colonial Negro*).

May the French ulcer love you and the Lord hate you. (*Arabian curse* for an enemy who tries to ingratiate himself through honied words. The ulcer, of course, stands for syphilis.

The French speak as fast as coffee grinders. (*German*).

You had better spend your money before the French return. (*Dutch*).

He lies like a French bulletin. (*Dutch*).

That is a French oath. (*Dutch*). To be totally discounted.

The effort was as much needed as in casting a Frenchman into hell. (*Dutch*). He would have eventually found his place there, anyway.

Only a dog or a Frenchman walks after he has eaten. (*French*).

The friendship of the French is like their wine, exquisite but of short duration. (*German*).

He is freezing like a Frenchman in Moscow. (*Russian*). The Napoleonic campaign is in mind here.

To a hungry Frenchman, a crow is welcome. (*Russian*).

When the Ethiopian turns white, the French will love the English. (*English*).

They [the French] do everything; they know nothing. (*Italian*).

Any German going to Paris must half a fool be. (*German*).

The French write other than they speak, and speak other than they mean. (*German*).

The French eat with their eyes. (*German*).

Frenchmen and women can live without bread but not without words. (*German*).

Frenchmen and sparrows run from loneliness as the mouse runs from the cat. (*German*).

French pox and a leather vest wear for life. (*German*).

French pox and pennilessness are two serious diseases. (*German*).

The Englishman is a tippler; the Frenchman is a cur, the Dutchman is a peasant. (*Spanish*).

GEORGIANS

The wit of an Armenian is in his head, that of a Georgian in his eyes. (*Armenian*).

GERMANS

No matter where you put him, the German is all over the place like a willow tree. (*Ruthenian*). That kind of tree can be quite a nuisance.

The German, as a petty master, is a petty scoundrel. (*Ruthenian*).

Where there is a German, there is deceit, and where a Gypsy, there is theft. (*Czech*).

He's German! Don't trust him. (*Czech*).

For company's sake, the German will hang himself. (*Polish*).

The German, though not too smart, will not fall off the bench. (*Polish*). When sleeping.

No German is afraid of losing his drawers. (*Serbian*). He wears none when sleeping according to the Serbs.

Be well on your guard that the Germans don't rob you. (*Silesian Polish*).

Stake nothing on the Germans for the Slavic tongue. (*Russian*).

God teaches man; the devil trains the German. (*Russian*).

Laugh to it like the German to the pancake. (*Serbian*).

Scorning all the world, in good German fashion. (*Russian*).

He is pleased with himself like the devil in German garb. (*Polish*). Literally (and perhaps correctly) it should be rendered, "He has fallen in love as the devil in German garb."

I sat there as at a German sermon. (*Polish*).

German goods are fragile and German words deceptive. (*Finnish*).

Be on your guard against the German queue. (*French*). This caution applies to the possible complications with Germans in business, and dates from the time when a German who thought himself insulted would start a feud, involving the kin of the alleged culprit until all seemed avenged.

Three things are in a poor plight: birds in the hands of

children, young girls in the hands of old men, and wine in the hands of Germans. (*Italian*).

He blusters like a Prussian trooper. (*Lithuanian; Polish*).

The slit is greater than the German. (*Yiddish*). The allusion is to the vent in the back of the coat, with an association of the anus too.

As jump as German's lips. (*English*). This simile which means "as true or exact as a German's word" — ironically, of course — is quoted as early as 1546, and is therefore one of the earliest allusions to German traits. A variant of the same simile is "as just as German's lips."

The German may be a good fellow; but it's better to hang him just the same. (*Russian*).

The Germans carry their wit in their fingers. (*English, also French*). A variant is "The German's wit is in his fingers." The Italians say: "The German has his brains in his hands." The manual dexterity and technological bent of the Germans were universally recognized. Naturally the Germans will interpret this proverb as if it implied that they had the replies and solutions at their finger tips.

Where Germans are, Italians like not to be. (*Italian*).

What is good for the Russian is death for the German. (*Russian*).

Sweep along like the Huns. (*American and English simile*).

> **The Germans in Greek**
> **Are sadly to seek;**
> **Not five in fivescore,**
> **But ninety-five more.**
> **All save only Hermann,**
> **And Hermann's a German.** (*English academic*).

This jingle, originally penned in Greek by an Etonian friend of the celebrated classical scholar, Richard Porson, has

often been quoted in its Englished version by British pro-
fessors who agreed that the Germans achieved little distinction in Greek studies.

The German can stand anything but a fillip. (*German*).

The German lives on sauerkraut. (*German*).

**The Germans gorge and swill themselves to poverty, disease,
and hell.** (*German*).

Four Germans to a bushel of hops, and yet they say "heavy."
(*Polish*). The Russians and Poles did not consider the
Germans to be physically strong.

**Once a German is in a rage, not even a paternoster will bring
him out of it.** (*German*). In spite of the recommended
maxim about saying the Lord's prayer when aroused to anger.

**With the Germans friendship make, but as neighbors do not
take.** (*German*).

**When a German calls the other "monsieur," it is not that he
deems him a sir, but as a rule, he thinks him a fool.**
(*German*).

**The Westphalians are like dogs — nine days blind; but as
soon as their sight begins, they can see through an oak
plank, provided it has a hole.** (*German*).

**When the Russian steals, he does it that he might have enough
for himself for a single day, but when the German steals,
he takes enough for his children and the morrow.**
(*German*). BISMARCK is reported to have made the statement
in an interview with JÓKAI, citing it as a proverb.

The German pays, while the Hungarian rules. (*German*).
Originated in Austria, in 1866, this dictum inveighs against
the preferment of Hungarians in official circles.

The German lies as soon as he becomes polite. (*German*). This
saying is supposed to be a compliment to the Germans.

A German doesn't need to jump into the water; he can swill to death [*ersauffen*] in a glass of beer or wine. (*German*).

The German woman excels in the shed; the Czech woman will have people fed, and the French woman is best in bed. (*Czech*).

The English write profoundly; the French gracefully; the Italians divinely and the Germans muchly. (*Italian*).

The German is hard to get into a temper, but harder still to get him out of it. (*German*).

The German must have a braid. (*German-American*). He is a slave to trifles and thus old-womanish.

Frankfurters and sauerkraut — nothing better to the German taste. (*German*).

The German proposes and the police disposes. (*German*). The *Verboten* injunction is probably referred to.

The German in a Czech council is like a moth in an expensive garment. (*Czech*).

The Germans have long syllables and short words. (*German*).

The German can stand all plagues but not thirst. (*German*).

The Germans are fellows with brains; that is why their society is not welcome. (*German*). It is possible to translate the first part differently, *viz.*, "clever boys," and therefore not seasoned.

The Germans raise up their hand, but soon it drops again to the sand. (*German*). Another saying, symbolic of the Nazi War.

It's hard to bring Germans under one roof. (*German*). The Germans seem to think that they lack unity.

Nothing will arouse the German so long as he has his potatoes and smoke. (*Ruthenian*).

What a Pole drinks away in a single day cannot be covered by a German fortune. (*Polish*). The Poles rather boast of what the Germans would twit them with.

A Spaniard is equal to four Germans, three Frenchmen, and two Italians. (*Spanish*). This of course was a boast of several centuries ago.

A German Italianate is the devil incarnate. (*Italian*). The English have been similarly treated by the Italians. The religious differences are mostly at the bottom of this libel.

The German sprouts like the willow, wherever he is planted. (*Russian*).

As long as the world lasts, the Pole will not be a brother to the German. (*Polish*).

Peace with the German like [peace] between wolf and sheep. (*Polish*).

Rather Turkish hatred than German love. (*Croatian*).

Where the moth is in the cloth, the wolf among the goats, the fish without water, the student among the girls, and the German in the council of the Czechs, things will never turn out well. (*Czech*).

What will the German not do for money? (*Danish and Swedish*). The slur dates possibly from the Hanseatic treaties, when the Scandinavian nations were at a disadvantage. The Swedes, taking this as an established fact, are led to lament their own folly in the admission that while the Germans do everything for money, the Swedes will be content with a drink, which, to a certain extent, is not to their discredit, in that they appear to spurn the yellow metal.

If anyone is born a German, God has sufficiently punished him. (*Russian*).

To curse a German relieves one's heart. (*Russian*).

The German provides his estate with wet goods, so that it might not burn. (*German*). A sort of German bull, this saying is, when we come to think that the "wet goods" are quite inflammable.

So many Russians, so many canes; so many Germans, so many canines. (*Russian*).

He's like a German. He can't understand a reasonable man. (*Lithuanian*).

Yes, try to speak to him, when he's a German. (*Czech*). Who will not or can not understand.

Dumb are the Germans beyond the hills; dumb the fish below the surface; us the Lord gave bread and speech. (*Czech*). Play on the name *German,* which, in the slavic languages, means *speechless.*

It were not a bad thing for Germany, if fools had a bath-house there. (*German*). A concession that all is not first rate there.

In Germany, it's like in the large lakes, where the carp devour the small fry. (*German*).

She jabbers English that a sow could not understand. (*American-German*). This was the reaction on the part of the German press in North America to the German newcomers and their children who thought that in the United States their language was English.

The Germans have devised their perpetuum mobile more felicitously than the mathematicians, in that their wine-cups and glasses always keep moving. (*German*).

In Spain, the reputed simplicity of the Germans is now thought of as little as the Spanish *bon mot*. (*German*).

Hungarians, trust the Germans not;
Be their promise ever so hot,
And though they give you a seal
On it as large as a wheel —
There is absolutely nothing to it.
May Jesus Christ smite them dead! (*Hungarian*).

They are a bit Prussian. (*German*). "Prussian" here has the connotation of unwilling to meet one half way, dissenting, uncoöperative.

The German will soon be as smart as the Lithuanian. (*Lithuanian*).

The Russian can learn even from the German. (*Russian*).

When a snake warms himself on ice, a German will begin to wish well a Czech. (*Czech*).

Wherever there are three Germans there are always four opinions. (*German*).

Wherever Germans are, it is unhealthy for Italians. (*Italian*).

The Irish, the Irish,
They don't amount to much,
But they's a damned sight better than
The dirty, dirty Dutch. (*American folk jingle*).
In this rhyme, cited by Mencken, the Dutch are to be understood as Germans, as also in the following American folk expressions.

There are three kinds of Dutch; the Dutch, the damned Dutch, and the hog Dutch. (*American*).

The Dutch companee is the best companee
That ever came over from old Germanee;
There's the Amsterdam Dutch and the Rotterdam Dutch,
The Potsdam Dutch and the other dam Dutch. (*American folk jingle*).

Rather die with Denmark than rot with Prussia. (*Danish-German*). The slogan of the inhabitants of Schleswig-Holstein, when in 1867, the question of the *Anschluss* came up.

God guard us against the health of the Germans [drinking] **and the malady of the French.** (*French*).

I make as much of it as a German of fresh water. (*Italian*).

If the truth in wine is hid, as the proverbs tell you,
Then the German has discovered truth, or will surely find it.
    (*Latin epigram*).

In German fashion, to nail the tablecloth to the table.
    (*Italian*). So that the tippler might not involuntarily bring everything down with the tablecloth.

He walks on German ground. (*Swiss*). Of one whose soles and heels are run down.

The Polish nobleman has an older pedigree than the German baron. (*Polish*).

He has forgotten his German. (*Swiss*). Of a reticent person.

I'll make you laugh the German way yet. (*Italian*). See *ridere alla tedesca.* The Germans appeared to be crying when laughing, and *vice versa.*

The Saxon [i.e. *German*] **travels in the rain; the wolf strikes in the mist.** (*Estonian*).

The German is not praised; and for a good reason. (*Latvian*).

Send the pig to Saxonland [Germany], **wash it with soap; the hog returns and remains a hog.** (*Estonian*).

Out of four Wends a stable is built. (*German*).

So as to pen up the Germans in it. (*Wendish*). The play on Wend and Wand (wall) gives rise to the first part of this bi-national proverb; the second part is but the repartee by the Wends, in this case, the Slavs in general.

Everywhere there are people; in Rammotau there are Germans. (*Czech*).

You are worse than a Lutheran. (*Polish*).

A Lutheran's foot has six toes. (*Polish*).

Half German, half goat; monstrous creature of God. (*Polish*). In the original, there is a rhyme.

You are a Lutheran, not a man. (*Polish*).

If a German, then a heretic. (*Polish*).

Among Poles, a German can satisfy his hunger, but among Germans not even a dog can get food. (*Polish*).

When the Pole puts his hand on his sword,
The German's soul is on the way to the Lord. (*Polish folk-song*).

Among Germans, not even a fly can feed itself. (*Polish*).

French wrath and German cowardice. (*Italian*).

The German is [no] better than a Jew; he will not even give you a spoonful of water for nothing. (*Polish*). I assume that in BYSTROŃ's *Megalomanja Narodowa* (page 254) the word "no" in this proverb has fallen out, otherwise the comparison hardly makes sense, unless we take it in an ironical sense, that is to say, the German is a "better" miser or mercenary.

It's as grateful a task as to fight for Vienna. (*Polish*). The Poles claim they had taken part in the battle against the Turks at the gate of Vienna without so much as getting a "thank you."

Every German a general. (*Polish*). The proverb alludes to the disproportionate number of German officers who fought with the Poles against the Cossacks, Turks, and Tartars in the seventeenth century.

Don't try to persuade me as if I were a German. (*Polish*).

[170]

The German is as big as a poplar tree, but stupid like a bean.
(*Polish*).

The German is dumb; he buys everything. (*Polish*).

> The clever Germans are for all that a stupid lot;
> By the Pole in a poke, they have often been bought.
> (*Polish folk rhyme*).

The German is wise up to noon. He becomes stupid thereafter soon. (*Polish*).

The German is as sly as the plague. (*Polish*).

German concern through winter will burn. (*Polish*). German
tension never relaxes.

> Serve the German with all your heart;
> Your reward will be a f . . t. (*Polish*).

He talked it into him like disease in a German. (*Polish*).

Don't try to persuade me as if I were a German. (*Polish*).

It's the care [*i.e.*, business] of a German to flay a man.
(*Polish*).

The Germans are an industrious people, not like us. For five
groszens, they would drive a herd of lice to Warsaw.
(*Polish*).

She whines like a German old woman. (*Polish*).

He snores like an old German. (*Polish*).

He wheezes like a Prussian soldier. (*Polish*).

His teeth are worn off like a German's from the pipe.
(*Polish*).

God invented man; the devil, the German. (*Polish*).

Stiff as a Prussian who swallowed a cane. (*Polish*).

It's an old story that the German is haughty. (*Polish*)

One German—a beer; two Germans—an organization; three Germans—a war. (*Polish*).

The German is wise only if he has tobacco in his pipe. (*Polish*).

With the German, every piece of art must bring its groszen at once. (*Polish*).

Every German a business man. (*Polish*). The Poles thought of business as a sordid vocation.

He is rushing like a German to the fair. (*Polish*).

Wherever the German enters, he draws the nails out of the wall. (*Slavic*).

Greedy like a German. (*Polish*).

Were it not for our cattle and swine, the German would go hungry and bare. (*Polish*).

At the German's, it's always after dinner. (*Polish*). So that visitors would not be invited to stay.
"Gerrie, would you like some dumplings?" "Yes." "But out of your flour!" Oh, no. (*Polish*).

The German moans about his poverty
Yet at home the coins jingle merrily. (*Polish*).

Without a trick or a ruse, you'll not get the German off the sleeping bench. (*Polish*).

Only through cunning, the German will be beaten. (*Polish*).

The German has outwitted the whole world. With the Lithuanian his success stops short. (*Polish*).

He grasps at (*klammert*) something as the German at heaven. (*Polish*). Without the slightest chance, of course.

He totters like the Lutheran religion. (*Polish*).

He forces his way into church like a Lutheran. (*Polish*).

He lives like a Lutheran. (*Polish*). In self-indulgence.

He tramps about like the Lutheran religion. (*Polish*).

A Pole is no German. (*Polish*).

Peace with the German is like a wolf and a sheep living together. (*Polish*).

Just as the winter cannot turn to summer, so the German can't become a brother. (*Polish*).

Sooner will you catch a ray of the sun than reach an agreement with the German. (*Polish*).

German and Pole; dog and cat. (*Polish*).

As long as mankind lasts, the German will nail the Pole. (*Polish*).

What weakens the Pole, makes the German well. (*Polish*).

With the German, not even the devil can come to an understanding. (*Polish*).

They must be devoid of pride who invite Germans as godfathers. (*Polish*).

The Germans, masters; the Poles, cattle. (*Polish*). In bitter irony.

He who serves the German gets his fee from the devil. (*Polish*).

Once the German is allowed on the threshold, the whole hut belongs to him. (*Polish*).

The German will make no hole, yet he will suck the blood out. (*Polish*).

Don't approach the German without a cane. (*Polish*).

Trust the German as you would a dog. (*Polish*).

He is as grateful as a German. (*Polish*). Which means ungrateful.

Speak to the German, but with a stone in your pocket. (*Polish*).

Whoever trusts the German will surely feel the bludgeon. (*Polish*).

Jew, German and devil—children of the same mother. (*Polish*).

Swabian, churl, stupid fellow; when he understands nothing, he says "ja". (*Polish*). Almost invariably the name "Swabian" is a derogatory nickname for the German in general.

The German will hear his mother insulted [or cursed] and all he will say is "ja, ja". (*Ukrainian*). Without understanding, the German is ready to agree to everything.

He is half German and half Slovak. (*Hungarian*). A nobody; a low life.

Whereas the frog croaks, the German bleats. (*Polish*).

That fellow must be a German; he yells so. (*Polish*).

The German can speak Polish outside, but not in the city. (*Polish*).

Bare as the German mouth. (*Hungarian*). Devoid of a beard, but probably with a double allusion.

That gives as much warmth as the cravat to a German. (*Ruthenian*).

He has as much rest as a German hat. (*Hungarian*). Scarce any, because it is constantly used in greeting people.

The Germans live like wolves in the woods. (*Ukrainian*).

He would not be a German, if he were not greedy. (*Ruthenian*).

The Swabian is sly like a street-girl. (*Ruthenian*).

Speak to him, if you only know German. (*Hungarian*). To one who is "a hard nut".

German, German [originally, *Swabie*], why don't you keep your tongue chained? (*Polish*).

Speak German at home, but outside don't make a splurge of it. (*Polish*). Addressed to the German colonists in Poland.

Warsaw and Cracow
Polish capitals fine,
But the Germans in Berlin
Live like swine. (*Polish folk rhyme*).

The music here is like that at a German funeral. (*Polish*).

You can tell a German by his singing and a dog by his bark. (*Polish*).

The German believes in God as the devil does in his horns. (*Polish*).

The German creed is like an old cow. (*Polish*).

While the Pole consecrates, the Swabian [German] does a merry dance. (*Polish*).

The German has no mind for the soul. (*Polish*).

He came to a worse end than a German. (*Ruthenian*).

The Saxon [German] fears neither God nor devil. (*Rumanian*).

He is a lost soul, worse than the German. (*Ruthenian*).

Swabian, you big stiff! Your religion lies chained. (*Polish*). Like a dog.

A Lutheran will be in heaven, where the hen scratches. (*Polish*). In the muck. A rather infantile conception of heaven.

When a German marries a Polish girl, it is as if the devil were to unite with an angel. (*Polish*).

Marry a German, and you'll see that [their] women have hairy tongues. (*Ruthenian*).

The wind is coming from the pantaloon [*i.e.*, "German"] side. (*Polish*).

It's going to rain. (*Latvian*). When they hear German spoken.

Mr. and Mrs. German are Mr. and Mrs. Devil. (*Polish*).

The German and the devil come from one and the same family. (*Polish*).

The German never prays before the Saint,
Thus he has the devil's taint. (*Polish*).

Where the devil finds it hard,
The German becomes his best card. (*Polish*).

Even if he tempts no one else, the devil will force the German. (*Polish*).

Either the devil or a German must have split it. (*Ukrainian*).
When he finds something has come apart.

You just wait. I'll be going to Berlin soon, and will hang the son of Lucifer by the tail. (*Mazovian Polish*). Said to naughty children.

The German smells of the devil. (*Ruthenian*).

Oh you German, potato-man,
Following the girl to the burial ground;
You have no master, no God;
The horseshoe you use for the sign of the cross. (*Polish folk song*).

The German in the council hall; the goat in the garden; the wolf in the stable, the liar at court, and a woman in office—this is all pretty bad business. (*Polish*).

Cracks the birch, cries the German. (*Polish*).

Not every German wearing an upturned moustache need be feared. (*Polish*).

If I had a German, and the devil good shoes I'd change with him, and make him a present of all the Germans. (*Polish children's rhyme*).

Though a German, yet a good scout. (*Polish*).

A fine fellow, as though he weren't a German. (*Polish*).

A good soul; what a pity he's German. (*Polish*).

When what's back of the Russian is in front with the German, there is no getting to the point. (*Russian*).

Quick, wife, the cat-o'-nine-tails to give the German a lesson. (*Ukrainian*).

May this befall the Germans thrice. (*Ukrainian*). On meeting with a bit of ill-luck.

I have an axe covered with tin; when I start to clout, Poles and Germans pass out. (*Ukrainian*).

Our hills will be badly off, so long as a single German remains. (*Ukrainian*).

The German [or the Saxon] is calling me. (*Hungarian*). The equivalent of "My aunt is calling me", when, among the plebeian youth, someone has to leave for natural purposes.

One swine, seven Germans. (*Polish*).

The German, a swine; the Pole is fine. (*Polish*).

What's German is canine. (*Polish*).

A dead German, a dead dog; the difference is but slight. (*Polish*).

GREEKS

After shaking hands with a Greek count your fingers. (*Albanian*).

Greeks tell the truth, but only once a year. (*Russian*).

Whoever trusts a Greek lack brains. (*Italian*).

A Greek will survive where an ass will starve. (*Dutch*). The saying occurs also in German.

One Greek can outwit ten Jews. (*Bulgarian*).

A Russian can be cheated only by a Gypsy; a Gypsy by a Jew; a Jew by a Greek, and a Greek by the devil. (*Russian*).

All Greeks look alike. (*Yiddish*). This is the literal translation of *Yevonim,* but the transferred sense is *Russians* of the military caste.

When Greeks joined Greeks, then was the tug of war. (*Lee*). This line from Nathaniel Lee's drama *Alexander the Great* has become the oft-quoted "When Greek meets Greek, then comes the tug of war." In America, there circulated about 1912, the parody "When Greek meets Greek, they open a restaurant."

Three Turks and three Greeks make six heathens. (*Serbian*).

A crab is no fish, and a Greek no man. (*Russian*).

Beware of a Gypsy who has become a Turk and of a peasant who has become a Greek. (*Rumanian*).

GYPSIES

The Gypsy does not human feel, if he has no chance to steal. (*Russian*).

What seems to him in a poor plight, the Gypsy will take to preserve it right. (*Rumanian*).

Why, he could cheat a Gypsy, then all the more me. (*Croatian*).

A Gypsy's life, a growling life. (*German*). A dog's life, in other words.

He could trim a Gypsy. (*Czech*).

Drinking woman, Gypsy woman. (*Slovenian*). A woman who drinks will be promiscuous.

He is poor as a Gypsy; he hasn't a red penny to his name. (*Albanian*).

You can't find a closet in a Gypsy tent. (*Turkish*).

He would ask for the lees of the Gypsy. (*Greek*). The Gypsies are supposed to have the lowest standards, here.

He eats his religion as the Gypsy did his church. (*Rumanian*). The Rumanians tell the story that while the Gypsies had a well-built church, the Wallachians made theirs out of bacon and pork. At a time of famine, the Gypsies asked for an exchange of churches, which the Wallachians accepted, and proceeded to consume their church, so that ever afterwards, the Gypsies made use of any church or religion of the people among whom they lived.

That is as becoming to him as ploughing to a Gypsy. (*Polish*).

You make a poor Gypsy; you can't tell fortunes. (*German*). To a liar who is not skillful.

Used to misery like a Gypsy to the gallows. (*German*).

The Gypsy has three souls: one with me, the other with you, and the third with himself. (*Ukrainian*).

The Gypsy has two hides: if he has parted with the one, he still has the second. (*Ukrainian*).

Black as a Gypsy. (*Russian*).

Even if we are dark, we are by no means Gypsies. (*Serbian*).

Where the Gypsy stays, he will not steal. (*German*). He would be too cautious.

Three people, four horses, five Gypsies. (*German*). The discrimination is quite evident.

Gypsy truth is worse than an Orthodox lie. (*Russian*). That is to say, the Greek Orthodox Church.

Bargain like a Gypsy but pay like a gentleman. (*Serbian*). This scarcely witty taunt occurs in the Scotch, Negro, and other collections, but is applied there to the Jews.

"Work a little, steal a little," said the Gypsy to his son, when he taught him maxims of life. (*Serbian*).

A Gypsy was made king; and the first man he hanged was his own father. (*Serbian*).

Where a Jew could not go, the Gypsy crept. (*Russian Gypsy*).

A Gypsy once in his life tells the truth, but then he repents of it. (*Russian*).

Every Gypsy praises his own hammer. (*Rumanian*). Many of the Gypsies were blacksmiths: *cf.* Anvil chorus in the opera, *Il Trovatore*.

When you cut the Gypsy in ten pieces, you have not killed him; you have only made ten Gypsies. (*English*). Probably comparison with the worm is here intended.

Half-breeds call themselves Gorgio among the Gorgios and Gypsy among the Gypsies. (*English Gypsy*). The Gorgio as a house dweller is frowned upon by the typical Gypsy who detests such adaptation as unworthy.

Even the Gypsy praises his own horse. (*Hungarian*).

The Gypsy calls on his own children to serve as witnesses for him. (*Polish*).

They cried, "The wolf ate the dobbin," but the Gypsy ate the dobbin. (*Russian*).

HESSIANS

Blind Hessian! Can't you see? (*Prussian*). When people bump into one another.

When a Hessian comes into a strange house, the nails on the wall begin to tremble. (*German*).

HINDUS

The Indian wears seven veils which must be removed if his true face is to be seen. (*English*).

India will be ruined by false scruples; Tibet by false hopes. (*Tibetan*).

Sacred as Hindu gods. (*American simile*).

Sacred as the cow in India. (*American simile*).

HOTTENTOTS

Absurd as a Hottentot marooned on an iceberg. (*American simile*).

HUNGARIANS

Do not trust a Hungarian unless he has a third eye in his forehead. (*Czech*).

The Poles and Czechs are like two close leaves, but when joined by the Hungarian, they make three fine thieves. (*German*).

As base as a Hungarian. (*Polish simile*).

Where there is a Slav, there is song; where a Magyar, there is rage. (*Slovak*).

Sins are born in Hungary. (*Czech*).

ICELANDERS

Bold as an Iceland lion. (*Danish*). To the Danes, the Icelanders are a timid people. An Iceland lion would be a sheep.

INDIANS

The only good Indian is a dead one. (*American*). A slogan originating in the Colonial period, when the Indians became a real menace, massacring hundreds of the new settlers.

Naked as an Indian back. (*American simile*).

Straight as an Indian's hair. (*American simile*).

Silent as an Indian. (*American simile*).

Red as an Indian. (*American simile*).

Impassive like an Indian idol. (*American simile*).

To stare like a wooden Indian. (*American simile*).

THE IRISH

His pappy is a Paddy; his mammy—a Jew. (*English*). At one time supposed to be an outlandish union, and the offspring, therefore, a double half-caste.

Get an Irishman on the spit and you'll easily find two others to turn him. (*Irish*).

He that would England win, must with Ireland first begin. (*English*).

Get Ireland today and England may be thine tomorrow. (*English*).

Home Rule is Rome rule. (English catch-phrase, calling attention to the Catholic influence in Ireland).

The Irishman for a hand, the Welshman for a leg, the Englishman for a face, and the Dutchman for a beard [is commended]. (*English*).

The Irishman is never at peace except when he is fighting. (*Irish*).

An Irishman before answering a question always asks another. (*English*). In comparing the similar Jewish trait often observed, we note that the Irishman only wants to know why he is asked, while the Jew puts the onus on the questioner, *e.g.*, "Are you Jewish?" "Are you?" "Why not?"

Ireland will be your hinder end. (*Scotch*). The meaning is that "you will be apprehended for stealing or some other crime and flee to Ireland in order to escape from justice."

Like an Irishman's obligation, all on one side. (*English*).

More Irish than the Irish themselves. (*English*). This folk-phrase, a translation of the Latin "*Hibernicis ipsis Hibernior*," or the more modern "*Hibernis ipsis Hiberniores*," was applied to the Norman-Irish feudal lords who, while despising the Irish, were in reality very Irish in their make-up and outlook.

For the Irish there are no stars. (*English*). So engrossed are they in the trivialities about them.

When the Irish are good, they are very good, but when they are bad, they are most bad. (*French*). The German parallel must have been borrowed from the French.

Loveless as an Irishman. (*Scotch*).

The dirty, dirty Dutch
They don't amount to much,
But they're a damned sight better than the Irish.
(*American folk jingle*).

Hit him again: he's Irish. (*Manx*).

Take away an Irishman's religion, and you make a devil of him. (*Probably of English authorship*).

The Irish and the Dutch,
They don't amount to much,
But hooroo for the Scandinoovian! (*American Folk Rhyme*).

As sluttish and slatternly as an Irishwoman bred in France. (*Irish*). The shaft is directed mainly against France, it would seem.

An Irish game hath an Irish trick or vengeance. (*Irish*).

After misfortune, the Irishman sees his profit. (*Irish*).

Like an Irish wolf, she barks at her own shadow. (*Irish*).

Melancholy as Irish melodies. (*American simile*).

Potent as Irish whiskey. (*American simile*).

Resolute as a drunken Irishman. (*American simile*).

ITALIANS

An ass in Germany is a professor in Rome. (*German*).

Eat in Poland, drink in Hungary, sleep in Germany, flirt in Italy. (*Polish*).

Italy is a paradise for horses, a hell for women. [ROBERT BURTON].

Three evils, the Germans brought out of Italy; empty bags, diseased bodies, and a bad conscience. (*German*).

Italy is the paradise of the flesh, the hell of the soul, and the purgatory of the pocketbook. (*German*).

Italy is a paradise wherein each has his sinning occasion. (*German*). *Sündefall* may mean also "fall through sin."

Italy is a paradise inhabited by devils. (*German*).

The Italian takes the money from the Church, and the Church from all the world. (*German*). In the original *Gelt* and *Welt* rhyme.

The Italians are either angels or devils. (*German*).

Of all Christians the Italians are the worst, and those at Rome the very worst. (*German*).

Half an Italian is one too many in a house. (*German*). It is uncertain whether the German or the French version of this saying came first.

Italian praying and German fasting are worth a bean. (*Medieval Latin*).

To get around the Italians, one must get up good and early. (*German*).

To one Genoese, seven Jews and one Florentine. (*Italian*).

One Genoese will get away with nine Jews. (*Italian*).

Italy might well be called a paradise; for whoever gets there readily falls into sin. (*German*).

Make one sign of the cross before an Andalusian and three on sighting a Genoese. (*Spanish*).

He that hath to do with a Tuscan must not be blind. (*Italian*).

Italian devotion and German fasting have no meaning. (*Danish*).

The Italianized Englishman is a devil incarnate. (*Italian*).

The Italians cry, the Germans bawl, and the French sing. (*French*).

If there be a hell, Rome is built over it. (*German*).

Genoa has mountains without wood, sea without fish, women without shame, and men without conscience. (*English*).

In Italy, there is too much grinding, too much feasting, and too many fires. (*German*). The rhyme is *Geleier, Gefeuer,* and *Gefeier.*

Italians will not fight. (*French*).

Italy is the land of the dead. (*French*).

Crafty as an Italian. (*Serbian*).

"Italian faithfulness." (*Dalmatian*). The phrase is *Lacmanska vira.*

The Italian will kill his father for money. (*Illyrian*).

To place before one, Italian soup. (*Czech*). To poison somebody. There are other similar expressions like "To die of an Italian arrow." These sayings are redolent of Borgian days.

Italian blood does no German good. (*German*).

If lies were Italian, he'd make a good interpreter. (*German*).

To cook an egg, to make the bed for a dog, and teach a Florentine to do anything are three hard things. (*German*).

JEWS

A priest's property and a Jew's are always safe. (*Polish*).

In Wilno there are seven roads for the Jew, and three for the Poles. (*Polish*).

Do not trust the dog that sleeps, the Jew who swears, the drunken man who prays, and the woman who weeps. (*Polish*).

A woman's knees, a peasant's chest, a baron's ears and a Jew's heels are never cold. (*Polish*).

Deceive a Jew and he will kiss you; kiss a Jew and he will deceive you. (*Russian*).

If a Jew can have the rope free of charge he will let himself be hanged. (*Russian*).

To murder a Jew is to remove forty sins from off one's soul. (*Ukrainian*).

A real Jew will never pause to eat till he has cheated you. (*Serbian*).

Judas never sleeps. (*Serbian*).

Count like Jew, agree like brother. (*Jamaica Negro*). This apparently was taken from the Scotch. Similar versions will be found elsewhere.

What he has been deposing is enough to bring a whole synagogue to the stake. (*Portuguese*).

If you beat my Jew, I'll beat yours. (*German*). A German view of tit for tat.

The real *(buen)* Jew will get gold out of straw. (*Spanish*).

A Jew's horse will receive enough water and exercise. (*Spanish*). A sarcastic dart at "Jewish" exploitation. The original is "*Harto de agua y bien corrido.*"

As scrupulous as a Jew on the Sabbath. (*Spanish*). Another version is "as scrupulous as a Jew on Friday," since the Sabbath begins on Friday eve, and preparations must be made before then.

The Jews sold Jesus Christ; were he alive now, he would have been sold by the baptized Jews. (*German*).

Before the Jew dies, he is ready to eat pork. (*German*). Here Wander, who cites this saying, impatiently adds: "A Christian would eat dog's and cat's meat if he thought it would protect him against death."

A Jew would not lend a Pfennig on a noble pedigree. (*German*).

There is as much superstition and magic in a Jew as there are hairs on nine cows. (*German*). Evidently this observation dates back to the eighteenth century and earlier. Wander deems it relevant to remind his readers that in 1510, seventy Jews were burned to death because the consecrated wafers in the damp cellar of the Church were covered with the red *monas prodigiosa*, which to the ignorant dignitaries was an indication that the Jews poisoned the Host.

A Jew says left is right, and his hindmouth is his foremouth. (*German*).

A Jew remains a Jew, though he sleep till noon. (*German*).

It is dangerous to deal with Jews when they begin using Hebrew words among themselves. (*German*). Their Yiddish was so much like German that the customer could understand it.

There are three kinds of Jews: cropped Jews, *i.e.*, mass priests who crucify Jesus every day in their masses; Jews wearing gold rings, *i.e.*, merchants who are more usurious than the Jews themselves; and circumcised Jews. (*German*).

Jews and fleas are the most impatient creatures on earth. (*German*).

Jews and jurists make vile Christians. (*German*).

Jews and tradespeople are the devil's staples. (*German*).

No Jew can be surety beyond his own house. (*German*). Jews had to lend money even on stolen goods, *i.e.*, without inquiring into their source, so that no purchaser could be secure against the risk of losing the bought article, should it turn out to have been stolen.

That's fit to eat for an ill Jew. (*German*). Apparently the Jews were supposed to be fastidious about their food.

A Jew would take something like that to heart. (*German*).

Well, no Jew will let you forget that so easily. (*German*). In other words, a well-learnt lesson.

You would sooner find bacon at the Jew's [than sense, or money]. (*German*).

It's like baptizing a dead Jew. (*German*).

He kissed a Jew. (*German*). Said of someone with an unpleasant odor. The Dutch parallel is probably taken from the German.

He is related to the Jews. (*German*). Said of someone who is in debt, the creditors being naturally Jews.

Did you see a Jew? (*German*). A catch-phrase in response to someone who is trying to get some information from or is teasing the speaker.

He is driving Jews. (*German*). Equivalent to "he is a timid individual." The phrase is based on a story that when Napoleon arrived in Posen, the Jews came out to meet him, dressed as Turks. When they reached the imperial coach, their leader said "Don't be afraid, your Majesty. We are not Turks but masqueraded Jews from Posen."

Off with the Jew; he has eaten bacon. (*German*).

Why, that you can buy at the Jew's. (*German*).

You act like the Jew who asks the way, though he well knows it himself. (*German*).

The pregnant Jew-girl would give birth to the Messiah and was delivered of a little daughter. (*German*).

The Jew-tax and the whore's hire are both very high. (*German*). Jew-tax here means his high rate of interest.

A Jew dies when two p - - - crosswise. (*German*). One of the many disgusting infantile superstitions in the land of poets and philosophers.

Ragged Jews have the most money. (*German*).

Freshly baptized Jews and new-baked barons are recognized by the tone. (*German*).

Of the converted Jew, better is due. (*German*). The original is *Getaufter Jud' tut selten gut.*

A baptized Jew is an empty leaf between the Old and New Testament. (*German*). We can scarcely call this sophisticated witticism a proverb, but it is an aphorism which lends itself to wide currency. A prelate of Mayence (*Mainz*), himself a converted Jew, a few centuries ago left his heirs a piece of statuary—a golden cat chasing a golden mouse with the legend underneath "No more will a Jew be a good Christian than this cat will eat the mouse."

Jew and Mennonite—of Christians the blight. (*German*).

Tartar and Jew are of the same stew. (*German*). In the original, *Jud' und Tatar ist einerlei Waar.*

Woman and Jew—all one crew. (*German*).

Only a Jew can convince a Jew. (*German*). It is well to note that Jews think differently.

Jews and loaded waggons have a tough time on ice. (*German*). The Dutch have a similar proverb.

The Jews and the nobility stick up for their own. (*German*).

He is just like the Jew; you throw him out of the front door and he comes in again from the rear. (*German*).

No one needs to be reminded to be—te a Jewish corpse once it's in sight. (*German*).

Honest Jews have hair on their palms. (*German*). That is to say, "as few Jews are honest as have hair on their palm."

You must be something more than a priest and a Jew to braid the Lord a beard of straw. (*German*).

A Jew is always lucky, though he sleep till noon. (*German*). He can always make his pile.

When the Jew comes to a village, the dogs bark. (*German*).

Sleep in the beds of Christians but don't eat their food; eat the food of Jews but don't sleep in their beds." (*Moorish*).*

Water with worms is better than the favor of Jews. (*Moorish*).

A Jew, if he cheats a Moslem, is happy that day. (*Moorish*).

If a Jew laughs at a Moslem, know that he girds himself [*i.e.,* makes himself ready] for cheating. (*Moorish*).

Don't trust a Jew if he has become Moslem, even though he remains so forty years. (*Moorish*).

If the power returns to the Jews [*i.e.,* the power they possessed in the times of Sidna Musa, or Moses], go into your house and close it. (*Moorish*).

If the Jew is of gold, his testicles are of copper. (*Moorish*).

A Jew in a room is better than a vile man. (*Moorish*).

Make friends with a Jew, he will be useful to you in this and that. (*Moorish*).

Do good even to a Jew; God will save you from enemies and envious people. (*Moorish*).

Azzuna [name for a Jewess of high rank, such as the wife of a rabbi] gives birth to a child, and the rabbi [her husband] feels pain in his bottom. (*Moorish*).

What a pity that the Jew has his eyes. (*Moorish*).

---

*In this and the following sayings, *Moorish* is intended as a synonym for *Moroccan*.

The Jews on a spit, and the Christians on a fish-hook, and the Moslems on a flower. (*Moorish*).

When the Jew is destitute, he remembers his father's buttons [*i.e.*, friends]. (*Moorish*).

You went to the Jewish quarter and called, "O lovers of the Prophet." (*Moorish*). The meaning is you tried to curry favor in vain by appealing to the heartless and faithless.

He is a Jew. (*German*). Not as innocent as it sounds, the saying is applied to one whose transactions are closely calculated.

He can cheat a Jew. (*German*). In other words, so cunning that he can go a Jew one better.

No Jew will lend you anything on it. (*German*).

No Jew will give you anything for a "has-been." (*German*).

He is off with the Jew-lance. (*German*). Apparently the picture is of a Jew hastening to collect money. The original reads: "*Er rennt mit dem Judenspiess.*"

Have nothing to do with priest or Jew. (*German*).

The Jew has come upon a priest. (*German*). Both were regarded as unscrupulous and therefore both of a kind by the Lutherans.

Count like Jews and agree like brethren. (*Scotch*).

Haggle like a Jew; pay like a brother. (*Estonian*).

Trade has spoilt the Jews and the Jews have spoilt trade. (*German*).

A bankrupt Jew searches his old accounts. (*Greek*).

Nothing is worse than a poor Jew, lean pork, or a drunken woman. (*Hungarian*).

A Jew does not give anything for "perhaps," because a hare does not have a tail. (*Livonian*).

Bargain like a Jew but pay like a Christian. (*Polish*).

The Pole is deceived by the German, the German by the Italian, the Italian by the Spaniard, the Spaniard by the Jew, the Jew by the devil. (Polish).

In misfortune even a Jew can be looked upon as a brother. (Polish).

In want, to the Jews; in distress, to the priest; in fear, to God. (Polish).

Two cheeses and one Jew make three smells. (Polish).

Punish the Jew with a whip, and the peasant with money. (Polish).

My coat is studying Hebrew. (German). A German student's way of announcing the fact that his coat is in hock, as most pawnshops were conducted by Jews.

Among the Jews it is better to be a swine than a human being. (German). This utterance was ascribed to Augustus when the infanticide of Herod was reported, but the curious part is that Herod, although King of Judea, was no Jew himself but an Idumean.

Jews, beggars, and gamblers always receive their dues in full. (German). They have no means of redress anyway.

For Jew and raven, bathing is in vain. (German).

The Jew bodes Christian no good. (German).

The Jew will rate nothing cheap that he receives free. (German).

The Jew will take a box in the ear if he gets it for nothing, but will not give one, if he can't profit by it. (German).

The Jew knows how to thrive by taking from others a shive. (German). In the original, *sich zu nähren und andere zu scheren.*

Ruination of the Jew; salvation for Christian. (German).

The most favorite Jewish color is yellow. (*German*). The color of gold.

The Jew will have his skin yellow because it reminds him of money. (*German*).

The Jews killed a hog in the Temple of Moses, s—— in a stocking and made bologna. Is this not something curious? (*German*). One of the bright sayings to be found in Wander's monumental collection of German proverbs. This classic, in another version—apparently a nursery rhyme —was heard a good deal in the German settlements in Poland, applied to their neighbors, who poked fun at them for their sausage-eating propensities. As Lück records it in his *Der Mythos vom Deutschen,* etc., page 176, the folk-jingle runs:
Polack, Strolack, Dudelsack;
Strumpf gesch . . . . Wurst gemacht.

The Jews use double chalk in writing. (*German*). Marking up the debts.

The Jews are of as much use to a country as the mice to a granary and the moths to clothes. (*German*).

No Jew could pass that up. (*German*).

No Jewish oath is valid against a Christian. (*German*).

Never trust a Jew on his oath nor a wolf on the heath. (*German*). In the original, the words *Eid* and *Heid* rhyme.

Two Jews know what a pair of spectacles are worth. (*German*). The moral is that two bids are necessary.

Over Jews and fleas, many a woe-cry is heard. (*German*).

When one Jew cheats another, when one priest betrays another, and one woman deceives another, God in heaven laughs. (*German*).

When a Jew is to receive money, he will come an hour too

early; when he has to pay out money, he will come at least an hour late. (*German*).

He who would baptize old Jews will waste a good deal of water. (*German*).

He who buys from a Jew need offer only half of what it's worth. (*German*).

Whoever offers [for a Jew's article] only half of the value is already cheated. (*German*).

Whoever trusts a Jew and sells his bed will have to sleep on straw. (*German*).

Trust a Jew and deny God—you are forever lost. (*German*).

Whoever trusts a Jew on his oath, a wolf on pasture, and a friend on his conscience free, will be bewrayed by all three. (*German*).

He who bewrays a Jew sins as much as courting a die. (*German*).

Whoever deceives a Jew receives ten years of dispensation. (*German*).

Where there are Jews and coals, it's time to fetch the devil. (*German*).

So many Jews, so many thieves. (*German*).

Ten Jews with the longest noses chased by one recruit like blazes. (*German*). In the original, *Nasen* and *Hasen*.

A Jew spat on this. (*German*). This used to be said to German children when a hole was found in their shirt or dress.

The Jews wished that on him. (*German*). Said of someone who has a nuisance on his hands.

That is something no Jew could stand, even if he were as old as the hills. (*German*).

It doesn't matter; let the Jew burn. (*German*).

Whoever loves Jews hates Germans. (*German*).

The German cheats the Pole; the Frenchman, the German; the Spaniard, the Frenchman; the Jew the Spaniard; and the devil only the Jew. (*Polish*). Variant on page 192.

What suits the Jews does not suit the Syrians. (*Danish*).

His pappy is a Paddy; his mammy—a Jew. (*English*). At one time supposed to be an outlandish union, and the offspring, therefore, a double half-caste.

One Jew is equal in cheating to two Greeks, and one Greek to two Armenians. (*Russian*).

When you baptize a Jew, keep him under water. (*Russian*).

By birth a landlord, by deeds a Jew. (*Russian*).

A Christianized Jew and a reconciled foe are not to be trusted. (*Russian*).

A Russian can be cheated only by a Gypsy, a Gypsy by a Jew, a Jew by a Greek, and a Greek by the devil. (*Russian*).

That's where a Jew died. (*Italian*). According to Zingarelli's *Vocabolario della Lingua Italiana,* this is said when a gambler meets with disaster.

Poland is the hell of peasants and the paradise of Jews. (*Polish*).

All idiots, priests, Jews, actors, monks, barbers and old women think they are physicians. (*Medieval Latin*).

When a Jew smiles at a Moslem, it is a sign that he is preparing to cheat him. (*Moorish*).

The peasant earns the money, the noble spends it, the Jew gets it in the end. (*Polish*).

Only the devil can cheat a Jew. (*Polish*).

A Jew and a wolf are never idle. (*Yiddish*).

A Jewish miser will regret nothing more than having had to part with his foreskin. (*Russian*). The Poles have a similar proverb.

A Jew found meat selling at next to nothing; "it stinks" he said, because the price was too high for him. (*Arab*).

The Jew is needed; "Oh no," says he "This day is a holiday for me." (*Arab*). Because his services were not to be paid for.

Give the Jew a ruble, and he will devour the whole of a young sow. (*Russian*).

If the Jew knew that the sow had swallowed half a kopek, he would have made a meal of it. (*Russian*).

Offer a Jew a thousand rubles for his wife; he will ask for another ruble, and offer you in addition his daughter. (*Russian*).

If you set up a Jew as a blacksmith, you have to pay for the iron and the nails. (*Russian*).

Don't trust a Jew, though he come from heaven. (*Ruthenian*).

Back to the water with the baptized Jew. (*Czech*).

When milk becomes dearer, the Jew drinks his wife's milk. (*Russian*).

Don't believe the woman who weeps, the horse that sweats, and the Jew who swears. (*Venetian*). Another Italian version of this proverb is:

A Jewish oath, a clear night, and women's tears are not worth a mite. (*Venetian*).

One who deceives a Jew receives a seat in heaven. (*Dutch*). The Germans have a slightly different version.

Jews do not learn cheating; they are born with it. (*Russian*).

The Jew is a cheat to begin with. (*Polish*).

The Jew cheats even while praying. (*Czech*).

The Jew will cheat himself, when the idea strikes him. (*Russian*).

Our lice are on our heads; the Jew's are in his heart. (*Russian*).

A Saxon cheated a Jew. (*German*). As if to say that a man bit a dog.

Some Jew must have gotten his goat. (*German*).

Sooner owe the Jew than the peasant. (*German*).

I'm no Jew and lick no sow. (*German*). In reply to a common vulgar expression, indicative of impatience or contempt.

A baptised Jew is a circumcised Christian. (*German*).

Moses does not play because he has not the wherewithal. (*Spanish*). Moses, of course, is here the representative name for the Jew.

There is not a pair of ears for every Jew. (*Spanish*). I gather that the sense of this saw is that the Jew has no ears for the exhortations of the Jesuits.

No Jew a fool, no hare lazy. (*Spanish*).

Folks say there is a shortage of four kinds of people on earth: of priests, else one would not have six or seven benefices; of gentlemen, else every boor would not want to be a squire; of whores, else married women and nuns would not carry on the trade; and of Jews, else Christians would not practise usury. (*German*).

Gone is gone; no Jew will lend on it. (*German*).

He that would cheat a Jew, must himself be a Jew. (*German*).

I never give or take, like a Jew on the Sabbath. (*Spanish*).

When the Jew grows poor, he looks to his old accounts. (*Arab or Moorish*).

No Jews, no wooden shoes. (*English catch-phrase about middle of eighteenth century*). Some demagogue used this slogan to associate an improbable French invasion with the handful of Jews who then resided in England.

To look like a Jew. (*English simile*). Thomas Coryat, himself of Sephardic stock, who cites the idiom in his *Crudities* (1611), presents various interpretations, none of them too complimentary: "Sometimes a weather beaten warp-faced fellow, sometimes a phreneticke and lunaticke person, sometimes one discontented."

To use one like a Jew. (*English simile*). While this phrase is not unequivocal, permitting of both the subjective and objective senses, it really points to the abuse and oppression which the Jews suffered in England for centuries.

No Jew will get any sense out of that. (*Dutch*). There is a German parallel to this.

He wanted to seize the Jew by the feet, and got the devil by the horns. (*Polish*). The German parallel is no different in sense.

A Jew dies; my father was a Jew; I'd like to die. (*Portuguese*). This cryptic proverb which, in the original Portuguese, reads: *Judeu morreu meu pae judeu quero morrer,* so far as I can interpret it means "Just after my father died, I discovered that he was a Jew, would that I were dead too."

Jew Ikey, nose spiky, nose pointy, nose sh—ty. (*Silesian*).

You're like the wandering Jew. (*Silesian*). The *ewige Jude* is supposed to come often and stay long.

He sat like a Jew. (*German*). The ethnophaulism is not so much the remark, as the action to suit the words, namely turning the chair around, or going from seat to seat.

Witch's liver, Jewfat, three times black tomcat. (*Silesian*). The relic of some old incantation, or a children's jingle like "Eenie, meenie, miney mo".

He must have passed through the wilderness with the chil-

dren of Israel. (*German*). This is usually said about a de-formed or unprepossessing person.

Roguery lies in the Jew's heart, while he is alive. (*German*).

The Jew is written all over his face. (*German*).

A real Jew never sits down to eat until he has been able to cheat. (*German*). There is a Rumanian version of this.

A Jew is of as much use as the moths in clothing. (*German*).

A Jew will never cross the ice, unless horse-dung there lies. (*German*).

Jews and apprentices you'll find everywhere. (*German*).

When a Jew at Mannheim gets a wallop, the Jews in Berlin and Hamburg feel the blow. (*German*).

Teaching Jews to ply their trade. (*German*). A saying like "teaching grandmother to eat her eggs."

Where Israelites decamp, there is bound to be a golden calf. (*German*).

Here comes the Jew. (*German*). A cry to frighten children, often heard in the Tyrol about a century ago.

Only a Jew will say that. (*German*).

That fellow is a restless Jew. (*German*).

A Jew fell into the water. (*German*). The first line of a folk-rhyme which runs as follows:

> **A Jew fell into the water;**
> **I heard him bounce and clatter;**
> **And had I not come over,**
> **He would have drowned right there.**

A Jew must be sitting here. (*German*). A catch-phrase of a gambler, when he receives a poor deal.

He outjews the Jew. (*German*).

[199]

Yiddle, Yiddle, hepp, hepp, hepp,
Jews get fat by eating pork. (*German*). I have translated the word "*Jüdlein*" by "yiddle."

In Poland, a Jew and an ass are always hung side by side.
(*German*).

Three things are maddening: the jurist with his book, the
Jew with his demands [interest] and the woman with her
handkerchief. (*German*). There is a triple rhyme in the
original — *Buche, Gesuche, weissem Tuche.* The handkerchief suggests weeping.

Erger, Berger, Schossberger;
Jews are all a scoundrel merger. (*Hungarian*).

He, whose sweetheart is a Jewish girl, should tie a rope
around his neck and whirl. (*Hungarian*).

When the Jew buys a gabardine, he becomes an expert on
cloth. (*Yiddish*).

If Moses could not get along with the Jews, could the man
in the street? (*Yiddish*). In reality this self-incriminating
saying is a kind of Irish bull, because the person to get along,
also a Jew, is just as bad as he whom he has to get along with.

> **Before borrowing, the Jew**
> **Goes a-worrying,**
> **When payment is due,**
> **He send the other whistling.** (*Yiddish*).

When a Jew is clever, he is very clever, and when he is a
fool, he is very much of a fool. (*Yiddish*).

The Jew is stubborn. (*Yiddish*).

The Jew will not give up, though death stare him in the
face. (*Yiddish*). Literally, "though the knife grazes his
throat."

The Jew likes to haggle. (*Yiddish*).

The Jew loves commerce. (*Yiddish*).

The Jew likes to poke his nose everywhere. (*Yiddish*).

The Jew is afraid of his own shadow. (*Yiddish*).

His own fur coat frightens the Jew. (*Yiddish*).

A Jew at a fair is like a fish in water. (*Yiddish*).

Whatever he may be, the Jew is no fool. (*Yiddish*).

A Jew answers a question by asking another. (*Yiddish*).

A Jew's answer is always in reverse. You say to him, "Peace be with you," and he replies "Unto you be peace." (*Yiddish*).

A Jew may be a thief, but never a robber. (*Yiddish*).

Every Jew has his idiosyncrasy. (*Yiddish*).

One Jew will begrudge another. (*Yiddish*).

All Jews might be cantors, were they not generally hoarse. (*Yiddish*).

The Jews have little of anything, but of intelligence they each have enough. (*Yiddish*).

The Lord guard us against Jewish arrogance, Jewish mouths, and Jewish heads. (*Yiddish*).

The Jew is put out not so much by his own poverty as by the other man's wealth. (*Yiddish*).

Every Jew would like the front seat in his little synagogue. (*Yiddish*).

The Jew is all right to eat pudding with, so long as it is not out of the same dish. (*Yiddish*).

The Jew is all right to pray with. (*Yiddish*).

There is nothing worse than a drunken Jew. (*Yiddish*).

No limit is enough for a Jew. (*Yiddish*).

Jewish gossip will not be cleansed by ten ablutions. (*Yiddish*).

In order to perform a good deed, he is ready to bury a Jew. (*Yiddish*). The Irish bull here is derived from the fact that Jewish burial is one of the most important precepts.

Once a Jew always a Jew. (*Yiddish*). This proverb which anti-Semitic writers have perverted in the sense that "a tiger cannot change his spots," actually means that even a converted Jew cannot drop his obligations, and also that Jews must be willing to welcome one of their number if he has become penitent after sinning against them.

Don't give a Jew the price he asks. (*Yiddish*). He is apt to fret for not having asked more.

The food and the insult are like the garden of a Jew. (*Moorish*). "It is said that a Jew speaks badly of a person who has been kind to him, and well of one who has treated him harshly." (E. Westermarck: *Wit and Wisdom in Morocco*.)

He beat me and wept, he went before me and complained. (*Moorish*). According to Westermarck's *Wit and Wisdom in Morocco*, this is styled a "Jewish accusation" by the natives.

The girdling is Christian and the business is Jewish. (*Moorish*).

Mammon is the God of the Jews. (*Hungarian*).

The Jew knows how to skin others while watching out for his own skin. (*Czech*). In the original, the pun consists in substituting an *i* for an *e*. It might be rendered perhaps "From each a shive makes the Jew thrive."

The Jew will lend nothing on a past something. (*Hungarian*).

A baptized Jew and a tamed wolf are but reconciled foes. (*Czech*).

A blunted sword, a domesticated wolf, a reconciled enemy, and a converted Jew—are not reliable. (*Polish*).

Give the Jew an egg and he'll demand the bird. (*Spanish*)

Tochuelo is an old Spanish word, about which there is considerable doubt, but it probably means a rare species of bird.

Don't trust a sleeping dog, a begging tippler, a Jew who swears, and a woman who weeps. (*Polish*).

Blind, poor, and old is a Jewish curse. (*Dutch*).

A bad neighbor is a Jew-curse. (*German*).

Lost like a Jewish soul. (*German*).

Hardened [*verstockt*] like a Jew. (*German*).

He spits like a Jew who has lost his lawsuit. (*German*).

Unsalted, it tastes like a dead Jew. (*German*). Referring to pigs' knuckles. The pig is thus identified with a Jew.

Everything seems to be going left, as with the Jews. (*German*).

Jews and crows will not benefit by a bath. (*German*).

Half wishing, half listening, like the Jew Grama. (*German*).

He looks like a Jew who lost his forfeit. (*Italian*). Designates a scornful expression.

He keeps his word like a Jew. (*Czech*).

The Christian is deceived by the Jew like the devil by his grandmother. (*Czech*).

The fly, the dog, and the Jew are chased away ten times, and yet they are back again. (*Czech*).

Monk and Jew, never true. (*Spanish*).

The Jew starts his journey, and stumbles on the Sabbath. (*Greek*). Jews must not travel on Saturday, except on foot, and even then but a short distance.

It's raining all over again like a Polish Jew. (*East Prussian*).

It's going to rain. The Jews are all about. (*Ukrainian*).

A good Gentile is better than a good Jew. (*Yiddish*). There may be a play of words here, since the "guter-yid," is the khassidic rabbi who is supposed to effect miracles, usually for some offering.

The Gentile is not respectful of Jews until he receives the first box (or slap). (*Yiddish*).

The Gentile who speaks Yiddish is no desirable article, nor is the woman who is Talmud-trained. (*Yiddish*).

The Gentile has no subtlety. (*Yiddish*).

The Gentile mind draws back. (*Yiddish*).

When the Pole thinks, he seizes his moustache, when the Russian thinks he takes hold of his forelocks, and when the Jew thinks, he holds his hands behind. (*Yiddish*).

When the Gentiles celebrate, the Jews are beaten. (*Yiddish*).

Give a Gentile a finger, and he will want the whole hand. (*Yiddish*).

Better a Jewish heart and a Gentile head, than a Gentile heart and a Jewish head. (*Yiddish*).

Better in the hands of a Gentile than in the mouth of a Jew. (*Yiddish*).

May the Lord preserve us against Gentile hands and Jewish heads. (*Yiddish*).

God save us from Gentile brawn and Jewish brains. (*Yiddish*).

May the Lord deliver us from Jewish pride and Gentile passion. (*Yiddish*).

To live among Gentiles; to die among Jews. (*Yiddish*).

Don't start up with a Gentile. (*Yiddish*).

The less the Jew, the greater the luck. (*Yiddish*). The original is: *Mer goy mer mazl; i.e.,* The more like a Gentile a Jew is, the luckier he will be. Cf. *"Gentile luck."*

A poor Gentile is better than a rich Jew. (*Yiddish*).

The Gentile is taboo, but his saying is kosher. (*Yiddish*). The Russian and Polish proverbs have much sense, even in the eyes of pious Jews, who prohibited the reading of books other than religious works in Hebrew (and Yiddish). Twin parodies have sprung from this proverb: "The Gentile is taboo, but his penny is kosher," and "The Jew is taboo but his groszen is clean" (to Gentiles).

JUTES

He lies like a Jute. (*Danish*).

Jutland tobacco. (*Frisian*). A vile-smelling brand.

Have you been long in Jutland? (*Danish*). The response to a boaster or liar.

LITHUANIANS

The Lithuanian is stupid like a pig but cunning like a serpent. (*Polish*).

The Litts are here; winter is near. (*German*). The Lithuanians here mean jackdaws whose cry reminds the Germans of Lithuanian sounds.

A Lithuanian [Jew] doesn't die. (*Yiddish*). The Polish and Ukrainian Jews have been at odds with their Lithuanian brethren, always taking the opportunity of finding flaws in them. In the present case, the sense of the saying is that the Lithuanian, in a constant state of ferment, either dies a Christian, or else is proscribed to Siberia as a revolutionary, or if he is pious, passes the rest of his days as a Palestinian.

The Lithuanian should not be trusted by a German, though they be bed-fellows. (*German*).

No Lithuanian is loyal to the Germans, even though he sleep till midday. (*German*).

The Lithuanian comes into the world with a horse's bit in his hands. (*German*). The Lithuanian is known for his horsemanship, and has, among the East Prussians, an unsavory reputation for horse-stealing.

The Lithuanian goes into the woods riding, and comes out driving. (*German*). The Lithuanian in Prussia is a master wainright, so that he fashions a cart usually in the forest out of wood alone, without the aid of metal operations.

A Lithuanian is not worth a pareska. (*German*). The pareska is a cheap slipper.

Did hogs feed here or did Lithuanians have a feast here? (*Polish*).

Lithuanian sincerity, an aged woman, and Jewish honesty are of no account. (*Polish*).

The Lithuanian has fair words for all, but is square with none. (*Polish*).

MANXMEN

The Manxman is never wise till the day after the fair. (*Manx*).

MOORS

There is quite a difference between hearing "The Moors are coming" and seeing them come. (*Spanish*).

Washing the head of a Moor [or a Negro] is only a waste of time and soap. (*French and Italian*).

An old Moor cannot learn a new language. (*Spanish*).

When a Moor goes to the bathhouse and comes out black again, he must still pay the attendant. (*German*). The reply to one who would dodge payment because the results are unsatisfactory.

"You blackamoor," says the kettle to the ladle. (*German*).

A Moor living among whites would like to be a blacksmith. (*German*).

A Moor does not paint, be he ever so black. (*German*).

A Moor may dress in white but cannot whiten his skin. (*German*).

One Moor will not blacken the other. (*German*).

A black Moor is better than the devil. (*German*).

A Moor is recognized by his complexion and a fool by his speech. (*German*).

Black will take no other hue. (*English*).

You would have to beat a Moor for long before he shows white spots. (*German*).

Moors when bathing will not blacken the water. (*German*).

Whoever wishes to be well served by a Moor should feed him well, let him work hard, and whip him thoroughly. (*German*).

The Jew ruins himself with Passovers, the Moor with wedding feasts, and the Christian with lawsuits. (*Spanish*).

The more Moors, the better victory. (*Spanish*).

Three Moors to a Portuguese, three Portuguese to an Englishman. (*Hindu*).

The Chinese have two eyes, the Franks one eye, but the Moors have none. (*Chinese*).

NEGROES

The devil of the Negro is white. (*Bulgarian*).

If Negroes were really good, their faces would not be black. (*Moorish*).

God made the white man and the black man, but the devil made the Mulatto. (*English*).

They are as like one another as two Negroes. (*German*).

Just put a Mulatto on horseback and he'll tell you his mother wasn't a Negress. (*Negro*).

Some niggers have got so much religion they want to have Sunday every day. (*American Negro*).

Why does the Negress take a bath, since she never can become white? (*Spanish*).

No matter how much you wash the Negro, he will ever remain black. (*Rumanian*).

On Negro territory, the Mulatto is fair. (*Spanish*).

The Negro has gone to the bathhouse, and talked about it for a year. (*Spanish*).

Under the coverlet, the Negress is like the white woman. (*Spanish*). (*Debajo de la manta tal es la negra como la blanca*).

You are always like the Abyssinian Negro. (*Turkish*). That is to say, you will never change.

Mulattoes fight, kids die. (*Negro*). Mulattoes stage a duel just to ape gallant whites, but end up in slaughtering a kid and making a feast to celebrate the reconciliation.

If there were goodness in the Negroes, their faces would not be [black like] iron. (*Moorish*).

The price of a Negro is [only] salt. (*Moorish*).

It is a lucky house where there is neither a Mabruk nor a Mabruka. (*Moorish*). These are names, meaning "the blessed one," which are given only to male and female slaves.

Don't be familiar with a Negro of the Gnawa. (*Moorish*).

A white man [is made to obey] **with a wink, a Negro with a blow.** (*Moorish*).

People say to the Negro, the face that is ashamed [in others] **is in you black.** (*Moorish*). He doesn't blush.

If the Negro does not taste the stick Sunday after Sunday, he says that there is nobody like him. (*Moorish*).

If the Negro is generous it does not belong to his nature, and if he is stingy, that is his nature. (*Moorish*).

Don't trust the son of a Negro wife [legal concubine], **even though he is blind.** (*Moorish*).

A Negress will never give birth to a child that makes her happy. (*Moorish*).

The Ethiopian becomes not white by the hot bath. (*Arabian poetry*).

The Negro in the South works only under the master's whip. (*American*).

Gay as a Negro funeral. (*American simile*).

Useless as a safety razor at a Negro ball. (*American simile*).

Proud as a Mulatto in a Negro congregation. (*American simile*).

All niggers look alike. (*American*).

NORMANS

A Norman makes and unmakes his promise. (*French*).

A Norman—one who is accustomed to recall his promise. (*French*).

Whoever is a Norman is a vagrant. (*French*).

A manceau is worth one and a-half Normans. (*French*).
The normand was a coin, as was the manceau.

NORWEGIANS

He looks like a Norwegian goat. (*Dutch*).

A Norwegian Norseman from Norway. (*Swedish*). The
dyed-in-the-wool quality of the rugged men of the North
is here playfully brought out by their kinsmen.

OSMANLIS

The Osmanli goes hunting in a carriage. (*Turkish*).

The Osmanli has no right nor left. (*Osmanli*).

The Osmanli's bread is on his knees. (*Osmanli*).

**By the side of an Osmanli, beware how you look; by the
side of a secretary, beware what you say.** (*Osmanli*).
SEE ALSO *TURKS*

PERSIANS

**The Negro eats till he has had enough, the Persian till he
bursts.** (*Osmanli*).

Like Persian stuff, it comes out at both ends. (*Osmanli*).

**The difference between Arabs and Persians is the same as
that between the date and its stone.** (*Arabian*).

PICARDS

The Picard has his head too close to the cap. (*French*). Indicating that he is headstrong.

Head and feast of a Picard. (*French*). The original is *tête et fête,* allusions to his impulsiveness and the drinking penchant.

To find their masters, the dogs of Normandy look up; those of Picardy look down. (*French*). Evidently, overcome by drink. Reinsberg-Düringsfeld points out another subtle hint in the saying, namely that the Normans deserved to be hanged.

For a Picard, you are not simple enough. (*French*).

"Picard, your house is afire!"
"What of it? I've got the key in my pocket."
(*French*). Typical of the happy-go-lucky attitude.

Ninety-nine sparrows and one Picard make 100 thieves. (*French*).

These Picards are not backward when it comes to battle. At first they are hardy, but then become cowardly. (*Latin Medieval rhyme*).

POLES

Nothing to hand in Poland. (*German*). The original is *In Polen ist nichts zu holen.*

Things are run no better than in Poland. (*German*).

A Polish bridge, a Bohemian monk, a Swabian nun, an Austrian soldier, Italian reverence, and German fasting, are worth a bean. (*German*).

What an Englishman cares to invent, a Frenchman to design, or a German to patch together, the stupid Pole will buy and the Russian will deprive him of it. (*Polish*).

God save us from a Polish bridge! (*German?*).

A Jew thinks of wife and child; the Polish squire, of horse and dog. (*Yiddish*).

Where there are two Poles, there will be three parties. (*German*).

In Poland, the churches have their pastures. (*German*).

The overabundance in Poland is its ruination. (*Polish*).

Poland has three governors; one abroad, one in Warsaw, and the third abroad. (*Polish*). The joke circulated around 1860 when the governor and his successor were both travelling, with an acting governor only to represent the Czar.

Poland has a ministry with four *withouts*: A minister of education without schools, a cultusminister without churches, a minister of justice without justice, and a minister of the treasury without finances. (*Polish*). This condition was incidental to the suppressed rebellion; and the grim humor of the Poles was an outlet for their despair.

Poland is ruled in confusion. (*German*). There is also the Latin version *Polonia confusione regitur.*

A single Russian hair outweighs half a Pole. (*Russian*).

The Pole is a thief; the Prussian, a traitor; the Bohemian, a heretic; and the Swabian, a chatterbox. (*Latin and German*). This proverb, cited in Latin, was first heard in Poland (Sarmatia, then), probably during the Hussite rebellion.

Polack language—omnibus language. (*German colonists in Poland*). The original as quoted by Lück is *Polacksprache—Sammelsprache.*

One word out of every tongue in the world—that is what the Polack language represents. (*Polish-German*).

The duck must be a Polish animal, because it always quacks "tak, tak, tak." (*German*). *Tak*, in Polish, means "so" "indeed," and is thus very often heard in conversation.

The Pole has a large mouth, but there is nothing back of it. (*German*).

He makes an appearance like a Polish nobleman. (*German*). "Putting on a big front."

He moans like a Polack. (*German colonists in Poland*). When a worker is heard sighing at work.

He eats everything like a Polack. (*German colonists in Poland*).

What the Pole now has (or is), **the German has forgotten.** (*German*).

Sluggards have it nowhere better than in Poland. (*German*).

What the German has excogitated, the Pole has only imitated. (*German colonists in Poland*).

A one-eyed Pomeranian sees more than three Kashubes. (*Pomeranian German*). The Kashubes or Slovintzis are a Polish offshoot living around Danzig and in Pomerania.

In Poland, a bagpipe stirs up the whole village. (*German*).

They are fighting over the Polish crown. (*German*). Quarreling over a fantastic or unattainable object.

The Mazurs have a black pipe. (*Lithuanian*). The Mazurs are a Polish tribe; and the pipe probably stands for the windpipe.

The Alps divide us from the Italians
    From the French, the rivers separate us
    The sea is between us and the English
    But only hate keeps us and the Poles apart. (*German seventeenth-century rhyme*).

      Where there are three Poles,
      There will be five opinions. (*German*).

How can we know a Pole? Run, and when you have looked back, you will see him following you. (*Ukrainian*).

Eight barons in the Oszmian district take one goat to market. (*Polish*). Extreme poverty.

Love without jealousy is like a Pole without lice. (*French*).

Give me, oh God, beforehand the sense which the Pole has too late. (*Ruthenian*).

Poland: The heaven of the nobility; paradise of the Jews, purgatory of the common man, and hell of the peasant, the gold-mine of foreigners, and the source of feminine luxury. Rich in wool, it is yet without cloth, grows flax in overabundance, and yet imports linen from abroad, favors all foreign goods and belittles its domestic products, boasts of its costly purchases and despises everything that is cheap. (old *Latin dictum*).

The Pole will sooner steal a horse on Sunday than eat milk or butter on Friday. (*German*).

Like a Polish boot; fits either foot. (*German*).

It rattles like a Polish cart. (*German?*).

Polish infantry is worth little. (*German*).

Two privates and four captains [in a Polish company] . (*German*).

Polish scares; but the Ruthenian fears them not. (*Ruthenian*).

Get a move on you, Pole; make room for the Ruthenians. (*Ruthenian*).

The Pole doesn't like being slain; his legs are still aquiver. (*Ruthenian*).

Why does the devil take the Polacks? Because they are glad to go along. (*Ruthenian*).

The devil has fashioned all the Polacks out of one last. (*Ruthenian*).

The Pole is there to oppress, and the peasant to endure. (*Ukrainian*).

The Pole becomes wise only after the harm is done. (*German*). The Poles and the Ukrainians have a similar saying.

Poles and Gypsies are one and the same. (*Ukrainian*).

May I be thrice a Pole, if this isn't so. (*Ukrainian*). A sort of oath which the listener sometimes affects to render more serious by exclaiming in a frightened tone, "Just think of your soul and don't curse it."

The loyalty of Poles, Jews, and dogs is identical. (*Ukrainian*).

May you croak in the faith of the Poles! (*Ukrainian*). That is regarded as an outrageous curse.

Mother, blindfold me so that I wouldn't see the terrible Poles. (*Ukrainian, among children*).

He is a Polish Englishman. (*Polish*). The phrase is similar to our "She's a Latin from Manhattan." The slur is not against the Englishman but against the Pole who poses as such.

The Pole often drinks away in one day more than the German can amass in a life-time. (*German*). The Poles say it, too, by way of a boast.

A Pole tells lies even in his old age. (*Russian*).

We are not in Poland where the women are stronger than the men. (*Russian*).

When God made the world, He gave the Poles some reason and the feet of a gnat, but even this little was taken away by a woman. (*Russian*).

As stubborn as a Polish horse. (*German*).

Things are like in provincial Poland. (*German*).

THE PORTUGUESE

A bad Spaniard makes a good Portuguese. (*Spanish*).

Take from a Spaniard all his good qualities, and there remains a Portuguese. (*Spanish*).

A Portuguese apprentice who can't sew, yet would be cutting out. (*Spanish*). The overconfidence of the Portuguese is ridiculed here.

PRUSSIANS

The Prussians have two stomachs but no heart. (*Low German*).

RUMANIANS

"We must show the Russians that we too are heroes," said the Rumanian and forthwith slew the Jew. (*German*).

How can we know a Wallachian? Show him a pocketbook and ask him to whom it belongs. (*Ukrainian*).

He left him as St. Paul did the Wallachian. (*Hungarian*). Rather brusquely.

RUSSIANS

If the Russian tells you, "it's dry," just put your collar up. (*Ukrainian*).

The Russian knows the way, yet he asks for directions. (*Ukrainian*).

The wolf is berated while the Russian nabbed the mare. (*Ukrainian*).

He swears like the Russian in the village. (*Ukrainian*).

He has become so Russian that he is ready to cut the heels off the living flesh. (*Ukrainian*).

Be friendly with the Russian, but take care that you always have a rock ready on your chest. (*Ukrainian*). The Pole and the Ruthenian say the same about one another.

The Russian looks like a crow, but he is slyer than the devil. (*Ukrainian*).

The devil you can ban with the cross, but of the Russian you can never get rid. (*Ukrainian*).

"Father, father, the devil is in this hut." "That's nothing, child, so long as it's not a Russian." (*Ukrainian*).

Cut the fields away before the Russians, and flee. (*Ukrainian*).

Please God that I don't meet a pope [orthodox Greek priest] **or run into a Russian, then there is nothing to fear.** (*Ukrainian*). Although Reinsberg-Düringsfeld attributes this "prayer" to the Ukrainians, it would be more logical for the Poles to show their aversion for the Russian priest.

Pshaw: the Russian is no great shakes. (*Ukrainian*).

Whoever goes to Russia must return home. (*Polish*).

If there is no magic in it, there is none in the Russian either. (*Polish*). That is to say, clever as it is, the Russians used no magic to devise it, and we can do the same.

The Cossack is like a child; sometimes he fills up on food, and sometimes on hope. (*Russian*).

The Cossack never drinks to that which is, but to that which is yet to come. (*Ukrainian*).

When the Turk comes, bread is cheap. (*Rumanian*). This folk-expression is really a slur on the Russians, for no sooner had they withdrawn, in 1854, than the Turks settled in Rumania, paying cash for everything.

The Russian steals, the Turk counts. (*Rumanian*). Both nationalities began to settle in Wallachia around 1854.

The Russians act out of terror and compulsion; the Germans out of obedience; the Swiss because they want peace; the Poles in order to have a free voice; the French for the sake of their king's glory and the English for the love of freedom. (*German*). This characterization dates, according to Wander, from 1776.

A Russian without the knout seldom does good. (*German*). The cat-o'-nine tails was often used on the Russian serfs.

Once the Russian has minced the meat, a German stomach will be found. (*German*). The Germans were known as "sausage fiends" in Russia.

[217]

Three Jews will be outwitted by a single Russian. (*Russian*). This is said to date from the time of Peter the Great, when he was approached to allow the Jews to return to Russia for which privilege they would pay 100,000 gulden. He was said to have replied that for their good, it would be better to wait, for "I know my Russians."

Scratch a Russian and you'll find a Tartar. (*English*). The French and the Germans have the same proverb.

What is good for the Russian is death for the German. (*Russian*).

You may praise a Russian a thousand times, but his eyes will still be blue. (*Turkish*).

The Russian is clever but always too late. (*Russian*).

Scratch a Russian and the bear will growl. (*German*).

Why, no Russian would think of it! (*German street expression*). Equivalent to "How can you accuse me of such!"

You'll get such a drubbing that you'll remember it a full Russian month. (*Polish*). The Russian month, following the Gregorian or Greek calendar, ends thirteen days later than the Julian or Roman month, hence was thought of as a long period.

How can we know a Russian? Go to sleep, and he will rob you. (*Ukrainian*).

Why are you so ravenous as if the Muscovite [Muskof] were pursuing you? (*Albanian*).

The faithless Muscovite has sold his soul to the devil. (*Polish folk jingle*).

The Muscovites eat children alive. (*Polish folk or children's jingle*).

A Russian is as sly as four Jews. (*Ukrainian*).

Don't let the Russian die and he won't let you live. (*German*).

Carry the Russian all day on your back, and in the evening he'll complain of being tired. (*Rumanian*).

In Russia all but God and the Czar steal. (*German*).

It's getting cold; the wind is blowing here from the Muscovites. (*Polish*).

RUTHENIANS*

Stiff-necked like a Ruthenian. (*Polish*).

Whoever would cheat a Ruthenian must be pretty clever. (*Polish*).

See Also UKRAINIANS

SAXONS

Don't yield to the Saxon but beat him well. (*Irish*).

Beware of the hoof of the horse, the horn of the bull, and the smile of the Saxon. (*English*).

The Saxons tolerate no evidence. (*German*).

Every Saxon will let the other take his oath where the evidence is not too favorable. (*German*).

Why should the Saxons be concerned when the Netherlanders have no bread? (*German*).

THE SCOTCH

A Scotchman and a Newcastle grindstone travel all the world over. (*English*).

A Scotchman, a crow, and a Newcastle grindstone travel a' the world ower. (*Scotch*).

A Scotchman is one who keeps the Sabbath and every other thing he can lay his hands on. (*American*).

*Ukrainians in Galicia, whom the Austrian and Polish reactionaries considered an independent nationality so as to reduce the claims of the Ukrainians (*divide et impera*).

If that you will France win, then with Scotland first begin. (*English*).

A Scotch mist will wet an Englishman to the skin. (*Scotch*).

Gae to Scotland without siller [silver], and to Ireland without blarney [fair words]. (*Scotch*).

Every English archer beareth under his girdle twenty-four Scots. (*English or Scotch*).

The Scot will not fight till he sees his own blood. (*English*).

The Scotsman is never at home but when he's abroad. (*Scotch*).

Three failures and a fire make a Scotsman's fortune. (*Scotch*).

Bare as a Scotchman's knee. (*American simile*).

Gie a Scotchman an inch and he'll take an ell. (*Scotch*).

Scotsmen tak a' they can get, and a little more if they can. (*Scotch*).

God keep the kindly Scot from the cloth-yard shaft, and he will keep himself from the handy stroke. (*Scotch*).

Crooked as a Scotchman's cane. (*English simile*).

We will not lose a Scot. (*English*). The sense is that no matter how slight the object, we do not want to risk losing it, if it is in our power.

You have a Scottish tongue in your head. (*Scotch*). In answer to those who wish to shirk a task by pleading ignorance, as if they couldn't ask.

The Irishman's wit is on his tongue, but the Gael is wise after the time. (*Gaelic*).

The Scots wear short patience and long daggers. (*Scotch*).

The Scotsman is aye wise ahint the hand. (*Scotch*). His wit comes too late.

As hard-hearted as a Scot of Scotland. (*English*).

A Scottish man is wise behind the hand. (*English*).

Judas might have repented before he could have found a tree to have hanged himself upon, had he betrayed Christ in Scotland. (*English*).

Scotsmen aye reckon frae an ill hour. (*Scotch*).

Scotsmen aye tak' their mark frae a mischief. (*Scotch*).
In these last two proverbs, the Scotchman takes himself to task for tactlessly referring to something which should not be brought up.

Nipping and scarting's Scotch folks wooing. (*Scotch*). *Scarting* is "scratching," with reference perhaps to the "itch," which the Scotch were said to be afflicted with. See "Ethnophaulisms in the English Language" of this DICTIONARY, under words "Scotch fiddle" and "Itchland."

Jews, Scotchmen, and counterfeits will be encountered throughout the world. (*German*). Here *Gelt* and *Welt* rhyme.

The Scotch are hellish women. (*German*). A rather recent pronouncement on the kilted bagpipers who inflicted much punishment on the Germans during the first World War.

He will dance his fling in socks. (*German*). "I'll make him run so hard that he will lose his shoes."

SERBIANS

Serbian impetuosity and Greek restlessness do no good. (*Serbian*).

Three Jews to one Levantine Serb in cunning. (*German, but probably originating in Hungary*). The original is "*Drei Juden geben erst einen Raizen. Raizen* refers to an Oriental Serb living in Hungary.

SLAVS (in general)

Night and day shall we pray that Slav and steer don't learn [the power of] their horn. (*Illyrian*).

Millet is no food; the Slav is no freeman. (*Hungarian*).

SLOVAKS

Potatoes are not food, Slovaks are not human beings. (*Hungarian*).

If you take a Slovak in to stay, he will turn you out of your house any day. (*Hungarian*).

A Slovak, that is to say not a person. (*Hungarian*).

THE SPANISH

The Spaniard is a bad servant, but a worse master. (*English*).

A man would live in Italy but he would choose to die in Spain. (*Probably English*). The contrast between living amidst pleasure and dying with all the rites rigidly carried out is the substance of this saying.

May my death come to me from Spain. (*Spanish and Italian*). In this saying, *Mi venga la muerte de Spagna,* the Spaniards pay a left-handed tribute to their own dilatoriness. The Italians seized on the proverb as if it originated with them.

Nothing ill in Spain but that which speaks. (*Spanish*). This condition, which bespeaks self-complacency, was attested to by the English traveller, Howell, in 1642, who, years before, found apparently nothing to criticise there. It is doubtful whether the proverb has been used by ordinary folk in centuries.

Succors of Spain, either late or never. (*Spanish*).

Jealous as a Spaniard. (*English simile*).

Proud as a Spanish grandee. (*English simile*).

[222]

According to the custom of Aragon—good service, bad guerdon. (*Spanish*).

When a Spaniard sings, he is either mad or has no money. (*Spanish*).

Have you got any Spanish? (*English*). In this way the English get even with the Spaniards for asking "Do you speak English?" when they wish to pair "money" and "English" as synonyms.

The only good that comes from the East is the sun. (*Portuguese*). A barb directed at Spain.

He speaks French like a Spanish cow. (*French*).

In a Spanish inn, you will find only what you have brought there yourself. (*French*). Although this observation comes from an individual writer, who apparently could not satisfy his French taste in Spanish taverns, it is often quoted.

The Spaniard is a Frenchman turned inside out. (*German*).

The Spaniard seems to be wiser than he is. (*German*).

The Spaniard would honor have, even if he must dig it from the grave. (*German*).

The Spaniard's war is more serviceable than his peace. (*German*).

Spanish and German slowness differ in that the former is dragging always ahead, while the latter drags behind. (*German*). Because of the obscurity of this epigram, the original is presented here: *Des Spaniers und Deutschen Langsamkeit unterscheiden sich so dass jene immer vor sich diese hinter sich geht.*

All Spaniards have sticky fingers. (*German*). In past centuries, the pots on the stove would have padlocks on them.

The Spaniards used to tug at their subjects in Sicily for

money; in Naples they would skin them; and in Milan, they would consume them. (*German*).

The Spaniards seem to be wise but are not; the French are wise but don't give the appearance of being so. (*German*).

The Spaniards are like body lice; once they are there, it is not easy to get rid of them. (*German*).

A Spaniard is no Spaniard if he is not a snob. (*German*).

A Spaniard will rather wear a torn shirt than a torn garment. (*German*). Most people would, I should think.

A Spaniard and a braggart are synonymous. (*German*).

A Spaniard may well be trusted but not farther than the nose. (*German*).

A Spaniard drops his courtliness only when the grave-digger has him in his power. (*German*).

A Spaniard is not to be trusted any more than if he had a cartload of earth on his mouth. (*German*).

"Spaniards no longer draw," said the Jew when a Spanish fly was prescribed for him. (*German*).

In Spain, the reputed simplicity of the Germans is now thought of as little as the Spanish *bon mot*. (*German*).

In Spain, all girls are called Mary, but they are not so named. (*German*). They are named after some particular attribute of Mary, *e.g.*, Dolores, or Concepcion.

Spain is the purgatory of all Europeans. (*German*). Because of its hot climate.

In Spain I reign over slaves; in Germany I rule over kings. (*German*). This was said to have first come from the lips of Charles V.

In Spain, the last flame which is to consume the world will have little to do. (*German*). The shortage of wood in that country has given rise to this remark.

Spain can supply the whole world with generals. (*German*). Yes, but not with *a* general.

Spain would be a fine country, if there were no Spaniards in it. (*German*).

If Spain had as many people as France, and France as many houses as Spain, both would have been on the road to recovery. (*German*).

When there is a fire in Spain, it lasts four days. (*German*).

He who would eat in Spain must bring his kitchen along. (*German*).

The German thinks of the past; the Frenchman of the present, and the Spaniard of the future. (*German*). Probably he is building castles in the air.

No laws can apply to German swilling, Italian dalliance, and Spanish pilfering. (*German*). This saying is attributed to Charles V, Holy Roman Emperor.

The Spaniards teach the Germans to steal, while the Germans teach the Spaniards to gorge and swill. (*German*).

Turkish sooner than Spanish. (*Dutch*).

Spain makes men and wastes them. (*Spanish*).

The Catalan sings well, if he is paid. (*Spanish-Castilian*). By way of retaliation, the Catalan replies "A gallego pedidor, Castelan tenidor," which may be translated rather freely thus:

When the Galician begs, the Castilian "ducks." (*Catalan*).

A chieftain must have Spanish feet so that he might rest where he stands. (*Polish*).

A rooster on a bench jumps like a Spaniard. (*Polish*).

He was given a Spanish fig. (*Dutch*). To wit: poison.

Three Spaniards make four devils in French. (*French*).

In Spanish style: a great advance and a beautiful retreat. (*Italian*).

[225]

He is slimmer than any Spaniard. (*Italian*).

Easterly winds and rain bring cockles here from Spain. (*English*).

SWABIANS

He's had the tough luck of the Swabian whose wife died on Good Friday, and who has another to take her place, but not before Easter. (*Swiss*).

Among the Swabians, the nun is chaste who has not yet given birth. (*North German*). Dating from sixteenth century.

A Swabian supper consists of three kinds of soup. (*German*).

The Swabian woman is dumb. (*Swiss*). Something incredible, because Swabians are regarded as chatterboxes, perhaps because of a play of words on their name. *See Supplementary Essay under "Linguistic Factors."*

One man is a match for seven Swabians. (*Alsace German*).

SWEDES

The Swedes had come, with fife and drum, seizing everything they could; breaking windows, they took the lead out, making bullets to shoot the girls with, while letting the boys off. (*German jingle*). This folk-rhyme (in the original) gave a picture of conditions in Germany during the Thirty Years' War, when the troops of Gustavus Adolphus invaded Prussia.

So long as the Swedes eat their dry crackers they can be trusted, but when they are on foreign fare, they become fierce. (*German*).

Against the Swedes, armor is a worthwhile prescription. (*German*). The word "*bewert*(h)" is not to be found in Grimm's Dictionary; "worthwhile" could not be far out.

Whoever would slap a Swede must be there to do it. (*German*).

Oh, something the Swedes left behind. (*German*). The Swedes were alleged to have left only the cobblestones behind when they invaded Germany during the Thirty Years' War.

May the Swede come upon you! (*German*). This curse dating from the Swedish-German wars, is equivalent to "the devil take you!"

The Swedes have come! (*German and Dutch*). Again an echo of the Thirty Years' War, when the Swedes struck terror into many a German heart.

There **is a Swede for you!** (*Silesian*).

You're a regular Swede. (*German*). Not in any flattering sense.

After it's all over, the Swede becomes wise. (*Finnish*).

He is an old Swede. (*German*). An experienced warrior who has been through the mill—a relic of the Thirty Years' War.

He perished like a Swede at Poltava. (*Russian*). There Charles XII of Sweden was defeated by the Czar, in 1709.

THE SWISS

No more money, no more Swiss. (*French*). The saying stems from the attitude of the Swiss bodyguards who refused to serve when their pay was not forthcoming. Thus the French branded them as mercenary.

A Swiss, like a fool, always sticks to his trade. (*French*).

He listens to reason no more than a Swiss. (*French*). To the French, the Swiss are a stubborn people.

You might just as well run your head against a wall as talk to a Swiss. (*French*).

O pshaw! Not a Kreuzer for a hundred Switzers. (*German folk rhyme*). This seems like a boomerang against the Swiss attitude expressed in the German *Kein Kreuzer, kein Schweizer* (No money, no Swiss).

Whether one has originally come from Switzerland minus brains or lost it in Swabia, has still the learned at odds. (*German*).

"Switzerland is very beautiful" said the maid "but there are altogether too many lakes and too few young men." (*German*).

A Swiss has two bad nights when he can't sleep; the one is when he has loaded his stomach, the other when he is awake thinking how he could fill it again. (*German*).

The Swiss must have some hole through which he gets out. (*German*). The ubiquity of the lackey and his servile profession are thus scorned.

It is too bad that Swiss must fight Swiss. (*German*). Swiss guards on opposite sides.

Fly Swiss; the Swabians are coming. (*German*). A catch-phrase of a century ago.

Let the Swiss alone in their callings and miscallings. (*German*). The German original rhymes—*Gebrauch* and *Misbrauch*.

If the Swiss dies today, he is dead tomorrow. (*German*). Probably the stolidity of the Swiss has inspired this saying.

When the Swiss take three steps forward culturally, they retreat two steps lest they lose an iota of their freedom. (*German*). This can hardly be a folk-saying, and has been attributed to Bodmer, himself one of the most cultured Swiss writers.

To take something apart with the Swiss axe. (*German*). The word *Schweizeraxt* is cited but not explained even in Grimm's Dictionary. I wonder if it is not a huge axe, so that the sense might be to put on a great effort for a small task, like using a truck to deliver a spool of cotton.

He is like a Swiss cow, which grazes on grass and flowers. (*German*). A reproach to those who are ready to criticize alike the worthy and the unworthy.

TARTARS

Desolate as in Tartary. (*Polish*).

When the Tartar runs, your head is at stake. (*Polish*).

A horse without a bridle, the Tartars in Podolia, and pills in the body are not without ill consequences. (*Polish*).

I strive for it as for the favor of the Tartar Khan. (*Polish*). Symbol of a superlative effort.

Woe to the civilian who is set upon by the Tartar. (*Ukrainian*).

The Tartar carnival is without end. (*Russian*).

I love courage, even among the Tartars. (*Russian*).

Age is respected among the very Tartars. (*Russian*).

The Tartar has no need of a guide. (*Osmanli*).

The Tartar sells his own father. (*Osmanli*).

The Tartar is born a pig, therefore he does not eat pork. (*Russian*).

Is there a Tartar who is chasing you? (*Osmanli*). To someone excited and impatient.

The Tartar who lives in a city believes himself in prison. (*Turkish*).

TELUGUS

If a Telugu man prosper, he is of no use to anyone. (*Tamil*).

TURKS

To a Turk, the inside of a town is a prison. (*Osmanli*).

Rugged as a Saracen. (*English simile*).

What does the Turk know of Bayram? He (can only) lap and drink whey. (*Osmanli*).

They gave a beyship to the Turk; and he first killed his father. (*Osmanli*).

The Turk and the young lion, together with the donkey, took counsel from the calf, because he [the Turk] was born of his [the calf's] mother. (*Osmanli*).

The Turk's sense comes afterwards. (*Osmanli*).

Where the Turk's horse once treads, the grass never grows. (*English*).

A horse is the ruin of the Osmanli; obstinacy ruins the Turk. (*Osmanli*).

The more you plunder a Turk, the richer he is. (*Montenegrin*).

A Turk, a parrot and a hare; these three are never grateful. (*Indian*).

Adam and Eve spoke of their love in Persian, and the angel who drove them out of Paradise spoke Turkish. (*Persian*).

No grass will grow where the Kurd's horse has rested its foot. (*Turkish*). The English say the same for the Turk's horse.

Never be in debt to a Turk, for whether you will be attending a wedding or the feast of Bayram, he will come to annoy you. (*Osmanli*).

A Turk on horseback thinks himself a prince. (*Osmanli*).

A Turk might become a scholar but never a man. (*Osmanli*).

An Arab eats until he has had his fill, but a Turk does not stop eating until he bursts. (*Osmanli*).

The Turk said: "Eat first and speak afterwards"; the Armenian said: "Eat and speak at the same time." (*Armenian*).

Turk and Tartar—twin godfathers. (*German*). Both devastated a large part of the world. And now a third is to form the unholy trio.

No cold without a gust; and without Turks no bad guests. (*Serbian*).

Not forever shall the Turks remain at the Danube. (*Ukrainian*).

Promises should not be made to a Turk or a child, or else they should be at once fulfilled. (*German*).

Many to the Near East soar who could at home do far more. (*German*). Around the fifteenth century, travel to Turkey was fashionable among the nobility.

Be on your guard against an old Turk and a young Serb. (*Czech*). The Germans have the same maxim.

Who would a Turk have sink, should get him brandy wine to drink. (*German*).

Wherever the Turk sets foot, no grass will grow there for good. (*German*).

Where the Turk doth set foot, for a hundred years the soil brings forth no fruit. (*German*).

No grass grows in the trail of the Turk. (*Arab*).

No Turk could endure that. (*Dutch*, also *German*).

That were too cruel even for a Turk. (*Dutch*). Too cruel punishment to be meted out even to such barbarians.

You can try that on a Turk, who has nothing to lose anyway. (*German*).

That fellow is even viler than the Turk. (*Serbian*).

The Turk holds his faith on his knees. (*Serbian*). He always falls down on his promises.

Even the Turk takes pity on his own.

He is having it as bad as the Turk at Neuhäusel. (*German*). A famous fortress in Austria which the Turks besieged in 1592 without making any appreciable progress. The saying then is equivalent to the information that X has tough sledding.

Like the Turk at a sermon. (*Italian*). Naturally at a Christian sermon.

Nude like a Turkish saint. (*Russian*).

As stupid as a Turkish horse. (*Galician*).

He walks by him as by a Turkish cemetery. (*Serbian*). Without so much as giving him a glance.

Worse than a Turk. (*Serbian*).

He is in the clutches of the Turk. (*Dutch*).

The answer to a Turkish question should be in Turkish. (*Persian*).

No measure to the ocean; no honesty in the Turk. (*Illyrian*).

In the forest, it's the wolf; in the field it's the Turk. (*Bosnian*). That we must guard against, or who is about to destroy us.

Gouge out the eye of the Turk and offer him a ducat; then you need have no fear. (*Serbian*).

The Turk's honor is on his knee. (*Serbian*). It rolls off on rising.

When I do what's unjust, God keeps me from laughing; when I do what's just, the Turks make it impossible to laugh. (*Bosnian*).

A "turn-Turk" is worse than a hundred [real] Turks. (*Dalmatian*).

That fellow is some Turk. (*German*).

There are no baser Turks than those turned Turks. (*Serbian*).

The turncoat is worse than a hundred Turks. (*Illyrian*).

Turks here, wolves there. (*Serbian*). Thus the Serbs found themselves between the devil and the deep sea.

To sue a Turk in a Turkish court. (*Czech*). What chance of justice was there in days of yore?

You must sing the Turkish song now that you have baited and lured the Turks. (*German*).

The Turkish curse fall upon you! (*German*). The curse really affected the Hungarians who, according to the imprecation, were never to be of accord among themselves.

Bad neighbours: a Turkish curse. (*Hungarian*).

TURKOMANS

A Turkoman on horseback neither father nor mother will lack. (*Persian*).

A Turkoman who hears the word "Paradise" mentioned asks: "Is there any booty to be had there?" (*Persian*).

UKRAINIANS

As in the Ukraine. (*Polish*). An outbreak of lawlessness.

The Ukrainian is the first-born of the cattle. (*German*).

The Russian sells the Little Russian's girdle for three groshens at the fair and throws the "bush" in free. (*Russian*). "Bush," i.e., the shock of hair, represents to a Russian the Ukrainian in a contemptuous sense.

See also RUTHENIANS.

Where the Waloons sit, the grass is not green for seven years. (*Flemish*).

THE WELSH

The Welshman keeps nothing till he has lost it. (*English*).

As long as a Welsh pedigree. (*English*).

His Welsh blood is up. (*English*).

Like the Welshman's cow, little and good. (*English*).

The Welshman had rather see his dam on the bier than to see a fair Februeer. (*English*).

Though he says nothing, he pays it with thinking like the Welshman's jackdaw. (*English*).

The older the Welshman, the more madman. [JAMES HOWELL].

A Welshman is a man who prays on his knees on Sunday and preys on his friends the rest of the week. (*Probably of English origin*).

In Wales, the cat is killed on Monday because it ate up the meat on Sunday. (*Irish*).

WHITE MAN

When the white man is about to leave a garden for good, he wrecks it. (*Yoruba*).

When black man thief, him steal half a bit; but when white man thief, him steal a whole sugar plantation. (*Jamaican Negro*).

De nigger is luckier than de white man at night. (*American*).

Ef yo' say to de white man: "Ain't yo' forget yo' hat?" he say: "Nigger, go get it." (*American Negro*).

Nigger be nigger, whatever he do. (*American Negro*). No

matter how praiseworthy, the white man will blame him just the same.

Nigger an' white man
  Playin' seven-up:
Nigger win de money—
  Skeered to pick 'em up. (*American Negro song*).

NATIONAL COMPARISONS

The following dicta are taken largely from Wander's great collection of German proverbs. Although many of them may be of German origin, a number of them appear in Latin and date from the sixteenth and seventeenth centuries. The characteristics of the various nations mentioned may not fit them today, although a certain residue still remains. They are not so much folk sayings as observations by the well-lettered cosmopolitan humanist, mainly of German origin, although a number bespeak an Italian source.

Probably not a few have come down to us from the medieval schools where the "nations" met in pre-university days, e.g., in Notre Dame at Paris, under Pierre Abélard.

Be on your guard against a red-headed Italian, a white-complexioned Frenchman, and a dark German.

In Spain, the women are slaves and in love; in Germany, frugal and frigid; in France, they love to doll up; in Italy—captives and cranky; in England domineering and extravagant.

The women in Germany love with their heart; those in England, with their mind; those in France with their understanding; Italian women with their body; Spanish women with body and heart; the Russian women, to give pleasure.

The Spaniard, in appearance, resembles the devil; the Italian is a man; the Frenchman is like a woman; the Englishman like an angel, and the German statuesque.

The angelic appearance of the Englishman seems to go back to the story of the angelic child sold as a slave and the comment of Gregory, who afterwards became Pope.

The Spaniard is (in matters of belief) superstitious; the German religious; the Frenchman zealous; the Englishman devout, and the Italian ceremonious.

The Spaniard is, as to dress, modest; the Italian, dismal; the Frenchman variable; the Briton smart, and the German imitative.

The Spaniard (in deliberation) is cautious; the Italian deliberative; the Frenchman impulsive, the Briton imprudent, and the German vacillating.

The Spaniard is necessitous; the Italian moderate, the Frenchman is a gourmet; the Englishman loves the table, and the German his drink.

As regards courage, the Spaniard is an elephant; the Italian a fox; the Frenchman an eagle; the Briton a lion; and the German a bear.

In disposition, the Spaniard is serious; the German genial; the Englishman moody; the Frenchman scornful; the Italian ingratiating.

The Spaniard is in attitude belittling; the Englishman haughty; the German benevolent; the Frenchman well-mannered; and the Italian polished.

In character, the Spaniard is settled; the Italian playful; the Frenchman boastful; the Briton mild, and the German earnest.

In religion, the Spaniard is a pious believer; the Italian worshipful; the Frenchman fervid; the Englishman variable, and the German superstitious.

In physique, the Spaniard is small; the German large; the Englishman stately, and the Frenchman graceful.

As to confidences, the Spaniard is dumb; the Italian reticent; the Frenchman loquacious; the Briton faithless, and the German forgetful.

The Spaniard is a theologian; the Italian an architect; the Frenchman all things; the Englishman a philosopher, and the German a jurist.

The Spaniard is deceptive; the Italian suspicious; the Frenchman lightheaded; the Englishman faithless, and the German faithful.

Domestically, the Spaniard is a tyrant; the German a master; the Frenchman not tied down; the Englishman a servant; and the Italian a prison warden.

As a servant, the Spaniard is servile; the Italian obedient; the Frenchman helpful; the Englishman a serf; the German loyal.

The Spaniard is submissive; the German reliable; the Frenchman faithful; the Englishman slavish; and the Italian respectful.

The Spaniard is subject to countless ills; the Italian is susceptible to infections; the Frenchman to French pox; the Englishman to lupus; and the German to gout.

The Spaniard lives in arms; the Italian in temples; the Briton in the navy; the German in fortresses.

The Spaniard seems to be wise, but is not; the Frenchman seems to be a fool, but is not; the Italian seems to be wise, and is so, while the Portuguese seems to be foolish, and is so.

The Spaniard sleeps; the Italian plays; the German smokes; the Frenchman promises; the Englishman eats, and the American boasts.

The Spaniard writes little; the German writes much; the Italian writes much and well; the Englishman writes excellently, and the Frenchman still better.

The Spaniard speaks; the Italian chatters; the Frenchman sings; the Briton weeps; the German howls.

The Spaniard speaks with God; the Italian with the women; the German with the horses; the Englishman with the birds; the Frenchman with his friends.

Charles V was said to have been the originator of this proverb, in that he was reported to have used different languages in his communion with different beings.

The Spaniard dies gently; the Italian in despair; the Frenchman reluctantly; the Englishman naively, and the German prepared.

The Spaniard is buried in his fatherland; the Italian in fire; the Frenchman on the battlefield; the Englishman in the sea; the German everywhere.

The Spaniard's wife is a slave; the Italian's, a prisoner; the Frenchman's, a mistress; the Englishman's, a queen, and the German's, a domestic.

The Spaniards are advised, belligerent, and grave; the Italians, spirited and vindictive; the Frenchmen, light-minded and passionate; the English, crafty tradesmen; the Belgians, soft and proficient in business and languages; the Germans, in general, honest warriors and beneficent, and the Franks especially valiant, vigorous, and with a penchant for wine and the truth; the Bavarians, mischievous junketers; the Swabians, prattlers and boasters light; the Misnians, lighthearted and rich; the Saxons, clever and pig-headed; the Rhinelanders, upright, hospitable, and open; the Bohemians, illiterate and rebellious; the Hungarians, crude in their mode of living; and the Poles, the poison of all nations.

This characterization, originally in Latin, was obviously composed by a German.

No laws can apply to German swilling, Italian dalliance, and Spanish pilfering. (*German*). This saying is attributed to Charles V, Holy Roman Emperor.

The Spaniards are birds under the sky since they strive for the higher things; the Genoese are fish in the sea as they seek their entertainment on the seas; the Swiss are cattle on the meadow for they live out of their cattle-raising; the Germans are wine-bibbers as they are addicted to drink; the French are men of all occasions.

The German loves his beer; the Frenchman his wine, and the Russian his gin (*vodka*).

German swilling, Italian treachery, and Spanish pilfering—they never fail, all three.

In Spain, the lawyer; in Italy, the doctor; in France, the flirt; in Germany, the artisan; in England, the merchant; in the Balkans, the thief; in Turkey, the soldier; in Poland, a treasury official; in Moscow, the liar—can always make a living. (*Polish*).

Bacchus scourges the Germans; woman is the vexation of the French.

Tell me which does the greater harm: VULVA VEL URNA (*Latin dictum about 1700*).

The Frenchman likes a woman to be agile and nimble—one who can dance well. The Spaniard prefers a graceful figure, and one who seems to be much in love. The Italian delights in a girl that is a bit lively, silly, and hesi-

tates a trifle, but a German likes a fresh and dizzy romp.
(*About 1700*).

The Italians call the English haughty, the French ranting,
the Germans populous, the Spaniards sly, the Hungarians cruel, the Slavs a ruined people, the Hebrews a scat-
tered people, and the Turks infidels.

Should a fly fall into his cup, the Englishman will take it out
and not drink; the German will take it out and drink;
the Russian will drink, fly and all.

A Roman *faremo*, like a Florentine *adesso*, like a Spanish *á la
magnana*, and an English *by and by*, or a German *gleich*
and a French *tantôt* are just twaddle.

Red Italians symbolize cardinals; white French, archbishops
or Augustine monks, and black Germans, monks in general. (*Latin dictum of about 1500*). The point being that
these are unnatural colors for the respective nationalities, and
therefore bode no good.

The stone is a German disease; the gout a British malady.
(*German*). The first part is a reference to gallstones or the
stone in the kidney.

The Spanish language is majestic; the French, affable; the
Italian, corrupt; the Polish, ingratiating; the Greek, com-
pendious; and the German, terrible.

The devil seduced Eve in Italian,
Eve misled Adam in Bohemian,
The Lord scolded them both in German,
Then the angel drove them from Paradise in Hungarian.
(*Polish*).

> The beneficence of Lombards,
> The industry of Picards,
> Norman humility,
> And German equanimity;

French generosity,
And English reliability,
As Burgundian devotion,
Are not worth a notion. (*Picardy jingle*).

Trust, look out for whom?
No Saxon, no Dane, no Czech.

Thievish as an American
Drunk as a Pole or a Swiss
Jealous as a Spaniard
Vindictive as a Corsican
Quarrelsome as a German
Greedy or arrogant as an Arab
Treacherous or haughty as a Scot
Cold as a Dutchman
Tricky as a Greek.

If the devil fell to the earth and broke up into fragments, his head must have fallen in Spain, (thus it went to their [the Spaniards'] head); the heart would have fallen in Italy (land of banditry and treachery); the belly in Germany; the hands among the Turks and Tartars so as to rob and steal; and the legs among the French for dancing and prancing. (*Czech*).

Whoever could cure [convert] a Frank of his coarseness—a Spaniard of his pride—an Austrian of swilling—a Bohemian of lying—a Graner of [rag] picking—a Polack of pillaging—an Italian of wenching—a Frenchman of unfaithfulness—a Bavarian of jabbering—a Swabian of chattering—him I should deem an upright man. (*Attributed to Abraham á St. Clara*).

Spanish simplicity, Italian generosity, Polish orderliness,

Prussian court-life, Danish style, English freedom, German humility, French penitence, Scotch ease, a Muscovite promise, Turkish marriage-ties, Italian faithfulness, Jewish preaching, Aryan love—all of these are suspicious traits. (*Polish,* 17th century).

Thus, the Spaniard is a theologian; the Italian, a philosopher; the Frenchman, a poet; the German, a historian, and the Pole, an orator. (*Latin,* 16th century).

In Spain, thrives the practitioner; in Italy, the physician; in France, the barber; in Denmark, England and Scotland, the merchant; in Wallachia [Rumania] the thief; in Turkey, the soldier; in Poland, the procurer; in Moscow, the liar, and in Prussia, the landlord. (*Polish,* 18th century).

Martial Poland, alert Prussia, witty Netherlands, rich Flanders, neat England, amorous France, crafty Savoy, wily Italy. (*German*).

> In Poland one eats well,
> In Hungary one drinks well,
> Sleeping is best done in Germany,
> And loving in Italy. (*Polish*).

> The Mazovian is ready for a fight,
> Dress is the German's blight;
> The Pole is given to counsel
> While the Litt is prone to quarrel. (*Polish*).

> Every Czech is a musician;
> Every Italian a physician;
> Every German a tradesman
> Every Pole a Nobleman. (*Polish*).

The Englishman conceives it; the Frenchman realizes it; the

German improves it, and the Pole seizes upon it and buys it. (*Polish*).

The French are knights; the Austrians, cursed dogs; the Germans, beasts; and the Poles, reckless sports. (*Galician Polish*).

In settling an island, the first building erected by a Spaniard would be a church; by a Frenchman, a fort; by a Dutchman, a warehouse, and by an Englishman, an ale house. (*English*).

The French are crabs. When they become too hot, they turn red. The English spin. In all corners of the earth, their net is found. The Russians are children. They would have all they set eyes on. The Germans are fish — always thirsty and dumb. (*German*).

The German drowns his sorrows in drink; the Frenchman in song; the Spaniard cries over them; the Englishman laughs them down, and the Italian puts them to sleep. (*German*).

PART FOUR

ASPECTS OF ETHNIC PREJUDICE

ASPECTS OF ETHNIC PREJUDICE

INTRODUCTORY

The word-lists contained in this volume were originally intended to form the illustrative material of an essay in social psychology. An examination of the various source-books and dictionaries, however, soon made it clear that the essay would be but an appendix to the growing vocabulary. The average person would scarcely have thought that there were about one thousand such slurs against all nationalities in the English language alone.

To be sure, most of these slurs occur not in standard English, but in colloquial parlance and slang. That is, of course, to be expected. Prejudices are to be found, as a rule, among the common people, the illiterate, and low society. Furthermore, the more polished a person is the more apt will he be to conceal his prejudices or at least not flaunt them overtly. Nevertheless, a few hundred derogatory locutions have become incorporated into the general English dictionary, which give us an insight into the historical relationship between peoples, as well as the content of the popular mind.

Most of the international references in a complete dictionary like *Webster's New International* or the *Oxford English Dictionary* are of course what may be called objective terms, dealing with products, and, to a much less extent, cultural forms. The older the country and the larger it is, *e.g.*, China or India, the more fauna and flora, as well as other products, like colors, will be named in connection with it, particularly if it is remote. It is surprising, therefore, to find Canada, which is adjacent to the United States, and subject to about the same climatic and historical conditions, represented in the dictionary with over two hundred objective references. Still greater is the wonder that Japan, though a comparatively small country and practically unknown to foreigners, until a century ago, actually rivals China in the number of what I shall call *geographical* (as contrasted with psychological) references. Does the solution lie in the vast number of products that are different from those of any other country?

This particular question, which has its psychological aspect—for many commodities differ but in name, as in the case of Canadian maidenhair and American maidenhair, Canadian cheese and American cheese; and therefore national aggressiveness, propaganda, and other circumstances may account for the particular spread of a country's trademark—need not detain us here, since our problem is concerned alone with the *psychological* or *subjective* evaluation of national traits.

A PSYCHOANALYTIC HINT

The segmentation of international references may find a somewhat loose yet useful analogue in the psychoanalytic treatment of the mind as a topographical scheme. The objective or geographical allusions to other nations, dealing as they do almost wholly with products and commodities, will have been governed by the realistic *ego*. Perhaps, too, the recognition of cultural forms will also stem from this sphere, although in a higher stratum. The *id* will be responsible for the mass of prejudices, the result of blind instincts, destructive impulses, *Schadenfreude,* sex displace ments, etc., while the very thin area of the *superego* allows for the few commendatory references to traits in other nationalities.

It is noteworthy that the scouted "Chosen People," as may be seen by referring to the instances in this little com pendium, particularly the section on proverbs, often be littles itself and speaks well of the Gentiles. The Scotch come next in pointing out their own faults, and the Irish sometimes do not spare themselves. We may recall that Freud, in his *Wit and the Unconscious* (title as in English translation) mentions the Jews as the people most able to laugh at themselves.

From this very fact, namely, that while credit is given hardly at all to other nationalities, criticism is passed out freely in the form of jocose shafts and downright libels, which is only human, all too human, in the case of individ uals who see the mote in the other man's eye but not the beam in their own, we may gather that the national *id* is still in a primitive stage, and that the national *superego* has not begun to develop. The national group is still a child, varying in different countries from infancy to puberty.

One reason for the lag is the very structure of national education. While selfishness in the individual is discour aged in the home, the school, at games, and in church, national aggrandizement and aggressiveness are fostered under the guise of patriotism often by the very educators and mentors who frown upon personal aggressiveness. A concrete illustration of this contrast will be seen in the circumstance that libelling an individual is fraught with unpleasant consequences for the culprit, whereas maligning a foreign group is as a rule considered a patriotic service, if not an act of heroism, the principle underlying this perversion being that your own group will be raised in prestige as others are downed. Furthermore, patriotism of this type is not considered selfish, because the anti-foreigner is not supposed to profit by it personally. At times, however, we are forcibly reminded of Samuel Johnson's famous dictum: "Patriotism is the last refuge of a scoundrel."

Perhaps it would be equally proper to say that patriotism, or rather patrioteering, is the egoist's public-minded mask. One who is constantly proclaiming the virtues of his own nation, his own country, his own flag, is merely telling the world that his country is the greatest because he happens to have been born there.

So far the general introduction which contains the fundamental motive underlying national prejudices. It would take us too far afield to attempt a thoroughgoing analysis of prejudice *in abstracto*. Besides, the subject has been treated from so many angles, though not altogether satisfactorily, that it would be necessary to go over the same ground and examine anew every result or conclusion gained through the various approaches: historical, sociological, psychological, statistical, and experimental. It is rather my purpose to deal with the specific subject in hand, to wit, the slurs which have been accumulating in every civilized and probably uncivilized language too. Our task is, therefore, concrete. Having before us nearly 3,000 international slurs, or, as we shall designate them from now on, *ethnophaulisms* (ἔθνος a national group and φαυλίζω to disparage) if the coinage is acceptable, it behooves us to draw certain inferences as to their nature, reasons for coming into being, specific attitudes revealed, and certain historical and sociological interconnections

The investigation was begun with the naïve thought that no one else had ever written on this particular theme, at least in English. Only after the actual work on the dictionary had been under way, did I discover a very brief chapter on "Offensive Nationality" in *Words, Words, Words!* by the tireless and entertaining Eric Partridge, who may have been stimulated to tackle this topic as a result of his editing anew Francis H. Grose's pioneer *Classical Dictionary of the Vulgar Tongue,* which contains perhaps fifty derogatory references to half a dozen peoples, but principally the Scotch, the Irish, and the Dutch.

Partridge, who appears to be a twentieth-century Grose, but with greater erudition (in spite of occasional curious lapses)* and a dynamo, far exceeding his American counterpart, H. L. Mencken, takes but a scant seven pages, largely filled with illustrations, to preëmpt the subject of "offensive nationality," which incidentally is not, to my

---

*In his *Words, Words, Words!* (page 16), he speaks of Paul Carus as a "great French philosopher, who appeared in an English translation in 1900," whereas Carus was a German-American philosophical writer *in English,* who has built up the Open Court Publishing Co. in Chicago. Again, Rumania's most important philologist and lexicographer, the Jew, Lazar Șaineanu, is taken for a Frenchman by Partridge, because his name

mind, the correct term, since the nationality as such is not offensive. It is the speaker, rather, who offends; and a coinage like *ethnophaulism* would have been the apt heading for the chapter (or essay in its original form).

SEQUENCE OF DISLIKES AND RIVALRY

In these seven pages, Partridge has traversed the centuries to show the sequence of the offensive butt or target. The author tells us that the Greeks and the Turks were the outcasts in the sixteenth century, while from about 1580 to 1650, the Spanish people became the target. The Dutch came in for their innings in the seventeenth century, while the eighteenth and nineteenth centuries were the periods during which the French became very unpopular, and somewhat less so the English, Welsh, Scotch, and Irish. The Germans did not share the common obloquy until the first World War.

The clue which Partridge supplies to this sequential unpopularity is the focus of rivalry, but although the chronological data are of value in our search, we cannot aver that any incisive attempt has been made to interrelate the historical, psychological, and sociological facts. The insular approach of the Englishman, sound and learned though he may be, is all but too apparent in this kaleidoscopic view. The Englishman, even the pundit, seldom has

---

appears as Sainéan, in the French environment, to which he had betaken himself, after his native land refused to grant him the rights of a citizen. Partridge is correct in regarding Sainéan as "the greatest of all authorities on thieves' slang, general and French." (Partridge: *Slang Today and Yesterday*. page 14).

any use for particles, and despises accents (except in the one field which he happens to be studying, *e.g.,* the classics) thus ignoring interstitial matter relevant to the issue. English is to him the epitome of all languages. The circumscription of the world by Basic English seems to be a logical corollary of this insular, and at the same time, imperial, outlook.

Partridge cites the example, dating as early as 1528, to be found in the *Oxford English Dictionary*: "In carde playing he is a goode Greke," that is to say of someone that, at cards, he is a sharper or cheat. The slur still lingers in the French language. (See this DICTIONARY, French section). What has led to the spread of this prejudice is not stated, unless we are to gather that the story of the wooden horse at Troy is responsible for the ethnophaulisms in regard to the Greeks? Certainly rivalry does not enter in here as an explanation.

Nor can it be said to figure in the detestation of the Turks during the sixteenth century, when the Saracens were the bugaboos of both young and old. It was during the Third Crusade that the Turks were invested with all sorts of fiendish qualities, but is it legitimate to speak of the Turks ruling over Palestine, thousands of miles away, as rivals who must be brought to bay? Perhaps in a religious sense, the conflict could be understood, in which event, however, another factor is introduced, not generally subsumed under the word *rivalry*.

Rivalry may be understood in a twofold sense, and unless specified, it leads, because of its ambiguity, to dubious conclusions. Partridge seems to talk of national rivalry when he introduces the subject of the Franco-

English wars, or the trade jealousy between the Dutch and the English in the seventeenth century. It so happens, however, that the Jews who, for thousands of years, have not been a rival of any national group (except possibly at present, the Arabs) have borne the chief brunt of the world's criticism.

It may be maintained in defense of the above view that individual rivalry in business, the arts, or the professions is to be included under the same category, but here again, the Jews, in most countries, could not be regarded as compet' itors. During the Middle Ages, only usury was open to them, because it was prohibited to Christians. For the most part, the Jews were poor and could not take part in any of the normal activities and pastimes of the country that harbored them. If Spain, prior to the discovery of America, and Italy, during the Renaissance, did allow the Jews to thrive, then only individual, but *non-political,* rivalry could have been possible.

Perhaps a better argument against the rivalry theory could be furnished by the Negroes who have been pilloried in the English language, principally in colloquial parlance and slang, without there being a possibility of competition on any basis whatsoever, nor in any sphere.

It would seem that rivalry is a factor, but not *the* factor in the development and spread of ethnophaulisms. We must look elsewhere for the key to this universal tendency.

DREAD OF THE FOREIGNER

In Ernest Weekley's chapter on "Xenophobia" (*in Words and Names*) published a few months later than the essay by Partridge (who incidentally pays tribute to its approach), we come perhaps closer to the psychological reason for the gibbeting of foreigners. But Weekley, too, by virtue of his vast philological equipment and linguistic propensities, falls short of the issue, in spite of the broad humanistic sweep of his essay, since he allows himself to meander occasionally into territory beyond the scope of his topic as defined by his chapter heading, so that while his confession in the preface that he has allowed his "pen to run on without any close regard to the rather vague headings of the various chapters" disarms us, it scarcely helps us in our quest. Truly the short chapter of twelve pages might as well have been headed "National references" as "Xenophobia"; for what have "Irish stew, Scotch collops", "Welsh rabbit", "Attic salt", or even "I caught a Tartar" (where the joke is on the Irish captor who can't get rid of his catch) to do with the subject of "Xenophobia"?

Weekley is always entertaining and generally sound,* but being a philologist and etymologist *par excellence,* he is intent upon dispensing information without giving much thought to the steering ideas which center around a definite

*His mention of Yiddish as the *lingua franca* of the Israelites, thus causing his follower, Eric Partridge to lean in the same direction, and, worse, his failure to capitalize the word *Yiddish,* go to show that there are foggy pockets in Weekley's lucid mind, but his scholarship is thereby not impugned. Of course Yiddish is no more a *lingua franca* than is English, which may also be considered a conglomerate, abused by millions, in fact the majority of English-speaking people; and the Israelites, Weekley should know, no longer exist. Indeed, those Jews who would prefer to be called Israelites rather than Jews are the very ones who either have never spoken Yiddish (the Sephardim and West European Jews) or else wish to drop it like a time-bomb.

problem. It is as if a great deal of material were dumped on a building site without a blueprint ever having been considered.

METHODOLOGY

Our first step then must be to define the boundaries and to keep within them. We are dealing exclusively with disparagements of other national and racial groups, including, however, the few critical references to one's own group, if for no other purpose, to serve as a minor control.

Abiding by this principle we must note (a) the historical period and conditions (b) the political and commercial relations between the countries involved (c) the propinquity, geographical and ethnic, of the nations and (d) chief of all, the content or grade of the slur. What is more, each of the circumstances must be viewed in the light of the others.

To take one instance: the hatred of the Turks, which reached its culminating point about the middle of the sixteenth century with their invasion of Central Europe, was a complex attitude, composed of religious, political, and psychological elements. Partridge would content himself with pointing out the rivalry between the Turks and the Western nations including England, during the Third Crusade, but he is oblivious to the fact that the epithet "Unspeakable Turk" was employed by no less a man than William Gladstone, not in the sixteenth but toward the end of the nineteenth century. That was the time when Turkey was no rival of any of the major European states, and certainly not of the British Empire. The phrase expressed a moral revulsion against the atrocities which were being perpetrated against the Greeks, the Serbs (Yugoslavians), and the Armenians. Similarly at the time of the pogroms against the Jews, during the latter part of the nineteenth and early part of the twentieth century, the Russians had earned for themselves the same adjective, "unspeakable." Only the Nazified Germans, who have outdone the Turks and the Russians a hundredfold, have remained "speakable" (about) under their various nick-names of Alboches, Boches, Huns, Gerries, etc.

The political and commercial relations are important in establishing the cause of the rancor. Certainly through the period of the Hundred Years' War, English feeling against the French would run high; and the latter were none too favorably disposed toward England.

Economic rivalry, on the seas, as well as wars, would account for the jocose and disparaging, although hardly contemptuous, allusions to the Dutch. There will be more said on this score in the breakdown of ethnophaulisms according to countries. We must bear in mind too, that the stock of phrases is an accumulation through centuries; and relations must have undergone various changes during that time, so that, unless we can trace definitely the origin of a specific expression, it would not do to treat it under some general explanation, like war and rivalry, or xenophobia.

No matter how bitter the conflict between two nations, there is a mutual respect for valor, if circumstances warrant it. In other words, as we shall presently see, *the evaluation of a foreign people or alien element is the core of the folk locution,* whether favorable or unfavorable. It is nearly always unfavorable as applied to any other nation, but there are degrees of such criticism, ranging from mild disapproval, or pleasantry, to violent hatred, as in the case of the Americans against the Japanese after the attack on Pearl Harbor and upon the execution of the captive airmen who raided Tokyo.

One of the outstanding factors in fostering enmity between national groups is propinquity. But whereas geographical contiguity has, for obvious reasons, often been taken into account, ethnic propinquity has scarcely, if at all, been thought of.

At first blush, we might have expected offshoots of the same racial stock to be closely attached to one another. What happens, however, is just the opposite, as witness the continual struggle between the Russians and the Poles, the Spaniards and the Portuguese, or the ill-concealed animosity between the Irish and the Scotch. The Jews and the Arabs, too, although at one time living together amicably under the rule of a wise kaliphate and the aegis of learning and enlightenment, have not trusted one another for centuries. And need one mention here the Chinese-Japanese feud which had been going on for ages? Whether it is for the same reason that brothers or sisters will often "fight like cats and dogs," or because, as seems more probable, the cognate groups are usually in close proximity to one another and an attempt is consequently made by the more aggressive to swallow up the weaker of the two, the fact in itself is worthy of study.

Lest someone should seek to adduce a negative instance in the relationship between the United States and England, it may be proper to point out that all of North America (omitting the local French and Spanish groups of an older origin) may be considered as an outgrowth of the mother country, while the newer immigration, with the exception of the Irish, would be likely to maintain the same balance that characterizes the Anglo-Saxon outlook, to the extent that it is not definitely affiliated with some foreign ideology.

The quale of the slur is really the crux of our investigation. Here many questions may be asked: (a) Is there anything valid about the criticism? (b) Do we come across specific differences, or is it a case of the pot calling the kettle black? (c) Why are there many more international references in some languages than in others? (d) What constitutes a slur? It is curious in this connection that to refer to a member of a nationality by the same term (untranslated) as he is known among his own kind is more or less of an insult. *Yid* and *Polack* are respectable designations among the Jews and Poles respectively, yet good manners would not permit the same appellations bandied about in English. The same may be said about *Dansker, Russky,* or *Svensker.*

Before we can ever attempt to answer these questions, it is necessary to analyse, more or less, the various segments of ethnophaulisms.

BREAKDOWN OF NATIONAL SLURS

If we examine a sufficient number of such derogatory locutions, on a comparative basis, we shall be forced to perceive certain results and perhaps gain some decided conclusions. Let us then discuss a number of characteristics of specific national slurring tendencies as well as the content of these slurs. There are doubtless many interesting observations to make about Arabian, Chinese, Hindu, or Japanese derogatory references, but unfortunately they lie beyond the ken of this writer. It is not sufficient, however, as has been done in the past, to confine ourselves exclusively to ethnophaulisms in English, or to deal with American phrases of this nature. Nevertheless we shall begin with these.

AMERICANS

The comparative paucity of phrases among other peoples relative to American traits can well be understood. In the first place, the United States formed only a century and a-half ago. Secondly, the geographical remoteness from other independent nations tends to shut out invidious comparisons. Thirdly, the heterogeneous constitution of the American people has prevented Europeans from saddling it with specific traits, aside from those which are characteristic of a pioneer and fast-growing community. Europe has been looking upon the United States very much as a middle-aged adult regards a bumptious adolescent. The Yankee is the only representative of the great Western Republic to the world.

Now if we were asked whether there is an American type, as there is a Russian, Polish, or French stereotype, we would be hard put to find the earmarks of such except, as already stated, in terms of technical speed and opportunities; for even the democratic traditions are no different from those of the old-country republics or the finer monarchies. Nor can the Yankee be taken as a symbol of the 130,000,000 Americans, most of whom do not resemble him.

It is different when we change positions and consider the slurs produced in the United States against other nationalities. Although many, if not most of them, are of a jocose nature, there are easily more than a hundred offensive nicknames and phrases embracing at least a score of the numerous nationalities which have found a haven at these shores. With so many different ethnic groups rubbing shoulders, name-calling is inevitable. Indeed some of the uncomplimentary allusions come from the very nationality to which they are applied.

Of the minor ethnophaulisms, national tastes for certain food form the basis of a considerable persiflage. The Italian is a *macaroni;* the Hungarian is a *goulash,* and the Frenchman a *frog-eater. Rosbif* represents an Englishman in France, and *chili con* characterizes the Mexican in the eyes of many an American. These names are harmless. The ethnophaulism, on this plane, means only: "How can one be so fond of such an uninteresting or unpalatable dish?"

THE BRITISH

In the British Isles, the story is different. John Bull does stand for a more or less well-knit complex of traits which have been analyzed by many writers, Ralph Waldo Emerson and William James among them. Certainly the Irish do not display the same set of qualities, nor do the Scotch. These three nations, originally sprung from the same ancestral matrix; foes for many a century and neighbors from time immemorial, whose histories are inseparably bound up with each other, form a sort of eternal triangle, in spite of the hotly contested divorce of Ireland. We cannot discuss the one nationality without the other two.

There is much to say about English, Scotch, and Irish proverbs as well as upon their mutual libels. As might be expected, the antagonisms are mainly directed against each other, but while the Irish and the Scotch will not spare themselves in their criticism, the English seldom record a self-disparaging remark. "*English*," writes Partridge in his *Words, Words, Words!* "is the rarest of all 'nasty nationalities' considered in this article; it is used in only two connexions, *English burgundy,* which meaning porter . . . . and *English Malady* or *English Melancholy* (that typically English complaint, the 'spleen'), these terms being seldom employed later than the year 1800."

If Partridge means that the English are the least nasty of nationalities, in their opinion, then we certainly concede the point, but that hardly needed saying: for this is *mutatis mutandis* true of every other ethnic group. What interests us more is the fact that the English have received a fair mead of opprobrium at the hands of, or in the mouths of, other nations. It is true, however, that in comparison with the Scotch and the Irish, they have been rather self-indulgent. They seem to have exhibited a genuine bourgeois self-complacency—or perhaps diplomacy—in this respect. The Scotch and the Irish have not fared so well in English lore and speech.

Let us see what particular traits are singled out for criticism among these three peoples. The English are generally taken to task for a species of hypocrisy (on the continent), for callousness, and aggression in a quiet way. They themselves admit being somewhat *difficile,* or at least offish.

The Scotch are charged with being hard-hearted, close-fisted, calculating, and so thoroughly indoctrinated as to cling to a rule that serves no useful purpose. The Irish, on the other hand, are taunted about their imputed uncouth habits, low standards, their inefficiency, temper, and irre-sponsibility. Irony or antiphrasis has been applied to the Irish more than to any other people, *e.g.,* "Irish theatre," "Irish promotion," "Irish dinner," all of which is to be taken in the opposite sense.

It would be an unfair omission to ignore the Welsh from our sketchy survey; for although they did not play such an important role historically as the Scotch and the Irish, their political and geographical conditions have been very similar to those of their Celtic cousins; and they have infiltrated into England in the same proportion, wielding considerable influence as individuals. The Welsh some-how have gained a reputation for deceitfulness and un-reliability in fulfilling agreements. Partridge's conjecture that all this may be due to a very old nursery rhyme, "Taffy is a Welshman, Taffy is a thief" seems like a flash in the pan. A single nursery rhyme scarcely accounts for deep-rooted prejudices.

As to shafts at other nationalities than their own satel-lites and associates, there are many, of course, but they are not so clearcut, nor so cordial as those directed against the Scotch and the Irish. H. L. Mencken in his *magnum opus** tells us that "the English have relatively few aliens in their midst, so in consequence they have developed noth-ing comparable to our huge repertory of opprobrious names for them." Here Mencken shows signs of inadequate in-formation; since, if the English have borrowed our *dago* for the Italian, we have borrowed far more from them.

*H. L. Mencken: *The American Language* (4th ed.) page 297.

To be sure, there are no organized foreign groups on the scale we have them in the United States, but, to compensate, the English have had long wars with nearly every major country in Europe. They have been able to travel to foreign lands more readily than Americans; and as traders and empire builders, they have, thanks to their great navy, compassed the world, seeing all sorts and conditions of men. Even their writers would be conversant with the characteristics of the most distant colonial natives; and in their sketches, stories, and poems would be apt to incorporate a term or phrase that would eventually become a folk usage. It is enough to take account of the Dutch allusions in the English language, both standard and slang, to satisfy ourselves that the English have not been so exclusive and insular as Mencken would have us suppose.

THE DUTCH AND THE GERMANS

Again we have a combination of two peoples and languages, which, although related, have otherwise little in common, yet through some quip of fate their fortunes have been inseparably bound up with one another in English parlance.

To begin with, even the tyro will have noticed how many times the word *Dutch* occurs in English conversation and narrative as compared with the word *German,* or even the more opprobrious epithets, *boche,* Hun, etc. The disproportion is all the more surprising because Holland is a small state while Germany has been a major power in the world. To understand this paradox, it is necessary to resort to history, both political and linguistic.

It is sometimes difficult for us to visualize that a country like the Netherlands could at one time have been a rival of England, yet about four centuries ago, the Dutch and the English were either allies or foes, and the naval and colonial competition was stiff and lasting. Germany, on the other hand, broken up into a number of small principalities and duchies, hardly existed as such until the comparatively recent consolidation. Such were the conditions during the most formative period of the English language and its literature.

Probably in England too, but certainly in the United States, the Dutch and the Germans have been confused because of the similarity of the sounds in *deutsch* (German) and Dutch. Pennsylvania-Dutch is really a misnomer due to this identification. Thus a man speaking *deutsch,* or *deitsch,* as the early immigrants from southwestern Germany called it, would be labelled a Dutchman: and when an editor recently reproached some of the German refugees for extolling the virtues of their Germany, he impulsively wrote "hard-headed Dutchmen." The Dutch comedian on the vaudeville stage of a few decades ago would be impersonating the German rather than the Dutchman. In the *Oxford English Dictionary,* we find *Dutchland* as an archaic form of Germany.

The confusion, or perhaps rather diffusion, has not been peculiar to America. In England, the term *Dutch* would stand as a generic name for the whole Germanic stock, sometimes even including the Scandinavian peoples.

Evidently the anglicized form of the German adjective, *deutsch,* was at the bottom of this substitution.

There is no doubt in my mind that at least some of the Dutch slurs were intended for the Germans, but there is no way of disentangling them, so that often the Dutch are "in dutch," while the Germans are allowed "to take French leave." "Double Dutch" is a fling at the Dutch language, but "Dutch sale," "Dutch concert," and "Dutch defence" are probably directed at the Germans. All nautical phrases in which the word "Dutch" occurs may be understood as coined at the expense of the Dutch.

It is not altogether clear why the Dutch have evoked a slightly derisive attitude in the English alone, although their wars with Spain and trade rivalry with Portugal must have produced considerable hostility in these countries.

More surprising is the fact that the Dutch have hardly anything retaliatory in this respect. The same word, in Dutch, stands for both English and angelic, as it does too in German. Aside from the fact that the English are not, to judge from some of the Dutch idioms, regarded as sufficiently painstaking or thorough, there is almost nothing disrespectful to be found in the Dutch language against them. The French and the Germans, on the other hand, do present a problem to the Dutch, who think of the former as sloppy, superficial, and frivolous, and of the latter as surly, gruff, and disagreeable. The French civilization, because of its influence in Belgium, naturally is a stumbling block to the Flemish and Dutch culture. As to Germany, the behavior of the Prussians, Westphalians, and Saxons in the Netherlands (especially as Spanish mercenaries) would evoke in the Dutch a dislike for the German temperament which all the wars with Spain did not succeed in calling forth.

Apart from the reproaches which the Germans unidentifiably share together with the Dutch, their psychological presence is not altogether lost sight of in the English dictionary. In such phrases as *German silver, made in Germany, German measles,* there is the undertone of *Ersatz.* It is as if German technicians were bound to find some substitute for even such a simple thing as an ailment. Lessing's epigram about the quest of truth being greater than its attainment appears to be transformed into such a maxim as that we ought not to be satisfied with the genuine unless we can achieve the spurious. The old simile as "jump as German lips" is a telling indictment, when we learn that *jump* means "false."

On the other hand, it may be that finding a substitute before we need it is an insurance against the day when such will be urgently required.

The relative absence of derogatory allusions to the Germans has to some extent been accounted for by their politically loose organization. Prussia represented the whole of Germany to a non-German. Some phrases at the expense of the Prussians have, to be sure, crept into the English language, but all things considered, the Germans have been treated rather chivalrously by their neighbors and, at one time or another, enemies. Achievement in the arts and sciences, in philosophy and technology, has of course earned the respect of the world for the nation as a whole, but there are probably other reasons, one of them being the great exaltation with which the individual members speak of their people. Only a few philosophers, like Nietzsche and Schopenhauer and poets like Hölderlin and Klopstock (for Heine was a Jew), dared to call attention to some of the outstanding German vices.

Whether, as Joachim Joesten hints in his brief article,* "others, at present violently opposed, have not yet contrived to forge linguistic weapons against their new enemies" remains to be seen. May it not be too that the Germans, because of their excellent social control among strangers, whom they impress by their efficiency, cleverness, and suave manners, contrive to cover up many of their faults. Nevertheless the Italians and the Russians by no means flattered them in their proverbs, and Lück has devoted a large volume to an extended discussion of the German in the light of Polish folklore, mythology, and belleslettres, which is anything but favorable. In this volume, Lück, only a year prior to the Nazi global war, is at pains to prove that the Germans have been shabbily treated by the Poles almost from time immemorial, that the German settlers in their Volksinseln (Germanpeople colonies) had much to complain of, and that the Germans were never so petty toward the Poles, etc. Polish writers would even refrain from capitalizing the N in Niemiec (German) as is often the case in our own country with the name "Negro." The numerous jokes and folk rhymes about one another are disgustingly coarse and point to a sense of humor on the coprophilic level of the infant, where the

*Joachim Joesten: "Calling Names in Any Language." *American Mercury*, 1935, vol. 36.

anus, defecation, and feces figure prominently. Indeed, Lück (page 242) is so impressed with this sort of folklore, that he sees the need of a doctoral dissertation entitled, *"Die Arschologie der Volkstumsfront"* ("The Arsology of the Nationalities Front"). Freud might have found much therein to corroborate his doctrine of anal eroticism.

It is somewhat of a revelation to find that the Poles ascribed to the Germans divers physically repulsive habits; moreover that the Polish *littérateurs* painted the Germans in colors none too bright. Lück's thorough treatment of German-Polish relations includes not only the folkloristic elements, but the philological, the historical, economic, and literary reactions upon one another.

At one stage Lück, lamenting the abuse of the Germans in Poland, speaks of the Polish practice of calling a dog by the name of Bismarck, which, he declares, is "certainly an unusual honor for a dog." Such an act of disrespect for a national hero, he contends, would hardly be thinkable in Germany under like circumstances. Yet this same pleader for justice and fairness, in Poznan (!), is not so fastidious himself when he has to mention the Jews; and Yiddish is known to him only by the name of *"Jargon-language."*

The Germans, on their part, have been most catholic and consistent in their contempt for other nations, or, as an Irishman might say it, most impartial in their aversions. The list of abusive epithets, including *die dummen Schweden,* (the "dumb" Swedes); *russische Schweine,* (Russian pigs); *polnisches Schwein,* (Polish hog); *schmutzige Franzosen,* (dirty Frenchmen); *Scheissfranzosen,* (the muck French); *Judensau,* (sow of a Jew); *Stinkjude,* (stinking Jew); and *verhasste Engländer,* (hateful Eng-

lish), may be extended considerably. It is true their attitudes are not proclaimed from the house-tops, but they
make themselves manifest just the same.

THE FRENCH

The vice that is laid universally at the door of the French
is that of lechery or perversion. The innuendo shuttled
back and forth by the English and the French is evident
in the fact that what the English call *French letter* is labelled
by the French *capote anglaise,* which again reverts to a
French origin in the slang name for this article. (See this
DICTIONARY, page 34.) Whether the English or the
French invented the condom, intense love-making in a
variety of forms is surely associated more with the French
than with any other nationality.

In addition, the English, who have had long accounts
to square with their neighbors across the Channel, credited
the French with faithlessness and an unwillingness to
meet obligations or even to face reality. The phrase "taking French leave" has become a standby in several European languages.

The French, on the other hand, have retaliated by emphasizing the money-mindedness of the English, as if they
were all a nation of shopkeepers and bill collectors. Nor
are the French very respectful of their minor playmate,
the Swiss, nor of the Spanish people, as may be seen from
the French section in this DICTIONARY. The Germans,
sometimes as Prussians, come in for their drubbing, but
the Irish, the Scotch, and the Dutch, all three of whom are
so mistreated by the English, scarcely have made any

impression on the folk-mind of the French. Instead, the Greeks and the Turks (probably as a result of school texts and literary references, as well as of personal experiences with certain immigrants who happened to have given a poor account of themselves ethically, by reason of their sharp practices) caught the imagination, not in its favorable phase, of the French.

THE GYPSIES

The Gypsies have universally gained a reputation for roaming, irresponsible and free living, as well as downright cheating and thieving, yet they too have had their defenders and patrons, as may be seen from a little-known book by Richard F. Burton, called *The Jew, The Gypsy, and El Islam*. Burton, whose features would indicate that he had Romany blood, places the Gypsies above the Jews, for whom he entertains an inexplicable aversion.

THE ITALIANS

The rôle which the Italians played in the Renaissance must have saved them from continental shafts of criticism at the time and later. The delightfulness of the climate and the scenic beauty, as well as the magnificent structures and art treasures upon which the tourists would sate their eyes, would naturally condition them against adopting an attitude of belittlement. The associations were too pleasant. Nor were there any aggressive wars on the part of the Italians to make them hated. Even the recent Fascistic rapaciousness was not identified with the people. At worst, Italians were bracketed with the French as sex-centred, although in a somewhat divergent manner.

At the conclusion of the Nazi war, we may have some pointed remarks circulating in Germany about Italian unreliability, and during the Libyan campaign, the constant retreats of the Italians drew some persiflage from columnist and cartoonist, but the censure on that account was not really in earnest.

On the part of the Italians, the English, the Germans, and the French seem to have elicited a few critical terms and sayings.

THE JEWS

Thus we come to the chief of scapegoats in history—the Jews. For two thousand years this People has been singled out almost in every country of their sojourn as deserving of special contempt. There were, to be sure, cases of tolerance in some countries, as during the kaliphate and the Moorish occupation of Spain, the reign of Alfonso XI and Pedro I in fourteenth-century Spain, and João I and Affonso V in Portugal. Italy and Poland, too, showed, during the later Renaissance, a broadminded spirit. We may well wonder, however, whether the very temperateness of the rulers did not cause a reaction among the masses, incited by the clergy and especially fanatical hoodlums.

We are somewhat taken aback to learn that standard Spanish retains more terms insulting to the Jews than any other language, with the possible exception of German, and that, although Spain had not harbored any Jews since 1492, its proverbs still harp on the Jewish gut. Perhaps to justify the extreme cruelty of the Inquisition, the Jews had to be painted as devils to the growing children, while the Marranos, the ostensible Christians, presented a particular problem and called forth the suspicion and distrust of the benighted populace. The German proverbs alone mention the Jews more frequently, and are even less delicate toward them, while Grimm's dictionary lists about a hundred derivatives (in compounds) of *Jude*, most of them derogatory to the Jews. The two countries (Spain and Germany) that have sinned most against the Jews revile them most, which is in keeping with the dynamics of motivation.

It is evident that God knew what He was talking about when He told King Solomon, as the author of *Kings* (I: vii, 9) relates, that He would make of Israel "a proverb and a byword among the nations," but the irony of it is that this happened not because the Jews abandoned their Deity and worshipped strange gods, but for the very reason that they clung to their rigorously monotheistic creed. Had they adopted the religion of the peoples among which they sojourned, this DICTIONARY would have had fewer pages.

What is it that is held against the Jew? First of all, he is a nonconformist in religion; then he is shrewd in business and not too fastidious in his methods, resorting to ingenious ruses in order to circumvent the law. Usury had been his mainstay for centuries; and he is said to thrive upon exploitation. Socially he is supposed to be a bounder, and politically he has been rocked in a revolutionary and subversive cradle.

When a nationality is thus earmarked, what does one mean? Surely it cannot be taken for granted that every member of the group is thus tainted. What it might signify is that there are a majority of individuals who fall under that category, or that more of that nationality display such and such characteristics than any other nationality.

With regard to the Jews, anthropologists are all but agreed that they do not constitute a pure or homogeneous race. There can, therefore, be little, if anything, in the hereditary stock to account for the objectionable traits. Community tradition and historical conditions have often been invoked by those who do not believe in original tendencies; *e.g.,* the Jew is alleged to have developed a superior business sense because money was the only thing with which he could buy protection, or because other than commercial occupations have been closed to him.

This development through generations, however, cannot be accepted as a theory in view of the intransmissibility of acquired characteristics. Can we say, then, that an individual, at the age of forty, has been able to cultivate shrewdness because of the community spirit or because of his own security aspirations? I should think that every Gentile who makes good in the commercial world is guided and goaded by the same considerations. It has long since been pointed out that the Jews have been blamed by their detractors for diametrically opposite proclivities and activities, like capitalism and communism, which, in itself, serves to explode the libel at either extreme.

Hardly anything can be more illuminating in this regard than the fact that the Grimm of the German proverb, F. Wander, after citing in his mammoth compilation of German sayings, libel upon libel against the Jews, casts off, for the nonce, his impassive reserve, and tells us point blank: "I have been cheated by Christians on a number occasions, never yet by a Jew." And Wander, who had done considerable travelling, visiting the United States, too, was well advanced in years when he gave us this important bit of information.

The Jew is probably no shrewder nor sharper as a trader than the Greek, the Armenian, the German, or the Yankee, but that there are Jewish mannerisms, a Jewish idiom in the transactions of those who have not become imbued with the standards and policies of modern business I am willing to concede. It should be borne in mind, however, that some of the founders of these standards and framers of codes have been Jews—Bamberger, Fuld, Filene, Gimbel, Kirstein, and Klein, who in his mammoth dress establish-ment boldly allowed the customers, most of whom were Jewish women, to be their own salesgirls, choose the dresses and pay for them on a self-service plan. Klein died a millionaire; and very rarely was there any occasion for a reprimand on the part of the store supervisors, much less an arrest.

My reason for dwelling on anti-Jewish libels is apparent. Here we have the crux of the question; and the conclusions come to with respect to the most maligned people can be applied to other groups.

Prejudice against the Jews is not confined to the masses alone. I have come across Nobel Prize men and scientists, who pride themselves upon their objectivity, liberalism, and broadmindedness, investing the Jews with dubious quali-ties—among them aggressiveness in a collective sense, ethnocentricism, clannishness, a superiority attitude, etc. On the other hand, there are many thousands of common folk who either overrate or at least do not saddle the Jews with all sorts of vague faults.

When an intellectual, therefore, once, playing his trump, called out that after all the whole world could not be wrong, that the Jews must be guilty of some of the charges levelled at them, the answer is that the *whole world* is not accusing the Jews. Comparatively few have set down their bill of generalities, or are responsible for the ethno-phaulisms detrimental to the Jews. The crowd has simply picked them up as it would a popular song or any catch-phrase. It would be too much to expect children to examine critically the slang terms they employ in their daily vocabu-lary. If someone, perhaps even a Jew, coins the expression "Jewish perfume" for "gasoline", the chances are that such *Schadenfreude* would appeal to the majority of the youth, and though fifty million people should utter this phrase, there is still no valid reason for the coinage, except that it serves to work off some exuberance; and the Jews, many of whom own automobiles, make a good target. In other words fifty million times zero is still zero.

There are scores of educated people who believe that the Jews, or at least some one sect or another of theirs, ingests Christian blood at Passover; and hundreds of thousands of Americans are under the impression that the Jews have precipitated the war with the Axis. Had not Japan at-tacked Pearl Harbor, and had the conflict started by a direct clash with Germany, the Jews would have been the victims of wholesale slander, if not of physical violence.

The canards current both in the United States and Eng-land about Jews evading combatant service can easily be spiked by scanning the newspapers or by referring to the statistical data, but no facts will convince the prejudiced. The British historian, J. B. Namier, tells of his encounters with people in England who kept reminding him of Jewish slackness on the war fronts, which cases, when reduced to their simplest and barest terms, were tantamount to asking, "How is it that not all the Jewish troops are at least wounded, and those wounded manage to recover, while a good many non-Jewish Tommies are either killed out-right or die of their wounds?"

In his *A B C's of Scapegoating*, G. W. Allport treats this subject with keen psychological insight, defining scape-goating as:

A phenomenon wherein some of the aggressive energies of a person or group are focused upon another individual, group, or object; the amount of aggression and blame being either partially or wholly unwarranted.

Three layers of scapegoating, *viz.*, predilection, prej-udice, and discrimination, are further demarcated in a clear-cut manner, and the following are thought to be the underlying factors of the whole complex process:

(A) thwarting and deprivation; (B) guilt; (C) fear and anxiety; (D) self-enhancement; (E) conformity; (F) tab-loid thinking.

Against this analysis, it may be urged that the Jews themselves have furnished us with a host of phrases and proverbs (reproduced in this book) which serve to in-criminate them in the eyes of the world. In other words, what better proof of guilt is there than confession?

To a psychologist this argument is very naïve. It takes no student of criminology to understand that *even an in-dividual's confession* of murder will not be accepted unless the *corpus delicti* can be found. Pathological admissions are not so uncommon as supposed. In the *group*, where the incrimination applies, as a rule, to other members and not to oneself, the confession becomes quite understandable, especially when we recognize that there is such a thing as Jewish anti-Semitism, and when it is further considered that no underdog so low but would point his finger at another, relegated to a still lower stratum. This well-known principle is at the root of the inferiority doctrine. Minor nationalities, themselves oppressed, will nearly always vent their frustrated feelings on more helpless minorities.

The subject of Jewish anti-Semitism has been dealt with in at least a dozen monographs and essays, principally in German, English, Yiddish, and Hebrew.

There is no reason in the world why a suggestible Jew should not be beguiled by an unfriendly majority into believing that his fellow-Jews, and even he himself, are inferior to the Gentiles, and particularly to the ruling element in the country they happen to inhabit.

In regard to the self-accusatory proverbs in Yiddish, we ought not to lose sight of a rather important circumstance, to wit, that while non-Jews, who live on their own soil, often make unflattering statements, derived from their experience with their own kind, without necessarily mentioning their own nationality, the Jews were obliged to make a distinction.

Thus, when the Frenchman says "*a prêtre cousin germain; au rendre, fils de putain*" (At borrowing a close cousin; at returning, the son of a whore) he is presenting a universally observed, although too generalized, fact, based on what he found to be the case in his country, inhabited preponderantly by Frenchmen. The Jew, who

has occasion to repeat the proverb "When he goes borrowing, the Jew will be worrying, but when the loan is due,
he sends the other whistling," does not mean to say that
the non-Jew is any better in this respect, but in all probability, from historical and literary descriptions in the past,
even worse, as indeed the French saw would indicate. It is,
however, an injunction or appeal to the would-be bor-
rower, or, *post factum,* a release of pent-up indignation
similar to an oath.

Yiddish proverbs—and this has not been recognized
apparently—are more than mere sayings or maxims. They
frequently serve to redirect the affect, and are therefore
abreactions, something like lightning rods. Thus if an
Englishman encounters a man hard to deal with, he might,
if belonging to the upper stratum, take leave under some
pretext which will conceal his real attitude; or else, if he is
of the lower type, he will indulge in a billingsgate sermon.
The Jew in the small town, for whom the slightest deal
might have meant the difference between a meal or no food
for his family, was neither inclined, nor could he afford, to
swear at his bargainer, his only satisfaction being the quo-
tation of a proverb like "With a Jew you can only eat
pudding, and that too not out of one dish." This is scarcely
in the category of a proverb but rather an elaborate
expletive.

THE MOORS

Hardly anyone nowadays speaks about the Moors except in a historical connection, but in comparative parœ-
miology they play a considerable part. A medley of
different stocks, coalescing after internecine wars over

centuries, they expanded their dominion in North Africa, bringing their Arab culture and Mohammedan religion into Spain, which flourished under their rule and influence in the eleventh to thirteenth centuries. Gradually Christian Spain began to throw off their yoke until they were banished or burned, together with the Jews, under the reign of Ferdinand and Isabella. The Moors declined steadily since as a people of power and culture and disintegrated into a number of tribes inhabiting Morocco, Tunisia, and Algeria, under the sovereignty of, first, Turkey, and, later, France. With Schiller we might have said "The Moor has performed his task, the Moor can go."

Certainly as a political figure, the Moor counts for naught at present, yet he still has an interest for us both as the producer and target of certain ethnophaulisms. Because of his dark skin, he was often set off from the other members of the Caucasian race, his hue calling forth both derision and fascination, and his prowess eliciting nothing but admiration. One finds no inferiority feeling in Othello; and the exploits of the Chieftain, which the genteel and beautiful Desdemona had found "passing strange" and "wondrous beautiful," so that she wished that "Heaven had made her such a man" were characteristic of many an Othello.

Sometimes the Moors would be classed with the Negroes because of their swarthiness, yet neither the Spanish nor the Portuguese were concerned with the color of their skin so much as with their being formidable enemies, and infidels to boot. The fact that they were allowed to dwell and prosper in Spain, if they embraced Christianity, after the royal edict of 1492, goes to show that to the fanatical

Isabella, at least, it was not so much what a man thought or did, still less what his appearance was like, as what he believed.

The Moors were apparently a bugbear to both Spain and Portugal, as the proverbs show. The Turks and the French who, of course, had a fighting acquaintance with them, nevertheless knew them rather as conquerors and saw none of the enviable qualities for which they were once noted. The Moroccans of the eighteenth and nineteenth centuries were but shadows of the Moor that inspired Shakespeare and Schiller.

If the Moors were not spared by the Iberians, the Turks, and the Arabs, in their folklore, they were in turn ready to reciprocate, although somewhat feebly, in that direction. Curiously enough, the Moroccan descendants of the doughty Moors vented their ire both physically and mentally on the Negroes and Jews. The former were the object of their contempt; the latter were the butt of their calumnies, as may be seen from the collection of Moroccan proverbs reproduced in this volume, most of which were culled from E. Westermarck's standard work *Wit and Wisdom in Morocco*. The savage thrusts are the result of a benighted state of civilization, superstition, and bigotry in religion. The Moors in their pristine glory treated the Jews almost on a par with themselves; and Jewish and Saracen achievements during the eleventh and twelfth centuries, as is well known, blazed the way for the European Renaissance.

THE NEGROES

If the Jews are the most universal scapegoat, the Negroes are both more fortunate and less fortunate in that they are seldom in a position which could in the slightest degree be regarded as responsible for the woes and miseries of a country or mankind, because—and this is the unfortunate aspect—they are held to be of insufficient intelligence to create any mischief. In the colonies, they are treated practically as subhumans, as if they were not worth discussing even in the spoken literature. In countries where their presence is not felt, as in Russia, Germany, and even France, their lot has not been too bad. We know of some outstanding men who were at least partly of Negro stock (Pushkin, in Russia, and Alexander Dumas, in France, for example).

It is in the United States, where the Negroes form about one-tenth of the population, and where in some localities they are in the majority, that the situation has become tense. It is not the actual discrimination and ill-treatment that we have in mind here, but rather the beliefs and opinions which frequently are the mainsprings of the physical, political, and economic abuse.

Were there only a few thousand Negroes in North America, their status would surely have been different in spite of their colored skins and often ill-shaped features. It is not that they constitute a minority, but that the minority, especially because of the contrasts, becomes so conspicuous. The Southern cry about keeping Negroes in their place implies unmistakably that they are thought to be inferior and unworthy of enjoying the same privileges as the Whites, particularly the progeny of the old settlers.

Nearly all the crimes in the calendar are fastened on them as a race, because of individual perpetrations. Uncleanliness is associated with the dark pigmentation. A body odor is supposed to be emitted even when not perspiring; and their mentality is rated as below that of the average White.

Here I must confess that on more than one occasion, I caught myself being surprised at the grades obtained by Negro students. As a graduate student, a bronze-colored student at Harvard was once introduced to me, who later said he was a native of the West Indies. I still recall my puzzled reaction, since I was under the impression that colored natives could hardly attain a grammar school education. (Perhaps the many stories about tribes in New Guinea, Fiji Islands, or Borneo unable to count more than ten were responsible for my naïve belief.)

When we examine the ethnophaulisms levelled at the Negro, we cannot help noting that in general it is only their color that is held against them. It was the prophet Jeremiah, over 2,000 years ago, who made the first recorded slur in this respect; and the world is harping on it in countless variations since. Outside of America, the Negro has not received many nicknames. In the United States, however, these sobriquets run into the dozens, but they deal again and again with the pigmentation of the skin, turning with a slight diversion in the direction of the inanimate, as if the Negro were a robot. The astonishing thing is that no specific accusations are pinned on him, collectively, as in the case of the Jew. His characteristics appear in a negative cast.

The Negroes are also the creators of proverbs. Since

there are so many different kinds of Negroes, who dwell in as many lands, their lore would naturally vary, but there is one theme running throughout, and that is the injustice of the white man, told with cutting sarcasm, for instance, "When black man thief, him steal half a bit, but when white man thief, him steal a whole sugar planta- tion." The Mulatto, who generally puts on airs because he is approximating the White more than the Negro, also earns the snicker of his less fortunate brother in such sayings as "Just put a mulatto on horseback, and he'll tell you his mother wasn't a Negress."

THE ORIENTALS

In the first instance to come under our consideration under this rubric are the Chinese and the Japanese. To judge by the meagre results obtained in my search of proverbs alluding to other nations in Chinese and Japanese collections, the Orientals are not preoccupied with others. The Chinese Wall was not only a physical structure; it was, to begin with, a *temperament*. Perhaps the adage "Chinese rulers do not concern themselves with Bar- barians" will give us a clue to this paucity of references to foreigners. It is possibly for this reason that they have been so tolerant to them. The moralistic form of Chinese maxims as well as of their humor seems to exclude the cynical or sophisticated ethnic slur.

Just as to us, "all Chinamen look alike," so to the Chinese all Europeans are red (the first contacts being with Germans, Russians, and Englishmen); all Europeans are "hook-nosed" (as compared with the short, tilted noses of the far Orientals) and all Europeans are "hairy-armed." In other words, the slur in this case is only the establish-ment of physical differences. The significance of the con-temptuous word "Teh", which was applied to Europeans, before it was forbidden by foreign intervention, is some-thing I have not been able to fathom. "Foreign devil" appears to have been the most universally employed ethnophaulism in China at the time of the Boxer War.

We do know, on the other hand, that the epithets "*fan kuai*," (in the North, it was "*yang kuei tse*") and "*yang weitz*," in allusion to all Occidentals, were definitely opprobrious, signifying, as they did, "foreign devil." Pos-sibly the early traders who were typical adventurers, to some extent, deserved the name.

Whether the same can be said of the Japanese is doubt-ful, yet the Japanese yield too is less than negligible. India, because of its closer contacts with the Arabs, the Turks, the Tartars, and the English, has been more outspoken. Korea offers us nothing in this field. Perhaps its proverb, "A man who stands behind a wall can see nothing else" tells part of the story.

On the other side of the fence (or the wall) *i.e.,* the European and American reaction to the Oriental, there is more to be said. "John Chinaman" has always been re-garded with considerable curiosity. Not so long ago chil-dren believed that the laundryman with the pigtail ate rats for supper, and such bywords as "chink," "a China-man's chance," "that's a Chinese puzzle," "all Chinamen look alike," together with journalese like "Celestial" and "Chinese wall," would produce in us the feeling that the Chinaman is, as the old song went, "a very, very funny

Chinaman." Their voluntary segregation into special districts (Chinatown) where American-born youngsters spoke their own language and where the stores displayed native products while the young women wore and are still wearing the traditional narrow slit gown would tend to emphasize the peculiarity.

With the Boxer uprising, the phrase "yellow peril" came into vogue; and, it sounds quite anachronistic now, but when the dormant Eastern giant began to awaken and stretch, turning the hoary Empire into a fresh Republic, there were warning cries in high American political circles. We were told to be on the *qui vive* not against Japan, the potentialities of which were discounted, but against swarming China. The adjective "yellow" became a synonym for "treachery"; and although Japan was included in this insult, the chief symbol seemed to be China.

A frank statement of the Chinese-American interaction appears in an article just as these pages go to press. The writer, a highly educated Chinese merchant, rather surprises us by the revelation that his race-fellows in America take it amiss not only if addressed by the casual factotum-name "Charlie," but even when referred to as Chinamen, although Irishmen, Englishmen, Dutchmen, and Frenchmen are not similarly affected, so far as we are aware: "I don't call you 'American-man,' so why should you call me 'Chinaman'?" is the way one student put his grievance.

"To the Chinese," we are told in this article, "the word 'Chinese' denotes refinement and an attitude of friendly respect on the part of the speaker. 'Chinaman' gives quite the opposite feeling. In short, a great many Chinese immediately form an unfavorable opinion of any Caucasian they hear using that word. He is suspected, usually with-out justification, of feeling contempt for the Chinese."*

The excessive politeness, the exaggerated compliments, bordering on insincere adulation, had been noticed by European travellers, and they could not help seeing in this racial trait a sinister design. *Pari passu,* there developed the American-Chinese detective novel with its lurid tales of mystery crime. The restriction of Oriental immigra-tion, although not the result of such influences, neverthe-less was abetted by the temper of the country. Books like Pearl Buck's *The Good Earth,* especially the superb film production, did much to counteract this prejudice, which has been on the wane since the United States found itself compelled to fight alongside China.

In comparison with China, Japan seems to have been a bit favored by both Europe and América. It forged ahead, adapting modern technique to its own needs and ends. It evolved a system of education which practically eradicated illiteracy, and its universities were soon turning out re-searches published both in English and Japanese that astonished the Western world.

Early in 1928, I received a communication from a Japanese student and university lecturer, telling me that my *Psychology of Character* was being studied in one of the classes in the University of Tokyo, and asking whether he could in any manner be of service. I was glad to have the information and the contact. There was an interruption in the correspondence, which was resumed in 1932. Although my correspondent employed a fairly correct Eng-

*Kong, W.: "Name Calling." *Survey Graphic,* June, 1944, vol. XXXII, No. 6.

lish, I was not always able to interpret the situation correctly, or, indeed, to discover the wherefore of certain expressions. I could not see, for example, why he should say
"I have duly received with a thousand pardons your favor
of Nov. 3." He did not write because he was unable to
furnish the data which he gathered for me as a result of
his offer, and he apologized profusely for his delay which
was due to the following incidents.

On leaving the University in 1929, I was en-
rolled in the army, and finished military service
two years later in 1931 during which I met with
some of the most lamentable accidents in my
life—one being the fire that destructed [sic]
almost all the works of my researches. I, from
your instruction, collected good many of the
Japanese works on, or rather, in the view point
of "temperament-typus" (*Katagi* in Japanese)
from about 1600 down to 1800, with their
copies and the extracts of the contents translated
into English. They were all reduced to ashes.
On leaving the army, I found myself penniless
and compelled to work hard from morn till night
for the life of a family of two parents and three
brothers and sisters and myself. I changed my
house three times. I have now only the title of
the works and their printing years. If you
would, for the time being of about half a year,
satisfied with the book names, I should be most
pleased. In the mean time, I am sure I can have
a little time and money and can send you the
copies rearranged with their contents translated.
Of course, I do not wish to make any ignoble

excuses myself. I know that you do not believe
me. Believe or unbelieve, I must do my duty and
keep my promise. All I ask of you is your pardon, and all I can say is, 'Wait, please, a little
more, if you would.'"

We have in this letter something typical, something
which sheds light on the Japanese sense of duty. The
anxiety to retrieve themselves at all costs, their humility
on such occasions, as when they have not shown themselves equal to the task, make the Japanese seem so
paradoxical to us Occidentals. "I am a poor student,"
which I took to mean in the material sense, turned out to
be a self-effacing remark about the writer's accomplish-
ments. When I suggested that he drop the task under the
circumstances, after having sent me a large number of
titles, both in English and in Japanese, for a projected
second edition of my *Bibliography of Character and Personality*, he wrote: "But I do not wish to have your
mind troubled about me. I beg you—please do not. I am
only doing my duty."

In another letter, he observes:

You say that Japan is now at war. I do not
think so. It is true (and I am sorry to say) that
China and Japan are not friendly with each
other. I believe, and from the bottom of my
heart, hope that some day they will come to
understand each other and shake hands.

This young man (born in 1902) who had undergone
four years of military training up to 1932, like his fellow-

students had a thorough knowledge of Japanese, Chinese, and English, was conversant with French and German, and could make out references in Latin and Greek.

These passages have been quoted because they reflect the cultivated Japanese mind; and now we can return to the specific subject at issue, *viz.*, the linguistic references to Japan and its people.

It is not altogether insignificant that when we compare in any complete dictionary, like *Webster's New International,* the terms and phrases which contain a derivative of "Japan" in it, with those referring to any European state, we shall find that Japan tops them all, yes, even vies with hoary China, which should have, by all the laws of logic, more space in our dictionaries. After all, Japan is a comparatively small group of islands only recently discovered to Westerners and to boot, so far away. How can we explain this disproportion except by supposing that Japan has been a protégé of the United States ever since Commodore M. G. Perry had broken the spell of Japanese exclusiveness in 1854, and also that there had been a great deal of traffic with that country? Curiously enough, however, the phrases involving the Japanese have, with such exceptions as the colloquial "Jap", or the common slur "yellow", all been of an objective, geographical, or commercial nature. It is evident that the Americans had a certain regard for the Japanese, until the attack on Pearl Harbor, and do not underrate their skill, endurance, and singleness of purpose to the point of death even now.

The Russians, at the time of the Russo-Japanese War, had a different approach. The Japs to them were *makaki i.e.,* little monkeys (*rhesus macacus*) and the then current phrase *makaki shapkami zakidayem* i.e., "we'll catch the little monkeys by throwing our hats over them" was a bit premature. The Americans know better.

THE OSMANLIS AND THE TURKS

It would be best to touch upon the Turks together with the Osmanlis; for even though the latter are seldom heard of, so many of the Turkish proverbs are labelled *Osmanli,* and, what is more, the Osmanli sayings as a rule poke fun at the Turks.

In order to understand the relationship, it is necessary to acquaint ourselves with the most elementary facts of early Turkish history, although much of it seems to be enveloped by a mist. Both the Osmanlis and the original Turks appear to be a conglomeration of small tribes, from Scythia, Turkestan, and the Mongolian neighborhood, as well as Arabia. It was not until the fourteenth century that a fearless and able leader, called Othman, conquered the people who had become known as the Turks, and consolidated his gains by establishing what afterwards under the aggressive expansion of his successors loomed as the Ottoman Empire. The Osmanli appellation, a tribute to the redoubtable conqueror, was adopted as the name of the nation, while Turk meant a "rustic", "menial" or any comical fellow. It was perhaps to pay off an old account, of six hundred years, that the first ruler of the Turkish Republic, Mustapha Kemal, in reverse formation, adopted the name of Attaturk.

Since the Turks were the vanquished people, we need not wonder that most of the proverbs and jokes of the ruling class were at their expense, an analogy to which is offered by the Norman treatment of the Anglo-Saxons during the twelfth and thirteenth centuries.

As for the reputation of the Turks (including the Osmanlis and Saracens) in Europe, the continual and savage strife between this warlike nation and the collection of Christian armies, under this or that Crusader, would be sufficient to brand the Turk, in the eyes of the enemy, as a devil incarnate; and Saladin became a name which was to strike terror in both child and adult. Centuries later, the enslavement of the Greeks, Bulgarians, Serbs, Rumanians, and the periodic massacres of the Armenians on the part of the Turks, did not add to their prestige.

"The Unspeakable Turk" then became a popular phrase shouted from the pulpit and rostrum, just as "the sick man of Europe" was echoed in parliaments and repeated in the press, until the Young Turks and Mustapha Kemal threw off the shackles of the moribund Sultanate and intrenched themselves at Ankara (close to the source of the original Turks) which became the seat of the new government, thereafter functioning as a normal nation after the European fashion!

THE PORTUGUESE AND THE SPANISH

The Iberian peninsula, probably because of the infiltration of foreign elements and clashes with many racial stocks, offers a goodly number of words and dicta tinctured with national innuendo. Both of these nations show in their lore a distinct animosity toward the Jews and the Moors. The French, the English, the Germans, and the Italians were scarcely known to the masses and therefore the few ethnophaulisms dealing with each are the conventional ones (interlinear, one might say). Occasionally even a flattering maxim is found, such as "War with all the world and peace with England."

The relation between Spain and Portugal is about the same as that between Russia and Poland. The larger state behaves like a bully toward the smaller.

In one of the Spanish-Portuguese wars, the street-girls, to show their devotion to the Spanish King, rendered service to their country in a unique way, when they sent a bevy of the most diseased of their profession to the Portuguese camp, close to Madrid, and within a week, six thousand of the enemy were *hors de combat*.

For some time, it was said, the Spaniards were the object of such hate among the Portuguese, that a Portuguese priest could hardly be found to give communion to a dying Spaniard.

The Portuguese, in the eyes of their blood-brethren, were Spaniards without their virtues. Portugal, in spite of her explorers and navigators, was a second-rater to Spain, but it did not serve as a scapegoat. That function was reserved for the Jews, who still are a cipher to the Spaniards of the lower classes. The Spanish and Portuguese dictionaries even now continue to include words and phrases that are decidedly offensive, as the Spanish-Portuguese section in this book will disclose; and as for proverbs, there are scores of them vilipending the two peoples that had raised Spain to its height of glory, politically, economically, and culturally.

The remarkable thing about this lore is that a period of 450 years has elapsed since the Jews were banished from Spain. For centuries the Spaniards did not know what a

Jew looked like, and yet the insinuations have clung to this day. The persistence on the part of the Sephardic (Spanish-Portuguese) Jews in preserving their Ladino dialect all these centuries in foreign countries contrasts rather ironically with the doggedness of their former compatriots in reviling them.

An eloquent account of this inexorableness in the face of time on the part of the Spaniards is described in a recent book on the Majorca Chuetas whose ancestors, on pain of exile or death, became converts to Christianity.

> There is a special poignancy about the story of the activities of the inquisition in Majorca and the Jewish converts to Christianity—who are today known as Chuetas—which distinguished it from the activities of the inquisition in other parts of Spain. For today, despite the five-hundred years which have passed since the forbears of the Chuetas were converted to Christianity, they are still an ostracized group in Catholic Majorca. They have not been completely assimilated into the island's life. Nowhere in all Spain has the identity of a small group been preserved so tenaciously over such a long period of time as in Majorca. It is a singular phenomenon that to this day the Chuetas are sometimes referred to as Judios (Jews) and Hebreos (Hebrews), and denied complete social equality, and sometimes economic opportunity, with the other natives of Majorca.
>
> The Chuetas constitute one of the tragedies of the modern world, living among an island-people who seem unable to rid themselves of

their provincial and fanatical prejudices, which the activities of the inquisition have played no small part to perpetuate. Up to our day the Chuetas remain a pariah-folk in the Mediterranean region, isolated in a Catholic land, among peoples whose faith they share, and whose life they have enriched by poets and writers. This anomalous situation is in large part a relic of the Spanish zeal for unity of the faith, inspiring the establishment of the Spanish Inquisition, and which, beginning in the fifteenth century, has not altogether spent its force in our times, a century after its extinction.

. . . . . .

With the birth of the New Spanish Republic (1931), it would appear that such outmoded prejudice would have vanished like smoke. Republican Spain, apparently, has not yet succeeded in obliterating an ancient prejudice held against a group of people persecuted on account of their Jewish antecedents.*

What about the attitude of other nations toward Spain? For the most part, the Spanish have been twitted internationally about their touchiness and inordinate pride verging on haughtiness, their foppishness and their fanaticism, so that even Italians close to the Throne of St. Peter would wish to live in Italy but die in Spain. Aggressiveness in lovemaking has been attributed to the Span-

*B. Braunstein: *The Chuetas of Majorca* (Columbia University Oriental Series) 1936. For the pejorative meaning of *Chuetas*, see Spanish-Portuguese section, this DICTIONARY.

ish, too. The Portuguese are seldom differentiated from the Spanish when it is a matter of temperamental rating, although it is recognized by the more informed that they are comparatively phlegmatic.

Since the Latin-American peoples are of Spanish-Indian or Portuguese-Indian stock, with a New-World tradition steering their destiny, much of what has been said of the mother nations applies to them, except that the Indian admixture and democratic setting serve to modify the intensity of the religious fervor and its social consequences. The folklore and vocabulary of these countries are still too young to reveal definite attitudes except toward the Americans and the English (the Gringos) and the Polaccos (Poles, as a euphemism for Jews).

THE SCANDINAVIANS

There is not much to report on Scandinavian slurs. The Danes, the Norwegians, and the Swedes, although at odds amongst themselves at different times, do not seem to have shown any real disrespect toward one another. Good-natured banter, relative to their super-patriotism, or "rooting" for their own country, is implied in some of their catch-phrases, like a "Norwegian North-man from Norway," or a "Swedish appointment." They have, of course, adopted some of the current ethnophaul-isms from their neighbors, e.g., "Polish Parliament," which the Germans use in a sense similar to our *bedlam,* and their similes include the Turks and Finns, the Irish, and the Scotch, the Dutch, and the French, but not the English. The Germans figure as exploiters.

As for the attitude of the rest of the world toward the Scandinavians, although the scars they left on the continent can still be traced in the folk locutions of Germany, Poland, Russia, and Finland, they are not deep. We are apt to forget that small as Denmark and Sweden are, they have in the past engaged in some spectacular warfare. Even England, sometime during the tenth and eleventh centuries, was under the sway of a Danish conqueror, while the brilliant campaigns of Gustavus Adolphus, in the seventeenth century, made Sweden the most feared country in the world; and had he not been killed in his thirties, Europe today might have been differently situated. It is also to be noted that while the average army would have lost courage in the knowledge that their beloved chief no longer could lead them, such was the morale of Gustavus Adolphus's troops that they became all the more exasperated and routed the enemy on his own soil.

The indomiable Charles XII who, at the age of 20, defeated in turn Frederick IV of Denmark, Peter the Great of Russia, and Augustus of Poland, did the same for Sweden at the beginning of the eighteenth century as his illustrious predecessor, perhaps with greater judiciousness, had accomplished during the Thirty Years' War, which the Germans did not forget so easily, as is evident from such folk expressions as *ein schwedischer Trank* (which see in the German section of the DICTIONARY). It is characteristic of the Swedes that although either of these warriors might have with greater justice been honored with the attribute *Great* than most of the other continental "greats", no attempt was made to apotheosize these modern Alexanders on the part of their subjects.

In England and the United States, the nicknames, like *Scandiwoogians, Swensky, squarehead,* imply no scorn, any more than "the old sweat", which Weekley believes, and with reason, to be the English adaptation of "der alte Schwede."

THE SLAVS

Our first thought about the Slavs has probably been the Russian bear, an ungainly and burly creature without too much intelligence. The Englishman or American who has had the occasion of seeing or hearing the word *muzhik* or *katzap,* must have visualized, in most cases, a broad-shouldered, square-faced, unkempt black-bearded man, uncouth in manners, but tractable. The Germans were prone to see in the Russian a simple barbarian, and in the Pole, a pretender. Both to them represented a rather low stage of civilization.

Indeed, the most tragic of all the slurs or ethnophaulisms I consider to be the word *slave.* Little do we realize, unless we are conversant with a particular field of history or philology, that what has become a synonym for an abject bondsman connoted at one time the *glory and fame* which the Slavs, in so designating themselves, boasted of. When the Germanic hordes during the Middle Ages waged an annihilating war against the Slavonic tribes, reducing them to captivity in Teutonic style, the *Slavs* simply became *slaves.* In this instance, the Slavs were not renamed. That were not so bad as to have their original denomination become a byword of such a character.

It is something of poetic justice, however, that the Slavs (Russians and Poles) have no name for the Germans except *Niemets,* which means "dumb," "can't speak." Not that the Germans could not speak, but their language was unintelligible to the Slavs, just as we say "that's Greek to me." The quip of fate becomes clear when we further are reminded that the word for speech in Rusian, *slovo,* is virtually the same as that for "glory" or "fame." (Compare *fama,* i.e., report, reputation, glory, and φημί, to speak, which are cognate in Latin and Greek.) Thus we see that quite unconsciously the Slavs repaid the Germans for changing their *speech-spread* (i.e., fame) to *slavery* by christening them, in turn, "unable to speak," or "the speechless."

After building up this traditional story, it is rather disappointing to have to present Lück's statement that the name *Slav* has nothing to do with either fame or speech, but is derived from the Gothic *slavan*—to be silent.* In brief, just as the Slavs called the German dumb, the latter regarded the Slavs as *speechless.* Our faith in Lück as a first class scholar, however, begins to waver when we read (page 264) his explanation of the word *tineff,* which, in Yiddish, means "trash," "muck." In 1663, the German settler, Timpf, was in charge of the mint in Poland, and was commissioned, because of the then state of the Polish treasury, to coin money which posessed no standard value. The Poles still say with

---

*Lück: *Der Mythos vom Deutschen,* etc., (see Bibliography) page 105. The Gothic word *slavan* is supposed to be cognate with our *slow,* which, according to Skeat's *Etymological Dictionary of the English Language,* is derived from a root meaning "blunt", "tepid".

reference to that episode: "A good joke—worth a timf."
Now, this fact occasions Lück to confidently assume that
when "the East European Jew calls all unreliable goods,
'*tineff*'," he is reviling poor old Timpf, the German, who
merely tried to improve the financial status of Poland.
In point of fact, any Jewish schoolboy could have informed
Lück that *tineff* was derived from the old Hebrew verb
taneff—to defile. But Lück was probably too eager to
catch the bird with two stones, simultaneously thrown . . . .

The Russians and the Germans, it appears, have always
been at loggerheads, as is manifested in their proverbs.
It is not scorn but fundamental hatred which bids us
"hang the German, though he may be a good fellow,"
while the German recommends drowning for the Russian.
The French have been held in mild contempt since
Napoleon's disaster in Russia. Flight, cowardice, inability
to endure hardships are the burden of Russian cavils
against the French. That the feeling was not deep-rooted
is evident from the aping of the French in Russian aristocratic circles to the degree of employing French as the
language of the élite.

The Poles, on the other hand, were treated as inferiors
by the Russians. Bulgaria, Serbia, and the smaller Slavic
divisions were looked upon as little sisters while Poland
was viewed as one step-brother by another. The foreign
dwellers in Russia who took to trading, *i.e.,* the Greeks
and the Armenians, were reviled as cheats. Other nationalities with which the Russians came in contact (the
Chinese, the Japanese, the Turks) receive a fair portion
of blame, but the "lion's share" of calumny was left for
the Jews. Both the Poles and the Russians appear to have

ASPECTS OF ETHNIC PREJUDICE

conspired in ascribing their troubles to Jewish practices. Of course, the reactionary element, the Czarist clique and the Holy Synod, were particularly active in devising slogans that proved hurtful to the Jews. The Poles could also afford to look down upon the Lithuanians who had declined in power and culture since Keistut and Yagello in the fourteenth and early fifteenth centuries.

The conventional slurs, which were merely adoptions from others, like "French malady," "English sickness," "Spanish influenza," are not lacking, but they are not to be considered specifically Russian or Polish.

The Czech culture, for a long time, had been buried under the Austrian incubus, but Bohemian sayings should receive more attention than they have been accorded. In any case their prevision of things to happen might be gleaned from the following proverbs: "Do not trust a Hungarian unless he has a third eye in his forehead," and "When a snake gets warm on ice, then will a German wish a Czech well."

The nicknames of Czechs, as they occur in the United States, like *bohunk, Chesky,* and *bootchkey* are merely harmless puerile teasing, of a verbal rather than an imputative nature.

THE GENESIS OF A PROVERB

Before taking up the question: How reliable is the average international slur, it is necessary to examine its origin. How do these ethnophaulisms come about? A folk expression is supposed to be a collective product, but obviously the originator is some individual. The individual is usually someone obscure, perhaps a peasant or artisan.

An epigram by a famous writer is hardly ever included in a collection of proverbs, but there is no reason why it should not be, provided it is in a folk vein and has been circulating among the masses. Thus Schiller's "The Moor has done his work, the Moor may go" contains nothing which the common people will fail to grasp the full sense of. It is pithy and is applicable to the humdrum situations which occur in everyday life. On the other hand, an aphorism like "Against stupidity the gods themselves strive in vain" is of a different texture, and is not likely to catch the fancy of the ordinary person.

It does not take a high degree of intelligence to invent a nickname or a mock-phrase or a statement like the Russian charge, "Deceive a Jew and he will kiss you; kiss a Jew and he will deceive you," or the Scotch self-incriminatory proverb (although it is more likely to have an English source) "Three failures and a fire make a Scotsman's fortune."

First, there is a certain attitude toward a particular group; the reproach, whether in the form of a catch-phrase, nickname, or proverb is bound to come. The man seeking his prey in a foreign group may go about it in the manner of the old Scottish judge who is alleged to have said, "Show me the man, and I'll show you the law."

Two things are to be kept in mind as responsible for the multitude of ethnophaulisms. First there is the tendency to magnify one's own group at the expense of another; for, as the Chinese say, "However stupid a man may be, he grows clever enough when he blames others; however wise, he becomes a dolt when blaming himself." The Biblical example of the beam in one's eye and the mote in the other's is turned picturesquely by the Negro into "Finger never say 'look here,' him say 'look yonder.' "

In his book *Megalomanja Narodowa* (National Megalomania), the Polish sociologist and folklorist, Jan St. Bystroń, ascribes the attitude toward other peoples to a sort of popular megalomania, which he identifies with imperialism. Even primitive tribes, according to him, regard themselves as the centre of the world, while all others are in the periphery. It may be added that each nationality thinks of its own language as an expressive, articulate medium, while members of other nations jabber, babble, or stammer, or speak barbarously.

The exaggeration of one's national ancestry leads people to believe that they are descended from the gods or from some universal heroes. The nationalization of God is a further consequence of this megalomania. Thus God favors their particular nation and will assist them to overwhelm their enemies; and if God is on their side, then their group must be not only dear to Him but sacred, too. Thus all laws and virtues are subordinate to the objectives and needs of that particular group and the state which it forms.

The theologian, Bystroń, declares that all this imperialism leads inevitably to paganism, as witness the Germans, but that corollary we need not accept, any more than the identification of imperialism and national megalomania. The most successful imperialists are the British; their national megalomania is most likely less than that of the Poles. Imperialism is national aggrandizement, a practical manipulation of national interrelations, while national megalomania may either remain in a theoretical stage, or undergo a conversion into national paranoia. The difference between national megalomania and imperialism, it seems to me, is that between egotism and egoism.

Perhaps the word megalomania is a bit too strong for this exaltation of one's country at the expense of its neighbors. "National adoration" might be a somewhat more appropriate term. Nor has it been appreciated that this national instinct serves a biological purpose, so far as the particular nationality is concerned, acting as an anti-toxin against the impulses of the individual to take the lines of least resistance in a national crisis, when, *e.g.*, renegades and traitors cannot resist the overtures of the conquering enemy. Without such national exaltation, the Quislings would be legion.

Another use of this mechanism is to stave off assimilation among minorities through intermarriage (with members of the dominant nationality in a country) as well as other environmental factors. The Jews have had to constantly harp on the *Chosen People* string in order to offset the attractiveness of apostasy and its advantages in a Christian or Mohammedan state. The very slur *shekets* or *sheyggets* (something disgusting), for a Gentile youth, was intended to serve as a conditioned reflex for the Jewish maiden over whom the non-Jewish lad would naturally exercise a strange fascination. The fact that no such disaparagement attached to the older Gentile (*goy*) should clinch the point which I am attempting to make. Nevertheless, despite all these ruses of the national unconscious, the "abomination" lost its repulsiveness for the Jewish girl in many cases, and as for *shikse,* the feminine of *sheyggets,* it even took on the bloom, if not the glamor, of

Gentile pulchritude, so that the original intent was definitely lost. Here we may be reminded of Shakespeare's
famous question about the name. The designation of
sheyggets or *shikse* held no terrors for, nor did it suggest
any repugnance to, the thousands of Jewish youths who
found the partner that satisfied them outside of their faith
and race. It was the triumph of realism—in the first stage
at least—over nominalism.

National exaltation does become akin to megalomania,
however, when it manifests itself to a high degree in a
country which is self-sufficient and not running the risk
of invasion. Such an outgrowth must necessarily reach
out into other territories and eventually cause aggression,
as was the case with Nazi Germany.

England, because of its comparative isolation, and its
advantage over Ireland, Scotland and Wales, was sufficiently protected against foreign inroads, and thus has
been perhaps the nation least addicted to what Bystroń
called "national megalomania," although its imperialism
has spread to the farthest corners of the earth; and its
dominions, again, because of their dependency on the
mother-country and relative unprotectedness, would tend
to heighten the incidence of British national exaltation.

What is it that nations say about each other? Usually
they fix upon some reputed fault and make a mountain of
it. No injunction or invitation to "please copy" is needed
for other nations to follow suit. All that the victim can
do is to hurl back the insult or seek redress by finding
some flaw in the opponent, or, what is more common still,
to pounce upon an underdog making him the butt of all
his abuses.

The other motive of the derogatory remark is securing a scapegoat, and where economic conditions are bad, or where disaster has overtaken a country or locality, it will not be long before the victim is found. Did not highly educated New Englanders discover in the "witches' " traffic with the devil the source of the evils that had then befallen the community? How much more then will the ignorant, and often besotted, peasant, in, let us say, Eastern Europe, find in the Jews the key to all his misfortunes, especially when the Czarist government or the Polish Endeks (supernationalists) would do their level best to spread defamatory propaganda? Nor would the local priests take a neutral position, especially before Easter.

Let us take a single instance. A peasant fancied or was led to believe that he had been taken advantage of by a Jew. Immediately, he will express his experience in the form of a generalization according to which every Jew is guilty of fraud. We do not yet know whether that particular Jew was at fault, but forthwith a whole people is libelled.

As a rule, the saying "give a dog a bad name and hang him" is true of the national mind. Just as children do not stop to investigate when a gawky, awkward, crippled, or overgrown fellow is being molested, but all join in the fun, so the folk-mind will not bother to inquire whether the nationality concerned is really to blame.

The fact that these indictments are numerous and are repeated in many countries does not make the charges valid, any more than the widespread ethnophaulism, *morbus Gallicus,* in its dozen or more translations, proves that syphilis or gonorrhea actually had its beginning in

France. Furthermore, since many nations fling back at one another the same accusation as "taking French leave," we must assume that they are just as bad, or that the vices cancel.

If the proverbs and other folk locutions were a true index of the libelee's acts, then the clergy would not come off too creditably. If we lent credence to the German sayings, the priests would emerge as a band of reprobates. Indeed the Nazis have drawn the logical conclusions and incarcerated many of them. Even among the Slavs, who are taught to revere the parson, the latter is taken down a peg in the folk expressions. The Bulgarian says "If you want to enjoy yourself for a week get married; if you want to have a life-time of pleasure, become a priest." According to the Russian, "the priest's eyes and the wolf's jaw will eat what they see," and the Pole echoes the refrain with such adages as "Children, chickens, priests, and women never have enough," or "The best beer is where the coachman and the priest go for their drink." The vituperation in Eastern sayings about women should discourage all contact with them. It would seem as if the more cruelly they were treated, the worse they were vilified.

IS A NATION A TABULA RASA?

Nevertheless, it would be a mistake to rule out of court all national differences. The scholar who discovered that the Jews were like everybody else, except more so, must have been mentally related to the Hibernian who wanted the world to know that "one man is as good as another and often a durn' sight better." Every nationality has its specific virtues and vices, excellences and defects, in that the majority exhibit propensities in a given direction not to be found in the average member of another ethnic group. The story about the contest in a seminar of research fellows, consisting of various nationals, who were given the task of writing on the elephant is more than a bit of pleasantry. It will be recalled that the Englishman took his gun, shot an elephant and brought the specimen for a concrete report. The Russian, after taking a glass of vodka, wrote all night on the question: "The Elephant: Does He Exist?" The Frenchman presented a disquisition on "Love among Elephants." The German shut himself up in the library and produced a history of the elephant since primitive days, in several volumes, while the Pole delivered himself of a lyric effusion on "The Elephant and Poland."

To affirm that there are national differences *does not mean that every member of a certain stock manifests these characteristics.* Nor are we attaching any value estimates to these differences. Moreover, we must concede that like individuals, nations will undergo certain changes at various periods of their lives. A warlike race may, because of conditions, grow pacific, and vice versa. At the same time, there is a kernel which remains fixed throughout the changes.

It is reasonable to urge that a proverbial contention or a catch-phrase slur is not acceptable without examina' tion, no matter how often it occurs and how universally or ubiquitously it is repeated; for a prejudice or slander multiplied a thousandfold does not become a demonstrable fact. Many of the slurs throw light on the subjects or carriers, rather than the objects or victims, of the libel. In some instances, no doubt, the accusation has some basis.

PREJUDICE AMONG CELEBRITIES

Prejudice, like disease, does not shun the great. A veritable encyclopedia could be compiled on the bias of celebrities. Not only the folk-mind, men of genius have shown remarkable prejudices which to people inferior yet fairer seem incomprehensible. Samuel Johnson's opinion of the Scotch is too well known. Thomas Jefferson detested the English, not merely their Government. In this loathing he was preceded by no less an Italian poet and scholar than Petrarch, who expressed himself in such emphatic language as: "Of all the barbarous nations, none is the more cowardly and ignorant than the English, excepting only the rascally Scotch." But Petrarch, born before Chaucer, was more justified in his estimate than Jefferson, himself one of the noblest Americans.

Chopin, Beethoven, and certainly Wagner were bitter against the Jews, although they owed much of their success, even their material well-being to them; and the great scientist, Thomas Huxley, said, "What a pack of liars! . . . . The Irish cannot tell the truth."

As for the comparison of the Greeks and Turks, the celebrated philosopher and historian, David Hume, than whom there were few men more sagacious and perspica-cious in his century, wrote, in 1741, "The integrity, grav-ity, and bravery of the Turks form an exact contrast to the deceit, levity, and cowardice of the modern Greeks." Yet we know from our own experience during the Nazi war, that this statement anent the Greeks is not true. These are only two or three of hundreds of instances. Such men, some of powerful intellect, could not all be right, nor is it possible that they are all wrong.

Some prejudices may be constitutional. I do not claim they are instinctive, or innate in the sense that we are born with a disposition to dislike a certain nationality, but rather that we come into the world with a set of traits which will make us disposed to appreciate or to deprecate certain qualities in others. Scotchmen and Irishmen may be able to get along with one another; and yet the average Scotchman will not respect the Irish, nor will the average Irishman like the Scotch. The reason will not be in their awareness of past feuds or in upbringing or in their religious differences, but rather in the constellation of characteristics which either appeals or is repugnant to them.

To partially corroborate this conclusion, I should offer in evidence the remarkable matching of likes and dislikes we find in so many notables. Thus, David Hume thought well of the Turks and berated their enemies, the Greeks. Carlyle cherished the Arabs and despised the Jews, hence he could say about the Nestor of German literature, "Blackguard Heine is worth very little." It is my conjecture that *few* intellectual Jews find Carlyle's works, even the pretentiously witty *Sartor Resartus,* anything but the handiwork of dull drudgery. Nietzsche, on the other hand, was a warm friend of the Jews; and, as we might have anticipated, the cult of Wagner, which at one time intrigued him, was bitterly exposed when he attained a more mature insight.

This see-saw attitude I have observed in cases too numerous to mention. There have been few who sustained their balance so as to like, *e.g.*, the Poles and the Russians, or the French and the Germans equally well; and here, as a caution, we are reminded of the adage that whoever cannot hate, cannot love. It is somewhat strange that a thorough investigation and analysis of the prejudices of the famous has not yet been made. The correlations might prove a revelation, and advance our knowledge of the problem of types, which psychologists are too apt to ignore.

ASSOCIATIVE AND ASSONANCE FACTORS

It would not occur to many sociologists or social psychologists that the very sounds and associations inherent in national designations may have something to do with fostering prejudices, yet it is my belief that such semantic conditioning does take place, as the following illustrations will serve to show.

For a long time I was under the impression that the Barbary Coast in North Africa was so named because of the barbarousness of the inhabitants. The piracy of Moroccan and Algerian seamen, the never-ending stream of heinous crimes that were being reported, the strength of the underworld in those countries, the feebleness of the authorities to enforce the law or to administer justice were enough to confirm anyone's picture of that region as a modern setting of Sodom. In reality, however, the Bar-

bary or Berbery states are etymologically remote from
our sense of barbarous, the word Barbar (or Berber)
happening to be the name of an Arab tribe inhabiting
the Northern part of Africa.

Another example is that of *Tartar*. The original name,
as is well known, contains only the final *r*. Why was this
word corrupted by the interpolation of a parasitic *r*? This
linguistic phenomenon, it seems to me, is quite common
(I have treated the subject of parasitic sounds extensively
elsewhere), and in this instance, probably the general tendency toward reduplication, *e.g.*, "hanky-panky", or assimilation, as in *convent* for *covent* (French, *couvent*) the
original form—is almost sufficient to explain the formation
of Tartar; but the specific perverse habit of the common
English-speaking person to add an *r* after a vowel or to
misplace it (the most annoying sample of this nefarious
practice is the way most American youths pronounce
("modern" as "morden") adds an auxiliary factor. In
addition to these mere technical influences, however, there
may very well have been the association of *Tartary* with
the Latin *Tartarus*, hell, since the Tartars had reduced a
large part of Europe to shambles, or in our slang, it might
be said that they were "raising hell."

Cockroaches, when they are not labelled *Prussians*, receive the name of *Schwaben* (Swabians) even in Germany.
Why should the Germans have singled out the Swabians,
if it were not for the close assonance of *Schaben* and
Schwaben? *Schaben*, or rather *Küchenschaben*, is the
standard German term for this unappetizing insect which
infests our restaurants.

It is not altogether unlikely, too, that the term *schwa-*

beln, which, in German, means "to chatter" or "prattle", is, aside from the fact that all Southerners would seem talkative to the Northerners of any nation, a pun on *Schwaben,* Swabians. In German and in Swedish, the word for Finn and the word meaning pimple are homo-phones (*Finne*). No matter whether there is a common source or not—in the mind of the people, the national connotation must be somewhat colored.

It is very well known that a coincidence loses its for-tuitousness and takes on the aspect of an incidence the more cases it involves. Let us take the homophone *Finne* which represents both a Finn and a pimple or a boil as our base. At first, we see no connection between the two, but when we discover that *uher* in Czech means both a Hungarian and a boil, that likewise, *mad'ar* has the same two meanings, that furthermore in Polish, *Wegier* shows the same "coincidence," ("Hungarian" and "abscess in animals") and when, finally, it occurs to us that the Finns and the Hungarians belong originally to the same general stock (Finno-Ugrian) we begin to wonder whether, after all, the homophones are not at bottom—synonyms; and when we, in addition, ponder the fact that for the Poles the word *Żyd,* a Jew, may also mean a boil, it dawns upon us that what it all amounts to is that to some of their neighbors, the Hungarians, Finns and Jews are just a "pain in the neck." If this is a coincidence, then it appears to "coincide" quite regularly.

The French phrase *exhiber son prussien* signifies to dis-play one's trousers' seat in making a headlong flight. The origin of this slang expression, at the expense of the Prus-sians, is obscure, but Henley and Farmer in their seven-

DICTIONARY OF INTERNATIONAL SLURS

volume [Dictionary of] *Slang and Its Analogues* trace *prussien* to the Romany word *prusiatini*, the posterior. Similarly the phrase *querelle d'Allemand,* a brawl over trifles, is explained by W. Gottschalk in his *Die sprich-wörtlichen Redensarten der französischen Sprache* (page 427) as harking back to the feuds of a family called the *Allemans,* in the thirteenth century. It may, of course, be that a German apologist will always find a loophole to suit his purpose, but the popular method of hanging aspersions or ridicule upon a national peg is patent.

Another of those suspicious coincidences is the fact that Βλάχος a Rumanian or Wallachian, in Modern Greek, is practically a homophone of the Greek word for a sluggard or dolt — Βλᾶκός

As usual, it is in the treatment of the Jew that we find our *locus classicus,* even in this linguistic region. To begin with, the very sound *Jew* is by no means euphonious. The original *Yehudi,* which is cognate with the Hebrew word for "praise" and "glory," has undergone all sorts of transformations through the Greek, the Latin, and the French, until, the liquid *Y* became a rough sibilant, and the *d* was chewed off altogether. The *J* in *Jew* is nearly always articulated as a *ch* by the man in the street.

In French, the word has fared even worse; for during the Renaissance, the name was at least *Juis.* The substitution of the final *f,* possibly to compensate for the corroded *d,* did not improve the sound. The explosive manner in which it is articulated suggests abuse; and I can understand why French Jews adopted the more ancient designations, *Hébreu* and *Israélite,* although I cannot approve of such cringing. We are here reminded of Heine's caustic observation, "When people talk about a wealthy man of my creed, they call him an Israelite, but if he is poor they call him a Jew."

In Russia, the name *zhid*, Jew, is not used except in a derogatory sense. Other appellations are substituted. And since Russia has been touched on, may there not be, in Italian, some slight repercussion of the word *russo*, snoring, on the name *Russo*, a Russian? Again the Russian slur-name for the Japanese, *makaki*, monkeys, (Latin, *macacus*) must have received some nurture from the resemblance of this name to some of the Japanese words.

In this connection, it is unfortunate for the Jews that the apostle who is credited with having betrayed his master bore the name of the founder of the tribe with which the Jews are identified. Had it been John, Peter, or James, the associative crest would not have formed, but Judas was bound to become a national symbol of the Jews, for all those who were only too willing to forget that the betrayed was no less a Jew than the betrayer. When we compare other national types in the world's literature with Jewish characters, we see cause for lament. Was there ever a more despicable character than Tartuffe? Yet who would ever think of employing that name as representative of the French? The Jews, however, have not been able to live down the literary prank that Shakespeare played in reversing the original *fabula* in the *Gesta Romanorum*, according to which it was the Christian who demanded his pound of flesh from the Jew.

All these assonances and associations may not play a dominant part in our consciousness, but they doubtless have a cumulative effect in stirring the emotions and heightening the imagination of all and sundry who had already been prepared to see the foreigner, and especially certain kinds of foreigners, in a given light, or rather shade.

HOW PERNICIOUS ARE THE SLURS?

This leads to the question whether the various ethno-phaulisms exercise an influence on the behavior of the people, or whether they are merely transformers of surplus energy.

My answer is that the aspersions implied do actually enter into the conduct of not only the average person, but even the outstanding man or woman who has not become immune to such prejudices.

Some years ago, the uncomplimentary references to Greeks in France had become so widespread that students from Greece would adopt their ancient name *Hellènes,* in order to divert the attention of their French critics. If a porter did not receive what he considered to be the proper *pourboire,* he might say, "There seems to be no one around today but Greeks." If someone anticipated him in some transaction, he might allude to it as a *grecquerie* or a *juiverie.* I could not help smiling when I heard an Eng-lishman living in a large French-Canadian community in the United States say, with a belittling gesture, as he looked at the name at the bottom of a letter, "Oh, French? I shouldn't pay much attention to that. I found them to be most unreliable." It would be interesting to know how the French immigrants have been looked upon in Greece. Certainly the Russians did not regard them in too favor-able a light.

A much more pronounced illustration of the connection between lore and practice is served by the plight of the Moroccan Jews. For centuries they have been subjected to all sorts of abuse, and the most impossible incriminations would be harbored not only among the benighted masses but even among the officials. An examination of the so-called wit and wisdom of Morocco would disclose to us in part the reason for the wretched state of affairs in that country even under the civilized but often corrupt French functionaries.

There is always to be expected a certain amount of superstition and prejudice in all proverbs, but the sayings of the Moroccans appear to place a special premium on a malicious cynicism in regard to subordinated elements. Jews, Negroes, and women are the special targets. To a layman, it would seem natural that the open acts of injustice or violence are the consequences of the beliefs, but while the causal relationship is assuredly established, we cannot be certain whether the practice was the result of the theory or *vice versa*. It may very well be that the low opinions were formed in justification of the bullying attitude, just as a hold-up man before robbing his victim will insult him in the vilest manner. More than once have I asked myself how the gangster can motivate his addition of insult to injury, (or rather his prefacing the injury by insults), but it is evident that by calling his prey a . . . . and . . . . etc., he is reversing the roles. It is as if he were in the capacity of a moral agent punishing the person about to be robbed for his well-known misdeeds.

Conversely, where there is little (if any) calumny of other nations, in the lore of a people, we shall always find a higher degree of respect for the foreigner. The jingo spirit, if not totally lacking, will be reduced to a minimum. Once we accept the fact of a correlation between the use of ethnophaulisms and actual ill-treatment of a national group, regardless of the sequence, since the process is probably reciprocal, we are before a very momentous question from a concrete angle, *viz.*, should national slurs be prohibited by law and the dissemination of collective libels be made a penal offence?

Thus, the philological and folkloristic data are moved into a new sphere, namely, the ethical and political universe of discourse, which eventually governs almost every human endeavor. The normative is often looked upon by the quantitative scientist as something superfluous or useless, but without the directive force of the values, either as an inner principle or an external agency, science, even in its most exact form, can only be putty in the hands of a ruthless dictator, as we, alas, have had the sad experience of witnessing but too acutely.

This problem, which already has become part of the agenda in Congress, will crop up again and again as the fascist elements in this country and England will gain momentum after the War. So many among the liberals and indifferents cannot bring themselves to believe that the great North American republic which was conceived in liberty, nay more, actually came into being, because of oppression elsewhere, as a haven for minorities, can some day turn into a reservoir of intolerance, where bigots and petty souls will seek an outlet for their pathological hatreds through restrictions of one sort or another, many of them veiled by abstract political lingo, but capable of singling out some specific group or groups for injurious treatment. We are prone to forget that (a) congressmen and senators do not always represent their constituencies (b) that often only a handful of legislators is sufficient to enact or defeat far-reaching measures (c) that the evil forces invariably possess greater vitality and are adept at the use of chicanery to further their wicked impulses. The nodding and napping usually takes place among the mild and moderate, who frequently, with all their seasoning in politics, do not sense the foulness in the air.

It is not possible discrimination that I have in mind so much as the lack of protection against onslaughts and actual discrimination, of which there is ample evidence today, even with a strong and fair-minded administration. What may be the situation when a weak but reactionary administration is wafted into office through the machinations of powerful alliances. Fascism, or rather the Nazi brand of it, prostrate in Europe, will rear its ugly head in this country, and the great Fathers, George Washington, Thomas Jefferson, Benjamin Franklin, James Madison and Abraham Lincoln will then be exhibited as spokesmen of the so-called "Christian Patriots" or whatever camouflaged name they choose to call themselves by.

On the other hand, it is not to be taken for granted that tolerance and broadmindedness can be legislated. We must also distinguish between slurs that are the material of folklore and deliberate libels and defamation which are bound to lead to physical suffering.

It would be undesirable, were it possible, e.g., to ban such designations as dago, kike, or mick, or some of the picturesque phrases which apart from the *Schadenfreude* they contain are jocose manifestations of the folk spirit. It would further be unfortunate if proverbs and maxims were to be anathema lest they offend some racial or religious group. In a sense, they portray the folk unconscious; and give us an insight into the collective *id* throughout the ages. Much of our language, particularly our slang, would be less colorful; and were we to adopt such a blanket policy, there is no telling where the matter might end. Surely jokes and anecdotes relative to various national groups would come under that head; the loss, then, to culture must inevitably be considerable, and moreover might seek compensation in other than the surrogate channel of humor; for when a bully cannot at least laugh at one whom he would like to consider inferior to himself, he might do much worse.

From England, it is reported that the popular humorous journal *Tit-Bits* announced that, in view of the great Jewish tragedy in Europe, it will no longer publish any jokes about Jews. One of the motivating factors is the desire of the publishers to furnish no material to anti-Semites in England. Laudable as the intention is, the discrimination is like throwing out the baby together with the bath water. Some national jokes are vulgar and slanderous and therefore should be eliminated at all times, and not only because of the growing propaganda at the present time. Other jokes, while somewhat fun-poking, the Jews can stand as well as other nationalities. Jokes featuring arson, short-changing, and the like, appearing in a Jewish setting, should not be allowed, tragedy or no tragedy in Europe. They are not jokes but libels in the sheepskin of humor.

In Europe, there were apparently attempts made by

some of the governments to curb slurring tendencies at least among minorities. In Poland, the designations *Moskal* and *Moskwicin,* which savor of some slight contempt, were placed on the index by Count Poniatowski, so that some of the Polish dictionaries do not include these ethnophau-lisms. In thumbing the voluminous Czech-German dictionaries of both Jungmann and Herzer, I was surprised not to find any derogatory allusions to Austria, although there were dozens of slurs on the Hungarians, Jews, Germans and others. Is it possible that Austria, which held the Czechs as in a vise for centuries, did not evoke some depreciatory remark from its victims? Perhaps the Austrians were subsumed under the Germans; for Austria is remarkably clear of such disparagement. It may be, too, that the affable and easygoing Austrians were distinguished from their Hapsburg rulers. Even the Italians, for long inveterate foes of the Austrians, merely cast at them the nickname *tedeschi* (Teutons or Theodosians). In any event, the clean slate is somewhat suspicious under the circumstances, although the Serbs and the Croats must have tucked away a few nicknames of the Austrians in their vocabulary.

In Russia, the word *zhid* (Jew) was considered bad form and an offense. The Soviet regime, with its outlawing of overt national prejudices, must have tightened the legal clamps around the slurring tendency, although one should hardly think that jail sentences would be meted out for bandying national nicknames. Probably the social taboo against such epithets would be a sufficient deterrent. And here we come to a query station; for it may be asked why with all the scores of nationalities in USSR, the principle of equality holds almost as an axiom among all the peoples, while in some of the much vaunted democracies there is no attempt made on the part of the government to invoke it even as a postulate.

It is evident that much depends on the regime or administration; for during the Czarist reign, prejudice had been rife to the point of being whipped up into violence. Certainly the attitude of the people as a whole had been changed on the subject, but the spur had come from without—education, public opinion, largely directed by a firm governmental policy. The *laissez-faire* policy in England and the United States has its advantages, but as we shall soon see, the liabilities perhaps far outweigh them.

It is not my intention to call down the furies on anyone who would make a certain nationality the butt of what is often a stale or flat joke. I can sympathize with that *enfant terrible* among a creative tribe of *enfants-terribles,* the Russian poet, Yessenin, about whom a characteristic story is told. Yessenin was standing at a tramway stop, waiting for a car. A friend happened to come along, and asked him what he was doing there. The poet ordinarily would have replied *"Podzhidayu tramvay"* (I am just waiting for a car), but the word *zhid,* which means "Jew", being a slur, forbidden by law, and to be replaced in speech and writing by the word *yevrey* (Hebrew), he replied nonchalantly, *"podyevreyevayu* tramvay", thus satirizing the law, by coining the verb *yevreyit* instead of the verb *zhidat* (to wait). Yessenin saw no reason for proscribing the designation "Jew" in Russian, but it is true, nevertheless, that the word *zhid* smacks of contempt; and it is next to impossible to change by decree the connotation of a word

in the minds of the people who were brought up to consider it as a slur. Not even a dictatorship can accomplish
that psychological transformation. At the same time, it
cannot but be recognized that with the average person,
who has no strong prejudices, the legal sanction is an important guiding factor, and should be resorted to in order
to forestall "excesses."

While Yessenin's whimsy may be understood, it is still
better to be too strict than too indulgent in this connection, as the following incident which took place only a
few days ago (February 17, 1944) goes to show.

A Jewish passenger in the subway offered a woman
(this time not a *lady*) his seat. The response was to the
effect that she would not allow a "dirty Jew" to offer her
his seat. Her torrent of invective and vituperation only
added to the insult, so that when the Jew-baitress, on
reaching her destination, stepped out, her victim, together
with a few witnesses, followed her and had her taken to
the police court, not an easy task. The magistrate was
apparently annoyed at the plaintiff (!) and asked the
woman whether she regretted the incident. The answer
was in the affirmative, whereupon the magistrate, with a
mild injunction to the defendant to be more careful about
her expression, dismissed the case, telling the plaintiff and
the lawyer that they had their satisfaction, and that he
would not countenance any insistence on the pound of
flesh.

In this instance, the magistrate revealed that his own
sentiments were not far from the woman's, and his own
behavior is open to question. In Nazi Germany, this type
of episode happened frequently. At one time, *e.g.*, when

[323]

a woman refused to take the seat a Jew offered her in the trolley car, a workman took her place. When it was time for him to alight, he turned to the woman and said, "There lady, you can take it now; I have Aryanized it." We would hardly think that it has come to such a pass in the Land of the Free.

INCONSISTENCIES OF THE LAW

It seems to me a perversion of common sense and law to hold a person responsible for criminal libel when he slanders an individual but immune when he vilifies a group in the most outrageous manner. Surely the consequences in the latter case are far more grave, tending to cause bloodshed on a large scale. If the damaging of a single reputation means so much in the eyes of the law, then why should the character assassination of a whole nationality, sect, or race be permissible under cover of a constitutional right which could never have been intended to embrace it? Whatever amends Henry Ford could have made in this instance, his instrumentality in the publication of *The International Jew,* which to this day is working mischief in many countries, cannot but be considered a criminal act. Certainly the author of that tissue of falsehoods should have been given a jail sentence, unless he could furnish the proof of his statements, which he would have found as difficult as squaring the circle.

I do not mean to say that opinions about groups should be curbed by law. Certainly freedom of speech must be upheld, but there is where we must draw the line—between *criticism* and *statement of fact*. General appraisals of

Negro, Jew, Catholic or Chinaman, no matter how much censure or belittlement they contain, must be tolerated. It is quite a different story, however, when particulars are presented as definite events. Either the assertions must be fully documented and *verified* or else it ought to be made clear that they are merely echoes of hearsay. Otherwise the authors or promulgators should be liable to punishment for spreading false rumors. I have in mind far more serious offences, but even the Pinckney diary forgery, purporting to show Benjamin Franklin's aversion to, and distrust of the Jews comes under this category. The mere denial by the people who were referred to in this hoax is not sufficient, for the pernicious propaganda will be read by millions, while the denials will be noticed by hundreds.

It has been thought that the wave of anti-Semitism, which is not only creating havoc among the Jews but fairly bids to make out of democracy a hypocrisy, dates in this country, at least, only from the advent of Hitler. Let me, therefore, make it clear that the soil had been fully prepared for the Nazis by numerous Jew-baiters who spawned their venom both by word of mouth and pen, during the last half-century.

The notorious author of *The Original Mr. Jacobs,* published in New York in 1888, gained such a success by this poisonous lampoon that according to his own statement in the "Introduction" to *The American Jew,* published a year later, "in less than three months this book has achieved a widespread circulation. It is at the present writing, in its twentieth edition, and its sale does not show any sign of abatement." Small wonder that this monomaniac, who describes himself as a Greek by birth and education, who built up a private school in New York, was encouraged to become a Jew-baiting institute all by himself, publishing each month a book, which was the prototype of Streicher's *Stürmer*.

I have before me *Judas Iscariot,* dated February 1889, and *The American Jew,* dated August 1, 1889. The former volume purports to be of the tenth edition, and the latter of the forty-ninth edition! Even if each edition should have had a run of only 2,000 copies, we can imagine the extent of the mephitic morass that the publications must have spread to. The paper was of the worst pulp kind and is now crumbling, yet subscribers were willing to pay $6.00 a year for this sort of matter (in the medical sense, rather). And these instigations to violence enjoyed the privilege of second-class rates at the post office.

In 1889, there were about 700,000 Jews in the whole of the United States, most of them of Spanish-Portuguese, Dutch and German provenance. The mass immigration had not yet begun. The anti-Semitic movement neverthe-less was in full sway, and the author of these abominations, which he calls books, requests his subscribers to support him in his fresh venture—launching a new periodical, "The Anti-Semite." In *Judas Iscariot* (page 290), he writes, "I announced, in the preface of the 'The American Jew' a monthly magazine to be called the *Anti-Jew*. This publica-tion I will surely bring forth."

What is the content of these publications which the American post office, founded by that liberal spirit, Ben-jamin Franklin, so generously accommodated. The mere enumeration of some of the chapters would suffice to con-vey an idea of the mentality of the author. Chapter *IV* is headed "The Jew Is a Liar." The next chapter reads, "The Jew Is Insolent." Then we have "The Jew Is a Perjurer", "The Jew Is a Usurer", "The Jew Is a Thief", "The Jew Is a Monomaniac", and finally a chapter entitled "The Jew Is a Murderer." From this last chapter I cite the following gem: "Who can wonder, after this, at the murders that Jews commit whenever they can perpetrate one with impunity?" (page 279). And a little farther, "I regard Jewish ritualistic murders as historically authenticated *and established beyond dispute* (the author's italics). There are positive proofs that Jews are bound to have Christian blood for Easter." If this is not enough, then let us read the next page where he repeats:

> Do Jews teach ritualistic murder? That they teach common murder is beyond doubt, and I can prove this from a number of Talmudical extracts; but I must candidly confess that it is beyond my power to prove by their books that they actually teach ritualistic murder. . . . . Scholarly ex-Jews give us a very valuable key to the mystery by telling us that it is a most sacred tradition, that fathers on their deathbed impart to one adult son, under the most horrible threats and imprecations not to divulge it . . . . I earnestly warn Christian parents and all friends of humanity to look out for their beloved ones about the time of the Jewish Easter, in March and April; especially I warn those who live down town on the eastern side.

In the name of free speech, these murderous words were allowed to have a wide circulation, and at reduced post-office rates. Here was a man who, for all his brilliance as a publicist and encyclopedic range of historical information, which he deliberately distorted, should have been committed, like any other dangerous paranoiac, yet the miasma which he kept spewing was obligingly spread through Government agencies, thus infecting millions of people, as indeed is taking place now in our very midst— and that is what makes the whole problem so actual today!

THE LOGIC OF PHOBIA

It is in these books, of 1888 and 1889, that the Nazi doctrine had already been preached. In the profuse caricatures which the author called illustrations, we have the stuff which went to make Streicher's *Der Stürmer;* and, if the Nazis fanned the antiSemitic fire in this country, it may also be said that they had exported a good many embers from the United States. The Aryan superiority myth, the blasphemous remarks about the Scriptures, yes, even the New Testament, and the slur on Jehovah might well have come from Rosenberg, Hitler, Goering or Goebbels. "Scientific deduction," writes this anonymous author in 1889, "has shown that the relationship between the Aryan and Jewish races is a more distant one than between the equine and the asinine families" (*Judas Iscariot,* page 141). This "scientific deduction" is based on the low birthrate in mixed marriages of Jews and Gentiles, if his tables are correct. We find here all the socalled physical stigmata of the Jew drawn by a certain Griboiedoff, and even the germ of the *"Protocols of Zion."*
The Nazi logical pattern by no means begins with Hitler

or Rosenberg. The reasoning is the same in all bigots and paranoiacs. In brief, the formula may be described as "The facts must be so because my hatred demands it." Before Hitler was born, the author of *The American Jew* (49th edition, page 34) dwells at length on a salient figure on Wall street who "practically rules the market," and he goes on to say that:

> Not the least mysterious peculiarity of this very mysterious personage is his origin. His parents were not Jews; it has not been found possible to trace any Jewish blood among his ancestors: he himself denies that he has any Jewish blood in his veins.
>
> But however this may be, account for it as you will, certain it is that the evil genius of the "Street" has Jew blood in his veins—is out and out a Jew (!)

This mental carriage marks, as I have had occasion to show, in my *William James,* the Nazi gospel which that brilliant English quisling, Houston Stewart Chamberlain, gave the world—also in 1889, *The Foundations of the Nineteenth Century.* From the ninth edition of this forerunner of Hitler's *Mein Kampf,* let me quote this gem: "Were it even proven that in the past there had been no Aryan race, it is for us to insist that such should exist in the future! For men of action that is the deciding standpoint."

When, therefore, it has been said of the Nazis that they are not at all certain whether or not Jesus actually existed, but they are absolutely sure that the Jews killed him, the story is scarcely to be taken as a joke; for it is typical of the Nazi mode of reasoning, and may be considered the Nazi bull *par excellence,* symbolizing their whole outlook on life.

THE PREVENTIVE PHASE OF LEGISLATION

"By their deeds shall ye know them" is of course true, but a commonplace; and as counsel is not valuable because it lacks the prognostic or predictive token. Perhaps many of the deeds which have set back the world worse than the Bubonic Plague would have been averted, if the maxim we had chosen to be guided by were "By their logic shall you know them," and if we, therefore, in *the interest of free speech* and the welfare of millions prevented the promulgation of their verbal brimstone. To millions in this country, it would seem as if the war against Fascism and Nazism is about ended. In my opinion, the real battle is yet to be won after the European citadel is demolished.

Because of the racy style, the fanatical zeal, and the intimate manner in which the author speaks about the Jew, posing as an authority and quoting the Talmud in the transliterated original, there is scarcely an average person who would not be influenced against the Jews, if the book fell into his hands. In fact, if he were not incited against the Jews, under the circumstances, he would not be an average person.

The anti-Semitic pamphlets and leaflets which have deluged the mails in this country during the past few years are really no different in character from the 1889 books cited.

From a broadside, published by the Nationalist Press Association, 147 East 116th St., New York, I cull the following gems: "Henry Ford, American automobile manufacturer, says: 'Corral fifty of the world's wealthiest Jews and there will be no more wars' ." "From authoritative sources we find, that President Rosenfeld (See 1939 World Almanac pgs. 638, 639) has seventy-two advisers around him of which fifty-two of them are Jews, and to make matters worse most of them are foreign born."

From the punctuation alone, (comma after "find" and not after "sources") and from the wording, too, ("fifty-two *of them*") it is evident that the scribbler was a German, or one who was educated in Germany. The insult to President Roosevelt—garbling his name—is characteristic of that type of individual. The pity is that not only have millions of these scurrilous sheets been distributed, but that the majority of the recipients must have been taken in by such brazen statements as "We are challenging Rabbi Stephen S. Wise, Samuel Untermyer, Louis D. Brandeis, Justice Felix Frankfurter, Bernard M. Baruch, Eddie Cantor, Alfred M. Cohen, or any Rabbi of recognized Jewish authority to disprove any statement contained in this pamphlet." The so-called quotations from the Talmud and other Rabbinical books, purporting to show that the Jew receives license to kill, enslave, rape, etc., have been proven on many occasions to have no foundation whatsoever, but the reader who is not especially bright reasons that the challenge could not have been made unless there were some basis to the charges.

At this writing a bill is before Congress to keep such, figuratively speaking, syphilitic literature out of the mails, but the Postmaster General balks at it, and cites difficulties and snags in the enforcement of such a measure which do not seem to occur to him when it is a matter of placing restrictions on a magazine that includes jokes or stories of a dubious nature. Was there ever a gnat so small to be strained and a camel so large to be swallowed than this procedure on the part of the Postmaster? Consider what harm could a flat joke with a suggestive lining accomplish as compared with an explosive libel viciously slandering a whole group? Yet we are told that in the one case, it will be difficult to determine the objectionableness of the contents and in the other case (the magazine) the wrong is palpable.

It is depressing to contemplate that while the Nazi regime was provoking the United States, and Hitler was behaving condescendingly toward our Administration, senators and congressmen were hobnobbing with his agents and tons of anti-Semitic literature reflecting the Nazi ideology were permitted to get into the mails on the franking privilege of legislators who should represent not only the people, but the spirit of the country. What will happen to us if the Reynoldses, the Rankins, the Hoffmans and the Thorkelsons should achieve the supremacy? Then the arrant and bigoted nonsense of J. O. Rankin and C. E. Hoffman, instead of being consigned to the pages of the *Congressional Record,* might be converted into action on the streets. It has happened before in 1933; and unfortunately we are not learning from the mistakes of the Weimar Republic which, too, protected demagogues in the name of the Constitution and free speech.

SPECTRES OF THE PAST

When we look, as the French say *à travers les choses,* can we be anything but disheartened over the fact that rogues and bigots can rise to high office, crush their rivals, and win the plaudits of not only the ordinary masses but of men of station and prestige?

A book of memoirs which has recently been published revived a tragedy and a horrible injustice which were all but forgotten—the Leo Frank case, that which was settled by "Judge" Lynch, nearly thirty years ago, in a particularly atrocious manner. It was a former judge of the Georgia Court of Appeals, who sat beside Judge Roan when the latter charged the jury—Honorable Arthur G. Powell— who turned our attention again to the terrible lot of the young man who was crucified ten times over for a crime that he had not committed. In his autobiography, *I Can Go Home Now,* Judge Powell writes:

> I am one of the few people who know that Leo Frank was innocent of the crime for which he was convicted and lynched. I know who killed Mary Phagan, but I know it in such a way that I can never honorably make the information public so long as certain persons are still living. . . . . I expect to write down what I know and why I know it, seal it up and put it away, with instructions that it is not to be opened until cer- tain persons are dead.

What an awful indictment of American justice and institutions when we come to think that the judges knew Frank to have been innocent, that Governor Slaton, who pardoned Frank, was aware of his innocence, that the then District Attorney, Hugh M. Dorsey, most likely was convinced of Frank's innocence, but had his heart set upon the governor's chair, which he succeeded in winning, thanks to his dogged prosecution of the case.

It was not difficult to play on the feelings of the jurors, painting the prosperous Northern college-bred Jew as the devil incarnate, and to force a verdict of guilty, on the testimony of the Negro janitor, who afterwards proved to be a felon and convict. The torments of that young man who had no blemish on his character must have been worse than martyrdom. To this add the physical tortures to which he was subjected; for even in prison he was attacked by a fellow-prisoner, who, seemingly revolting at the thought of being in the same jail with such a heinous criminal, plunged a knife into Frank's throat. And finally, when Frank's sentence was commuted, because Governor Slaton could not bring himself to allow an in-nocent person to be executed, Frank, hardly recovered from the all but fatal stabbing, was seized by a mob and beaten to death before being hanged. Not even Job could claim a fate as cruel as that meted out Leo Frank by the denizens of the State of Georgia, founded by the stalwart champion of liberty, General Oglethorpe.

Are the people in Georgia any different from those of other states? Probably not. Some in the lynching party may have been genial and well-disposed, although emo-tional, men, especially wrought up because of the nature of the crime. Who was responsible for the lynching? Partly the district attorney, whose business it was to make out of the accused a fiend, but the chief, and perhaps the real, instigator of the mob murder was Tom Watson, a demagogue who loathed the Jews and spread hate through his sheet which, in consequence of the Frank Case, multi- plied its circulation. Watson became rich and powerful after the lynching, and ended his days as a highly respected United States senator. When he died, he was accorded a semi-regal funeral, and the eulogies by some of his fellow- senators in Washington breathed of a sublimity that brought tears to the eyes of the listeners.

That man who was so honored by his peers was, in effect, the very one whose vehement incitations led to the lynching of an innocent man. It is as if he had plied a mob with denatured alcohol and then supplied them with fire- arms.

The fact that many ambitious men stoop to become affiliated with the Klu Klux Klan and other lawless organi- zations in order to receive their first start in politics is another sad commentary on our public life. It not only indicates what power these groups have but also that some of our subsequent leaders lacked the stamina to avoid pernicious alliances, even if they did reason: better to com- promise with the devil and win than to flout him and lose out!

It is because of this situation that we have more prej- udice in the United States than in some of the European monarchies, and what is worse, we apparently do less to invoke the aid of the law to stem it. For no matter how reasonable and sensible a measure appears to be, there will always be enough reactionary and subversive elements in Congress to oppose it. Furthermore, even when the bill passes and the law is enacted, it cannot be enforced.

IMPS OF THE PRESENT

Is there anything more desirable than the anti-lynching measure for the protection of the Negroes in the South, yet what a howl was raised against it by well-educated, cultured, and, from all appearances, high-minded men who, while representing the Southern Whites, should have thought of humanity first.

To take another instance, in spite of the directives of the President's Committee on Fair Employment Practice forbidding racial and religious discrimination, sixteen Southern railways defied the order and charged that the Committee was "utterly unrealistic" in attempting to solve delicate problems of interracial relations in the Southern States "by fiat."

Evidently not only much water will pass under the bridge but much blood will be spilled before the Whites in the South will recognize the rights of the Negro, and before Jim Crow will be a relic seen in museums. The school, the church, and the home must needs coöperate in order to bring about a modicum of tolerance of the races; and each individual will have to exercise some self-discipline in order to cure himself of such prejudices as are constitutional or due to the environment. Both kinds undoubtedly assail us under certain conditions.

In addition to the prejudices we harbor, there is the urge for a scapegoat—almost biological in its insistence. No amount of legislation could prevent the publication of diatribes against Catholics in the predominantly Protestant states; and again it may be said that there is no harm in the release of criticism. If, however, facts are cited such as that the Catholics have sought to bribe legislators in order to further a particular measure, or if "disclosures" like *Maria Monk* are published, the libel law should be invoked as in individual libel cases. The very airing of such accusations in court would have a salutary effect in that the public would learn the true nature of these charges, and also could evaluate future contentions of this type.

BIGOTRY AS A DISEASE

Prejudices are bacilli, but so long as they are not blown about and do not become infectious, they are relatively harmless. Once, however, they are imposed or, worse, propagated, they take on the form of an epidemic. We are all subject to certain prejudices, but should restrict them against individuals rather than against groups; for surely each group must contain a variety of individuals. There is no group which is either wholly admirable or wholly contemptible; and when we are annoyed by a specific trait which we ascribe to a particular group, we shall do well to single out a different trait which is to the advantage of that group. Thus we may not like the brusqueness of some people, yet their efficiency or pertinence is a compensation. Sometimes easygoing manners and methods irk us, but then we are comforted by the jollity or good-naturedness that goes with such a temperament.

We do not always understand racial or national collectives any more than we fathom individuals. Frenchmen, Germans, Chinamen, Poles have a different approach often from that we have been accustomed to. They may seem curt, unaccommodating, indifferent, condescending because we have had a different upbringing, or because we expect some group to cater to us in our feeling of superiority. Perhaps more is expected of a Negro than of a White, and if he does not coöperate, he is deemed arrogant or defiant. Kant's great maxim, great in its simplicity, occurs to us here. "Treat every one as a person," means that we are not to make of a person an instrument or tool for our benefit, as unfortunately most people are inclined to do. For our purpose, we may adapt Kant's dictum so as to read, "Treat every one as an individual and not as a member of a special collective." Once we have adopted this principle, we should not be guilty of saddling other members of a group with the unpleasant experience received at the hands of some one individual.

THE SYNECDOCHE COMPLEX IN BIGOTS

It is well known that Voltaire, Wagner, and other anti-Semitic celebrities have "taken it out" on the whole race, because of a grievance against some Jew or Jewess. Their mind is thus ruled by the metaphor of synecdoche, where the part is taken for the whole. I do not wish to imply that their aversion was the result of this experience alone. It is my belief that Wagner's anti-Semitism symbolized his hatred for his Jewish father, and may have included other causes as well, but the personal resentment in adolescent or adult life tended to accentuate the revulsion and to bring it to a white heat. Siegfried, Wagner's son, on the other hand, was the opposite of his father in this regard; and expressed himself emphatically in favor of the Jews. A Freudian might see in this, too, an unconscious reaction against his father.

Sooner or later it will come to be recognized that bigotry is a disease like smallpox, leprosy, cancer, or dementia praecox. Negro-baiting, anti-Semitism, Anglophobia or any other national hatred is a psychoneurosis pure and simple, and may attain the depth of a psychosis, a mono-mania, as in the case of the author quoted. In the preface to my *Psychorama,* I have had occasion to say "Scratch a Jew-baiter and find a hoodlum or a psychopath." Bigotry comes under the category of megalomania and paranoia, although there are people who make out of anti-Semitism a lucrative racket, but if there were not so many ordinary people inoculated with the virus, it could not be so profit-able to the racketeers.

President Roosevelt's recent declaration on the subject was tantamount to saying that he regards anti-Semitism as a perversion of human thought and action. It is a perver-sion indeed, but it is not rooted in ideas so much as in the emotions. It is an *affect* which points to a glaring mal-adjustment in the culprit. Every anti-Semite that I can think of was a dyed-in-the-wool reactionary, a person who had no understanding for the rights of others than himself and his own. Every reactionary is a Nazi *in embryone;* and that is the reason why, in the democracies, he was anxious to keep appeasing Hitler and his gang; and has been hoping for a negotiated peace, once war was declared.

That Fascism, which is the somewhat diluted non-German brand of the Nazi ideology, is rampant in this country is evident from the many endeavors which have been made by leaders in all walks of life to countervail its activities. What is particularly symptomatic is the fact that Catholics in good standing will heed the calls of the

Christian Front against the authoritative admonitions of archbishops and cardinals, and indeed even the Pope. Both the late Pius XI and the present Pius XII denounced anti-Semitism and have shown, by example, their kind sentiments toward the Jews, whom they protected against cruel onslaughts, yet why do the followers of Father Coughlin choose to place his opinion and injunctions above those emanating from the lips of Pontiffs? The query has been puzzling me for a long time, and should serve to illuminate the clinical picture of anti-Semitism, as an excrescence of a mental aberration in the aggressor.

I have dwelt on anti-Semitism more than on any other form of bigotry, because it is the most dangerous, the most universal, the most insistent, and the most deadly of all international ills. It can never be completely exterminated, so long as there are Jews, and so long as prejudice is a human foible, but it can be curbed to a comparatively harmless degree. To this end, a vast educational campaign must be launched, not merely a series of goodwill conferences. That Jews have faults is a truism. But only after it is proven that the fault-finders are flawless are the anti-Semites within their rights of advocating restrictions. As a matter of fact who are these castigators of the Jews, these Rankins and Reynoldses, Thorkelsons, Hoffmans, and Heflins, if not Americans of English, Irish, German, French or Scandinavian extraction, who must, therefore, plead guilty to the faults of their own racial stock? Or do they maintain that other nationalities than the Jews are perfect?

ABOVE ALL NATIONS HUMANITY

It may be somewhat of an irony to appeal to a slogan

which the originator, Goldwin Smith, scarcely heeded himself. The four words, "Above all Nations Humanity," carved in stone on a campus bench at Cornell University would have carried more weight had the man who uttered them seriously identified himself with the great cause which they purport to serve. Unfortunately, while the noted political scientist and essayist devised an excellent abstract motto; in the concrete, he did no more nor less than to place himself squarely on the side of reaction. On the subject of "Woman" he wrote, "But before man hands over the government to woman, he ought to be satisfied that he cannot do what is right himself"—obviously a sophistic turn of the real situation involved. On the Home Rule bill, he would not even approve a confederation in the United Kingdom, with Ireland one of the states. "It is not Ulster or Protestantism alone" he wrote "that desires the preservation of the Union, but almost the entire wealth and intelligence of Ireland, whether Protestant or Catholic" (*Essays on Questions of the Day,* page 305) "Civil war is a dreadful thing, but there are things even more dreadful than civil war," he continues. "Submission to the dismemberment of the nation by the sinister machinations of a morally insane ambition would in the end work more havoc than the civil sword."

From these passages, one can well imagine what Smith's attitude might be toward the Jews. In 1892, Goldwin Smith, writing on "The Jewish Question", almost justified the pogroms in Russia and revived all the myths about the Jews which he could ferret out from the limbo of bigotry. He was a pillar of what is sometimes oxymoronically called "higher anti-Semitism", a synonym for the anti-Semitism of the learned, who do not encourage violence outright, but by their very citations, dubious to say the least, rouse their readers against the Jews. Their citations are in reality incitations.

Goldwin Smith was neither a humanist nor a humanitarian in life or letters, yet his *devise* "above all nations humanity" may be adopted as the first step toward throwing off the incubus of hate and scorn that besets minorities in our still juvenile world.

His own doctrines proved him to be prejudiced against minorities. His education and erudition were no safeguard. The march of events demonstrated that allowing the women to have a voice in the government was no peril such as he had anticipated, and that not only was Home Rule achieved in Ireland without civil war, but something far beyond this "morally insane ambition," *viz.,* the establishment of a Free State came to pass without resulting in a calamity. Equally wrong was Goldwin Smith in his attitude towards the Jews. It goes to show once more that wrong-headedness is not the peculiar attribute of ignorance; that understanding and insight are gifts with which the untutored may be endowed and which may be lacking in otherwise very capable individuals.

NOT EDUCATION BUT ENLIGHTENMENT — OUR HOPE

There are those who practice Tertullian's *credo quia absurdum* quite literally. All that the great Church Father meant was that when a theological dogma was absurd, he could not accept it rationally, but must nilly-willy believe.

The mass of people who make it almost a rule to espouse the wrong cause are those who seem to possess a romantic flair for vivifying absurdities and then accepting them as real facts. They, and that includes many a college-bred man and woman, will believe in the Protocols of Zion forgeries, and yet deny that the Nazis have deliberately and in cold blood killed any Jews or Poles without provocation. They will take it for granted that the Negro is degenerate, lazy, and mentally deficient. They will fulminate against any progressive recommendation, *e.g.,* to give the franchise to Chinese residents who have met the requirements. They will propose puerile measures like the teachers' oath law, which is as arrogant in intent as it is futile in purpose.

It is difficult to know how to deal with wrong-headedness. Education, of the garden variety, is insufficient. It is the *ego* that needs training, and the question is how we can get to it.

Our aim, *prima facie,* might be to *enlighten* the public, so that they would elect the proper candidates to office, who in turn would frame salutary laws, but the knots in the democratic wheel prevent it from revolving smoothly. As yet we are hardly a democracy, but perhaps a demi-cracy. We shall attain the status of a full democracy when the various elements will consider not only their own self-interest, but the welfare of the whole nation. Then the laws enacted will, *ipso facto,* be for the benefit of all, and while prejudices will not become extinct, they will not be allowed to crystallize into overt restrictions. If public opinion will prove inadequate to nip them in the bud, legislation will attend to that task. The problem of priority between public opinion and legislation is as insoluble as the chick and the egg riddle.

A set of efficient and forward-looking legislators should not wait until an emergency forces them to act. They should not always ask themselves what their particular constituents wish them to do, or consult what their party has decreed for them, or vote.down some bill proposed by an opponent, but should have the good of all in mind. This conclusion seems too trite to state, yet it is so far from realization that one wonders again whether the weakness inherent in politics, and in the whole species *homo sapiens,* will ever be corrected so as to bring us closer to the goal of an equitable existence, or whether the Hobbesian jungle formula of *bellum omnium contra omnes* will always prevail on our sanguinary planet.

Perhaps we shall come closer toward a solution of this perplexing problem when public men, the world over, instead of drawing up a double code, one that is different for the individual and for the state, will, once and for all, recognize and act upon the simple verity contained in the message of that glorious American, Charles Sumner: "The true greatness of nations is in those qualities which constitute the greatness of the individual."

BIBLIOGRAPHIES

A NOTE ON DICTIONARIES

In the handling of dictionaries of various languages, a number of curious facts come to mind. It is remarkable, for instance, that French, which, a century ago, was considered the world's leading language, still has no adequate dictionary and that Littré's *Dictionnaire,* in four volumes, is more useful than that of the French Academy. It would seem that in compilations on a large scale, requiring whole-hearted coöperation and efficient coördination, the French lag behind.

It is consequently necessary to use many French dictionaries for a given purpose, since "two heads are better than one," *a fortiori* a dozen heads, even if without benefit of consultation. Nearly every dictionary has its little offering to make in the matter of international slurs.

On the other hand, in this connection, it is not so much the language as the compiler that counts. Some lexicographers are too prosaic to include transferred meanings suggestive of folklore. Bulky dictionaries may contain less of this material than smaller works.

In contrast with the skimpiness of the French dictionaries, the lexical opulence of the Swedish, Danish, and Dutch dictionaries is amazing, outstripping in the matter of completeness the colossal Grimm German dictionary, which, when completed, will probably fill more than 25 large volumes, and even the *Oxford English Dictionary,* which as a completed work has no equal thus far. Of the Danish academic dictionary, twenty sturdy volumes are now available, and were it not for the Nazi occupation, it might have reached the final letters of the alphabet.

Incidentally, what we see as a large and hefty volume does not always coincide with what the editors or publishers choose to call a volume. Thus one of the Grimm dictionary volumes, containing nearly 3000 double-column pages, is labelled a part of a volume. The *Oxford English Dictionary* similarly disregards the bulk and binding in its computation, its ten volumes, not counting The Supplement, representing really twenty massive tomes.

A study might be made of the lexicographic proclivities of certain peoples. The Russian academic dictionary has reached the ninth volume, but even these nine volumes lack parts here and there. The Poles, on the other hand, even a hundred years ago, produced a Linde who brought out, single-handed, a Polish dictionary (with German equivalents) in seven weighty volumes. A recent academic Polish dictionary, by Karłowicz and others, in eight volumes and a dictionary of Polish dialects (six volumes) not to mention smaller works of the same nature, reveal the ardor of the Poles in standardizing their language and taking stock of its literary treasures. The situation among the Serbians and the Croats is somewhat different in that, aside from the alphabet, Croatian and Serbian are practically the same; and the Croato-Serbian academic dictionary, in twelve volumes, though as yet incomplete, is a work of which any people might be proud. In giving priority to the Croatian element in the hyphenation, I am merely taking cognizance of the greater cultural achievements manifested by the politically lesser people. (In bibliography, the usual combination is Serbo-Croatian.) The Czechs, too, despite the resignation of their philologists, who practically despaired of hearing their language spoken in official circles, only a few decades ago, are fortunate to have had their Herzers and Jungmanns, although the productions in either case are bilingual (Czech-German).

Bilingual Dictionaries

Of all bilingual dictionaries, the best without doubt seems to be the Muret-Sanders Encyclopaedic German-English and English-German Dictionary, in four huge volumes. Next to it, is probably the Sachs-Villatte French and German dictionary, for though the earlier French-German dictionary by Abbé Mozin contains far more entries, it is apparent that the five volumes (including the supplement) are much padded. The Czech-German dictionaries of Herzer and of Jungmann are a monument to their patience and diligence, but they are not on the plane of craftsmanship displayed by Sanders, Muret, and Schmidt, who were masters of idiomatic rendering. Rigutini and Bulle's Italian-German dictionary belongs to the same class as the Sachs-Villatte French-German work.

In attaching the names of authors or compilers, we are often in quandary; for frequently a dictionary is known by the name of its originator, who may have died soon after undertaking the project. Occasionally, a work undergoes so many revisions, like the Baretti Italian-English dictionary of 1760, that the name is scarcely more than a trademark in a particular case. To append dates with either the Baretti Italian-English or the Velázquez Spanish-English dictionary is misleading. Publishers have lost track of the number of the edition; and there may be far less difference between two contemporary dictionaries than between the tenth and the original edition of a given dictionary. In vain do we look for the share which Surenne had in the Spiers-Surenne French-English dictionary. It probably was only the method of Surenne which was adopted in the work. That is true of the Ollendorff, Langenscheidt, and other series. Publishers sometimes like to attach their names to dictionaries which they bring out (Appleton; Harper; Harrap) thus pushing the compilers' names into the background.

Of the lone workers along bilingual lines, J. Brynildsen deserves more than passing mention for his dictionaries. Whether in the Dano-Norwegian and English or in the Dano-Norwegian and German combinations, he displays an intimacy with the languages and a resourcefulness that qualify him particularly as a lexicographer *par excellence*. It is somewhat odd that the international references, akin to ethnophaulisms, were more or less expurgated in the final revision of the Norwegian-English dictionary, prior to his death. This probably was rendered necessary because of the extensive addition of matter-of-fact words and idioms. The circumstance, however, goes to show that it is not always the most recent edition which serves our purpose best. Indeed, some of the older dictionaries yielded more slurs on other nations than did similar works issued within the last two or three years.

BIBLIOGRAPHY

A

ENGLISH DICTIONARIES

[ANON] A New Canting Dictionary, London, 1725.
Whether Grose made use of this dictionary or not, the majority of the terms are to be found in A Classical Dictionary of the Vulgar Tongue, although defined in different words.

BARRÈRE, A. and LELAND, C. G.: A Dictionary of Slang, Jargon and Cant, etc. London, 1889-90 (Ballantyne) 2 vols.

BERREY, L. V. and VAN DEN BARK, M.: The American Thesaurus of Slang. N. Y. 1942, (Crowell).
The most complete reference work of its kind in any country, so far as listing goes. The technical arrangement too is excellent, but, of course, it is no dictionary and frequently the shades of difference between the many synonyms cannot even be guessed. It contains the raw material for an encyclopedia of slang in many volumes. The number of slang words and phrases in English (including American), in my estimate, aggregates to 75,000, as a conservative figure.

BOWEN, F. C.: Sea Slang. London, [1928?] (Low, Marston).

FARMER, J. S. and HENLEY, W. E.: Slang and Its Analogues. London, 1890-1904, 7 vols.
A stupendous work, the best of its kind in English, it not only

cites sources but often presents foreign analogues. Sometimes, it assumes the functions of a thesaurus in listing synonyms; and occasionally it may be said to be overcomplete in that standard-English phrases are included, but usually, such only as are debatable.

GROSE, FRANCIS H.: *A Classical Dictionary of the Vulgar Tongue.* London, 1785.
Although it is by no means the first dictionary of English slang, it may be regarded as the pioneer work from our point of view, in that about fifty words and phrases suggesting international slurs are recorded here. The compilation of this little book was apparently thoroughly enjoyed by Grose. Several expurgated, revised, enlarged, or annotated editions were brought out subsequently, the most recent one containing explanatory material by Eric Partridge.

HOTTEN, J. C.: *A Dictionary of Modern Slang, Cant, and Vulgar Words.* London, 1859.
Judging by the number of editions which this work, first published anonymously, enjoyed, one would have expected it to be a more extensive collection.

MURRAY, J. A. H., BRADLEY, H., CRAIGIE, W. A. and ONIONS, C. T.: *Oxford English Dictionary* (originally published as *New English Dictionary*). Oxford, 1888-1933. 10 vols. in 20 and supplement).
The miracle of intellectual coöperation, beside which the *Encyclopedia Britannica,* even in its best edition, is a mere compilation, uneven in quality and uncomprehensive in scope. Although the Grimm German dictionary contains in its incomplete form more material than the *Oxford English Dictionary* it is much inferior to it as a guide and inadequate in its architectonic arrangement. The mastery of coördination and systematic collation of the relevant sub-items and senses

are a tribute to British lexicography. While the Grimm dictionary is a thesaurus, and a vast fragmentary anthology of German literature, it falls short of the purpose for which it was undertaken nearly a century ago.

PARTRIDGE, ERIC: *A Dictionary of Slang and Unconventional English*. New York, 1938, 2nd edition. (Macmillan).
In one sense, this work might be regarded as a thoroughly revised and enlarged edition of Farmer and Henley's seven-volume dictionary of slang (mentioned earlier) shorn of its academic paraphernalia and brought up to date, yet Partridge's work is monumental in its own right and bears the colorful personality of the compiler, who brought to the Falstaffian spirit of his predecessor, Francis Grose, an unusually informative and direct mind, impatient of the intellectual red tape too often found in scholarly works.

WARE, J. R.: *Passing English of the Victorian Era*. London, 1909. Ware has a flair for ferreting out some out-of-the-way information, but does not always go to the root of his find. His informants on Yiddish are not always reliable.

Webster's New International Dictionary of The English Language. Springfield, 1938, 2nd edition reprinted (Merriam).
This is still the best compact unabridged dictionary of the English language, rating next to the *Oxford English Dictionary* in comprehensiveness, and including considerable slang. *The Standard Dictionary of the English Language* is, I believe, third in rank.

WESEEN, M. H.: *A Dictionary of American Slang*. New York, 1934 (Crowell).
The most extensive dictionary of American slang, unless we count the *American Thesaurus of Slang* by Berrey and Van den Bark. The lists are classified according to the walks (or talks) of life.

B

FOREIGN, INCLUDING BILINGUAL, DICTIONARIES

CROATO-SERBIAN

FILIPOVIĆ I (and others): *Deutsch-kroatisches Wörterbuch.* Agram, 1869-70.

JUGOSLAVIAN ACADEMY: *Rječnik Hrvatskoga ili Srpskoga Jezika.* Zagreb, 1880-1937, vols. 1-12 (—PROV) T. Maretić, chief compiler.

POPOVIĆ, G.: *Wörterbuch der serbischen und deutschen Sprache.* Pančova, 1881.

ŠAMŠALOVIĆ, G.: *Rječnik Njemačko-Hrvatsko-Srpski.* Zagreb, 1929.

ŠULEK, B.: *Němačko-Hrvatski Rěčnik.* Zagreb, 1860, 2 vols.

CZECH

CHESHIRE, H. T.: *Czech-English Dictionary.* Prague, 1938.

HERZER, J.: *Českoněmecký Slovník.* Prague, 1901, 3 vols.

JUNGMANN, J.: *Slovník Česko-Německý.* Wpraze, 1835-1839. 5 vols.

DANISH

DAHLERUP, V. and others: *Ordbog over det Danske Sprog.* Copenhagen, 1918-41, vols. 1-20 (— SOR).

LARSEN, A. L.: *Dictionary of the Dano-Norwegian and English Languages,* Copenhagen, 1910 (rev. by Johannes Magnussen, 4th ed.)

BIBLIOGRAPHY

DUTCH

CALISCH, I.: *New Complete Dictionary of the English and Dutch Languages.* Tiel, Campagne, 1890-92, 2 vols.

DALE, J. H. VAN: *Groot woordenboek der Nederlandsche Taal.* 's — Gravenhage, 1924, (Nijhoff).

DE VRIES, M., and others: *Woordenboek der Nederlandsche Taal.* Leiden, 1882-1939, vols. 1-15; (— STOVER, but incomplete volumes).

FRENCH

BARRÈRE, A.: *Argot and Slang.* London, 1887 (rev. ed. 1889).

DELESALLE, G.: *Dictionnaire Argot-Français et Français-Argot.* Paris, 1896.

Dictionnaire de L'Académie Française. Paris, 1932-35, 8th ed., 2 vols.

GASC, F.: *Dictionary of the French and English languages.* New York, 1929.

HATZFELD, A., and DARMESTETER, A.: *Dictionnaire générale de la Langue Française.* Paris, 1920, 2 vols., 6th ed.

LARIVE and FLEURY (*pseudon.*): *Dictionnaire Français.* Paris, 1903, rev. ed., 3 vols.

LAROUSSE, P.: *Grand Dictionnaire Universel du XIX Siècle.* Paris, 1866-90, 17 vols.

LAROUSSE, P.: *Nouveau petit Larousse illustré.* Paris, 1941.

LEROUX, P. J.: *Dictionnaire Comique, etc.* Pampelune, 1735; 2d ed. 1786, 2 vols.

LITTRÉ, E.: *Dictionnaire de la Langue Française.* Paris, 1881, 4 vols.

BIBLIOGRAPHY

MANSION, J. E.: Harrap's Standard French and English Dictionary. London, 1934, 1939, 2 vols.

MOZIN (l'abbé): Dictionnaire complet des Langues Française et
Allemande. Stuttgart, 1856-1859, 5 vols. including supplem.,
3d ed.

POITEVIN, P.: Nouveau dictionnaire, etc. Paris, 1856-60, 2 vols.

SPIERS, A. (and SURENNE): French and English Pronouncing
Dictionary. New York, 1927, rev. ed.

GERMAN

GRIMM, J. and W.: Deutsches Wörterbuch. Leipzig, 1854-1934,
vols. 1-16; incomplete.

MURET, E., and SANDERS, D.: Encyclopaedic English-German and
German-English Dictionary. German-English part in 2 vols.,
Berlin, 1908.

VILLATTE, C. and SACHS, K.: Encyklopädisches französisch-
deutsches Wörterbuch. Berlin, 1880, 2 vols.

GREEK

LIDDELL, H. G. and SCOTT, R.: Greek-English Lexicon. Oxford,
1897, 8th ed.

MODERN GREEK

HÉPITÈS, A. T.: Dictionnaire Grec-Français. Athens, 1908-1910,
3 vols. The French-Greek part, in 2 volumes, appeared in
1911, 1914.

HEBREW

BEN YEHUDAH, E.: A Complete Dictionary of Ancient and
Modern Hebrew. Berlin—Jerusalem, 1908—? The ninth
volume brings the work down to, but not including, the letter

BIBLIOGRAPHY

P, perhaps a symbol of the publishing difficulties involved in bringing out this monument of labor and learning. In reality, this is a polyglot dictionary; for in addition to comparative Semitic observations, it contains The French, English, and German translations of every Hebrew term.

GESENIUS, W.: *Hebrew and Chaldee Lexicon*. London, 1859 (rev. by S. P. Tregelles).

HUNGARIAN

BALLAGI, (*i.e.* BLOCH) M.: *Neues vollständiges ungarisches und deutsches Wörterbuch*. Budapest, 1905, 2 vols. (The 4th edition appeared in 1875).

YOLLAND, A. B.: *A Dictionary of the Hungarian and English Languages*. Budapest, 1905.

ICELANDIC

CLEASBY, R. and VIGFUSSON, G.: *An Icelandic-English Dictionary*. Oxford, 1874 (Clarendon).

ITALIAN

BARETTI, G. M. A. (based on that of): *New Dictionary of the Italian and English languages*. London, 18—, 2 vols. The Baretti dictionary first appeared in 1760.

LYSLE, A. DE R.: *Il Nuovissimo Vocabolario Moderno, etc.* Turin, 1938.

MESTICA, E.: *Dizionario della Lingua Italiana*. Turin, 1937, 3rd ed.

PANZINI, A.: *Dizionario Moderno, etc.* Milan, 1935.

PETRÒCCHI, P.: *Nòvo Dizionàrio universale, etc.*, Milan, 1910, rev. ed. 2 vols.

BIBLIOGRAPHY

RIGUTINI, G. and BULLE, O.: *Nuovo Dizionario Italiano-Tedesco.* Leipzig, 1896, 2 vols.

TOMMASEO, N.: *Dizionario della Lingua Italiana.* Turin, 1865- 79, 4 vols. The 3d edition, in 7 vols., appeared in 1916.

ZINGARELLI, N.: *Vocabolario della Lingua Italiana.* Milan, 1933, 5th ed.

LATIN

ANDREWS, E. A. (based on Freund): *A New Latin Dictionary.* N.Y., 1907 (rev. and enlar.)

MEXICAN

I. R. B.: *Diccionario Mexico.* Mexico City, 1943.

NORWEGIAN

BRYNILDSEN, J.: *Tysk-Norsk (Dansk) Ordbog.* Christiana, 1900.

BRYNILDSEN, J.: *Norsk-Engelsk Ordbok.* Oslo, 1927, 3d ed.

POLISH

KARŁOWICZ, J. and others: *Słownik Gwar Polskich.* [Dictionary of Polish Dialects]. Cracow, 1911, 6 vols.

KARŁOWICZ, J.: *Słownik Języka Polskiego,* Warsaw, 1900-27, 8 vols.

KONARSKI, F. and others: *Dokładny Słownik Języków Polskiego i Niemieckiego.* Vienna, 1904, 2d ed. 1911 (A. Zipper, ed.) 4 vols.

LINDE, S. B.: *Słownik Języka Polskiego.* Lwów, 1854-1860. 6 vols.

MRONGOVIUS, C. C.: *Dokładny Słownik Polsko-Niemiecki.* Königsberg, 1835.

BIBLIOGRAPHY

PORTUGUESE

LACERDA, D. J. de: *A New Dictionary of the Portuguese and English Languages.* Lisbon, 1871.

MICHAELIS, H.: *A New Dictionary of the Portuguese and English Languages.* Leipzig, 1932, 2 vols.

SÉGUIER, J. DE: *Diccionário Prático.* Porto, 1931, 3rd ed.

PROVENÇAL

AZAÏS, G.: *Dictionnaire des idiomes romans,* etc., Paris, 1877, 3 vols.

DE FOURVIÈRES, R. P. X.: *Dictionnaire Provençal-Français et Français-Provençal.* Avignon, 1902.

HONNORAT, S. J.: *Dictionnaire-Provençal-Français.* Digne, 1847.

LEVY, E.: *Petit Dictionnaire Provençal-Français.* Heidelberg, 1909, 1923.

MISTRAL, F.: *Lou Trésor dóu Félibrige.* Paris, 1878, 1932.

RUMANIAN

ACADEMIA ROMÂNĂ: *Dicţionarul Limbii Române,* Bucharest, 1913-37, 2 incomplete vols.

ŞAINEANU, L.: *Dicţionar Universal al Limbei Române* [Craiova] 5th ed. [1925?]

ŞAINEANU, M.: *Dicţionar Româno-Frances.* Craiova [1925].

RUSSIAN

ALEXANDROW, A.: *Russian-English Dictionary.* New York, 1919, 6th ed. rev. and enlar.

DAHL, VL: *Tolkoviy Slovar Zhivavo Velykoruskavo Yezika.* Moscow, 1882, 4 vols.

BIBLIOGRAPHY

IMPERIAL ACADEMY OF SCIENCE: *Slovar Russkavo Yezika.* St. Petersburg, 1895, 9 vols. Incomplete.

MAKAROFF, N. P.: *Dictionnaire Français-Russe.* St. Petersburg, 1906, 12th ed.

MÜLLER, V. K.: *Russian-English Dictionary.* New York, 1944 (Dutton).

PAVLOVSKIY, I.: *Deutsches-russisches Wörterbuch.* Riga, 1911.

SEGAL, L.: *New Complete Russian-English Dictionary.* New York, 1942.

SERBIAN
See under CROATO-SERBIAN

SPANISH

BLANC, ST. H.: *Novisimo Diccionario Frances-Español.* Paris, 1870, rev. ed., 2 vols.

LAROUSSE, P.: *Pequeño Larousse Illustrado.* Paris, 1935.

MALARET, A.: *Diccionario de Americanismos.* Puerto Rico, 1925.

MACRAGH, E.: *Diccionario Amaltea, Inglés y Español.* Barcelona, 1933.

SALVÁ, D. V.: *Nuevo Diccionario Frances-Español.* Paris, 1901 (rev. by Gómez).

SEGOVIA, L.: *Diccionario de Argentinismos, etc.* Buenos Aires, 1911.

VELÁZQUEZ DE LA CADENA, M.: *A New Pronouncing Dictionary of the Spanish and English languages.* Chicago, 1942 (? ed).

SWEDISH

BJÖRKMAN, C. J.: *Svensk-Engelsk Ordbok.* Stockholm [1889?].

BIBLIOGRAPHY

SWEDISH ACADEMY: *Ordbok öfver Svenska Språket.* Lund, 1898-1939, vols. 1-15 (— LEU).

WENSTRÖM, O. E. and HARLOCK, W. E. *A Swedish-English Dictionary,* Stockholm, 1935.

YIDDISH

No dictionaries used, but compiled the list from memory and Bernstein's collection of Yiddish proverbs, cited in the next section.

C

A SELECTED BIBLIOGRAPHY OF PROVERBIAL COMPILATIONS

APPERSON, G. L.: *English Proverbs and Proverbial Phrases.* London, 1929 (Dent).
Apperson's collection differs from William Hazlitt's not only in its fuller offering, but in the academic nature of the book, with its classical parallels. The meticulous character of the workmanship may be gleaned from the fact that the author did not consult the *New English Dictionary,* until his progress had been close to the goal, so that whatever he included was the fruit of his own labor; but wherein is the consultation of other reference books and works on proverbial lore any different for our purpose from scanning the great Dictionary? Had he picked up the sayings first from the lips of the folk, it might have been the "fruit of my own labor," in other words tapping the original source.

BAYAN, G.: *Armenian Proverbs.* Venice, 1889.

BERNSTEIN, I.: *Catalogue des livres Parémiologiques.* Warsaw, 1900.
Describes the thousands of volumes on proverbs in his own library.

[361]

BIBLIOGRAPHY

BERNSTEIN, I.: *Yiddishe Shprikhverter.* Warsaw, 1912.
This first respectable collection in Yiddish, by the foremost paroemiographer of his generation, contains only 4000 proverbs. Many more sayings have been recorded since, but the Yiddish field has certainly not been cultivated; and the 121 specimens which Champion has reproduced in his *Racial Proverbs* are not representative of this collection.

BOHN, H. G.: *A Hand-Book of Proverbs.* London, 1855 *(Bell).*

BOHN, H. G.: *A Polyglot of Foreign Proverbs.* London, 1857 (Bell.). Probably the first work of its kind in English.

CAHAN, J. L.: *Der Yid vegn zikh un vegn andere.* New York, 1933. (Yiddish Scientific Institute).

CHAMPION, S. G.: *Racial Proverbs.* New York, 1938 (Macmillan).
This work, the fruit of 25 years of collecting, is the most ambitious work of its kind, at any rate in English; yet the compiler has, with the aid of 115 departmental aids, many of them authorities in their own national folklore, found only 26,000 proverbs worthy of selection from 186 languages and dialects. The first criticism to make of this work is that the title is a misnomer. It suggests that the proverbs are on racial topics, but in reality, the collection contains relatively few sayings with racial references. The volume should have been called "Proverbs from Many Peoples." A proverb may be racial when its content deals with race or nationality. Many of Champion's quotations do not even reflect the specific spirit or individuality of the particular people presented. In the second place, the disproportion is flagrant — extensive cultures poorly represented and low cultures padded. The same reversal manifests itself in the introductions — a page for the introduction to the French proverbs and about six pages

[362]

for the introduction to the Georgian (Grusinian) sayings
Numerous proverbs appear to be common to several countries,
and in some cases, it is obvious that the ascribed source is in-
correct, *e.g.*, Would the Poles, known for their intense patriotism and national sentiments, have originated the following
proverbs? "We are not in Poland where the women are
stronger than the men." "When God made the world, He sent
to the Poles some reason and the feet of a gnat, but even this
little was taken away by a woman." "God save us from a
Polish bridge"! Is it not likely that the Russians are responsible for the first two and the Germans for the third? And
is not the saying "The rabbi is dead but the scripture remains"
a Jewish rather than a Polish epigram?
Nevertheless, with all its faults — and some of them are due
perhaps to the multitude of collaborators — Champion's work,
especially on the technical side, is a considerable advance on
the books of proverbs we have had thus far in English, along
polygot lines.

CHRISTY, R.: *Proverbs, Maxims, and Phrases of all Ages.* (2 vols.).
New York and London, 1889 (Putnam).

CLARKE, JOHN: *Paroemiologia Anglo-Latina,* or *Proverbs English
and Latine.* London, 1639.
Clarke here compares, in parallel columns, the English proverbs with those collected by Erasmus in Latin. The correspondence is often so close that we wonder whether many are
not translations.

DÜRINGSFELD, IDA VON, and REINSBERG-DÜRINGSFELD, OTTO
VON: *Sprichwörter der germanischen und romanischen
Sprachen (vergleichend zusammengestellt),* 2 vols. Leipzig,
1872.
Although the parallels are extensively treated, the scope is
limited, and the national aspect is practically missing. This

phase, however, was covered very adequately in two small volumes under the title of *Internationale Titulaturen* by Reinsberg-Düringsfeld, in 1863. See under REINSBERG.

GOTTSCHALK, W.: *Die sprichwörtlichen Redensarten der französischen Sprache.* Heidelberg, 1930 (Winter).

GOTTSCHALK, W.: *Die bildhaften Sprichwörter der Romanen* (3 vols.). Heidelberg, 1936 (Winter).
Had the author translated the Romance proverbs instead of interpreting them homiletically and, occasionally, hermeneutically, the books would have been more useful. His search for parallels in German has led often to a narrowing of his field of operations. It is strange, for instance, that only a few proverbs should be cited from the Spanish and Portuguese, dealing with nationalities.

HAZLITT, W. C.: *English Proverbs and Proverbial Phrases.* London, 1869 (Smith).
The first comprehensive collection of English proverbs, it has enjoyed several editions. There are probably double the number of proverbs contained here than in John Ray's *Collection of English Proverbs.*

HERBERT, GEORGE: *Outlandish Proverbs.* London, 1640. On the title-page of this pioneer collection of 1032 English proverbs, only "Mr. G. H." appears as the compiler, but on the title-page of the second edition (*Jacula Prudentum or Outlandish Proverbs, Sentences,* etc.) the name appears in full. The number of proverbs might have been increased to about 1200. Why Herbert calls the proverbs "outlandish" is not clear from the booklet.

HALLER, J.: *Altspanische Sprichwörter und sprichwörtliche Redensart aus den Zeiten vor Cervantes.* Regensburg, 1883. An excellent comparative work.

BIBLIOGRAPHY

KING, W. F. H.: *Classical and Foreign Quotations*. London, 1889 (Whitaker).

KÜFFNER, G. M.: *Die Deutschen im Sprichwort*. Heidelberg, 1899 (Winter).
The author cites a bibliography of 77 references and has gone through 186 other works, but has apparently missed Wander's giant work. No wonder then that his yield is only meagre — 421 items, not counting the variants, of which there might be about a hundred. Why he did not use 174 items which evidently he had collected is left unexplained in the booklet. It is as if a man obtained his fish oil from a number of sardine boxes instead of from the whale, to which Wander's *Sprichwörter-Lexikon* might be compared. Yet it must be said that Küffner, making allowance for his natural bias and prejudices, is a careful investigator.

MARVIN, D. E.: *Curiosities in Proverbs*. London and New York, 1916 (Putnam).

MENCKEN, H. L.: *New Dictionary of Quotations*. New York, 1942 (Knopf).
Although Burton Stevenson's *Home Book of Quotations* contains at least half as much more material than Mencken's, I am not listing it because it has confined itself to purely individual literary quotations and has (perhaps rightfully) excluded folk expressions. It might be said, however, that Mencken's work is not merely one more dictionary of quotations. It shows considerable deliberation and planning, and certainly is the most judicious and balanced reference work of its kind, at least in English. Of what good are the hundreds of trite remarks about immortality, benevolence, or friendship that most of these compilations are filled with? Stevenson's volume stands half way between the compilative and the creative type.

MÉSANGÈRE, M. DE LA: *Dictionnaire des proverbes Français.* Paris, 1823.

RAY, JOHN: *A Collection of English Proverbs.* Cambridge, 1670. With the exception of John Clarke's *Paroemiologia Anglo-Latina,* this seems to be the first considerable compilation of proverbs in English, comprising, in the fourth (posthumous) edition of 1768, some five thousand proverbs. On the title-page of this edition, the author is referred to as the "late Reverend and Learned." From the point of view of the learned, the collection is truly respectable. Some misgivings, however, may be entertained as to whether clergymen would regard it as respectable. Fortunately censorship in those days was not too rigorous.

REINSBERG-DÜRINGSFELD, OTTO VON: *Internationale Titulaturen.* Leipzig, 1863 (Fries) in two slender volumes.
In this collection of proverbs, which was probably the first to treat of national attitudes, the favorable as well as the unfavorable reactions are given. A good deal of the compilation is devoted to individual states, provinces, counties, and even cities. The author, who traveled far and wide, is versed in considerable lore, particularly of the Balkan countries and peoples. As in most collections of proverbs by Germans, the stress is Teutonic.

ROBACK, A. A.: "The Jew and His Proverbs" (a series of eight articles) in *Canadian Jewish Chronicle,* vol. 1, 1914.

ROBACK, A. A.: *The Yiddish Proverb—A Study in Folk Psychology.* New York, 1918.

ROTHER, K.: *Die schlesischen Sprichwörter und Redensarten.* Breslau, 1928.

SEILER, F.: *Deutsche Sprichwörterkunde.* München, 1922 (Beck).

SMITH, W. G.: *The Oxford Dictionary of English Proverbs*. Oxford, 1935 (Clarendon).
This is the standard work on English proverbs, provided with an interesting introduction and an elaborate index by Miss J. E. Heseltine. Champion's criticism of its inclusiveness is valid only with respect to the appropriation of proverbs originating in other countries than England. It would seem as if all were grist that came to the English proverbial mill, but as for its comprehensiveness in regard to folk phrases, sobriquets, catch-words, etc., *The Oxford Dictionary of English Proverbs* is to be commended on its scope, until such time, at least, as there is a division of labor undertaken by other compilers.

TETZNER, F.: *Deutsches Sprichwörterbuch*. Leipzig, 1903 (Reclam).

WESTERMARCK, E.: *Wit and Wisdom in Morocco*. London, 1930 (Routledge).
A solid work, giving also the text in Arabic, by an authority with field experience.

WANDER, K. F. W.: *Deutsches Sprichwörter-Lexikon*, in 5 vols., quarto. Leipzig, 1870, (Brockhaus).
The most complete collection of proverbs in any language, citing more than a quarter of a million German sayings, and in addition about 60,000 foreign proverbs as parallels; for even though the Finns are said to have compilations aggregating nearly 2,000,000 proverbs, only a fraction of this number has been published. We may suspect too that there are far more variants than basic proverbs in the Finnish collections.
What is surprising, however, is that Wander should have included in this 9000-column work thousands of Yiddish proverbs, which I. Bernstein put at his disposal, as well as Tendlau's Judeo-German proverbs. It is a noble gesture on

the part of Wander, but there is apt to be confusion, as Yiddish proverbs have a Hebrew rather than a German background. One fears that the proverbs of other nations, too, have been incorporated in the various German collections somewhat indiscriminately.

D

GENERAL WORKS (MAINLY PHILOLOGICAL)

ALLPORT, G. W.: *The A B C's of Scapegoating.* Chicago, 1944 (Central Y.M.C.A. College).

BENEDICT, RUTH: *Race; Science and Politics.* New York, 1940 (Modern Age).

BOILLOT, F.: *Répertoire des métaphores et mots Français,* etc. Paris, 1929.

BRAUNSTEIN, B.: *The Chuetas of Majorca.* New York, 1936 (Columbia Oriental Series).
Although the author of this revealing study of persecution, visited on the Christian descendants by centuries removed from their Jewish ancestors, does not draw the necessary corollary, we may well infer what might happen if the Jews in any community, as a body, embrace Christianity.

BYSTROŃ, J. S.: *Megalomanja Narodowa* (in Polish). Warsaw, 1935 (Roj).
Bystroń has dealt in his miscellany of folklore, very extensively with the Polish ethnophaulisms, although scores which I found in the most complete Polish dictionary of Karłowicz *et alii* do not appear in Bystroń's book.

EFVERGREN, C.: *Names of Places in a Transferred Sense in English.* Lund, 1909.

JOESTEN, J.: "Calling Names in Any Language." *American Mercury*, Dec., 1935.

JOHNSON, J. W.: "Offensive Nicknames," New York *Age*, Feb. 1, 1919.

KLEINPAUL, R.: *Menschen-und Völkernamen.* Leipzig, 1885 (Reissner).

KLEINPAUL, R.: *Länder-und Völkernamen.* Leipzig, 1910 (Goschen). Both are excellent studies, the latter more popular. A tremendous amount of knowledge in the form of a feuilleton. Kleinpaul is one of the very few German philologists I know of who wrote in an entertaining and dramatic style, as if his erudition just gushed out of him spontaneously.

KONG, W.: "Name Calling." *Survey Graphic,* June, 1944, vol. XXXII, No. 6.

LÜCK, K.: *Der Mythos vom Deutschen in der polnischen Volks-überlieferung und Literatur.* Poznan, 1938 (Hirzel, Leipzig). Lück's book is by far the most comprehensive study we have in any language of relations prevailing between neighboring nations. Such investigations, when undertaken in a less partisan spirit, are of great value, linguistically, folkloristically, historically, and politically.

MENCKEN, H. L.: *The American Language* (4th edition). New York, 1936 (Knopf). Although not a dictionary, it is a linguistic declaration of independence. As usual, Mencken may be counted on to touch upon almost every phenomenon connected with language in a stimulating, even if not in a profound, manner.

MULERTT, W.: "Francospanische Kulturberührungen," *Volkstum und Kultur der Romanen,* 1930, vol. III.

MYERS, G.: *History of Bigotry in the United States.* New York, 1943 (Random House).

NYKL, A. R.: "Picaro," *Rev. Hispanique,* 1929, vol. LXXVII.

PARTRIDGE, E.: "Offensive Nationality," in *Words, Words, Words!* London, 1933, (Methuen).

PARTRIDGE, E.: *Slang To-Day and Yesterday.* New York, 1934 (Macmillan).

PARTRIDGE, E.: *The World of Words.* London, 1938 (Routledge).

POWER, W.: "International Libels," *Glasgow Record,* April 10, 1929.

SCHREUDER, H.: *Pejorative Sense Development in English.* Groningen, 1929 (Noordhoff).

SZAJKOWSKI, Z.: "Jewish Motifs in the Folk Culture of Comtat Venaissin in the 17th-19th Centuries," (in Yiddish), *Yivo Bleter,* 1942, vol. XIX.

VLEKKE, B. H. M.: "Over Moffen" (in Dutch), *Knickerbocker Weekly,* Dec. 15, 1941.

WEEKLEY, E.: "Xenophobia," in *Words and Names.* London, 1932, (Murray).

ZWEIFEL, MARGARET: *Untersuchung über die Bedeutungsentwicklung von Langobardus-Lombardus, etc.* Halle, 1921 (Niemeyer).

INDEXES

REGISTER OF PERSONAL NAMES

INDEX OF SUBJECTS

(*including languages and nationalities*)

Cornwall, England, 49, 53
Corsicans, 241
Cossacks, 94, 122, 138, 139
Cracow, 94
Cretans, 76, 77
Crimean War, 114
Croats, 82, 84, 108, 137
Cultural forms, vs. national products, 248-249
Cyprians, proverbs slurring, 154
Czechs, 301
  slurred in:
    Czech, 79
    English, 26, (by Americans), 22
    German, 108, 114, 154
    Hungarian, 116
    Polish, 124, 125
  proverbs slurring, 154

Dalmatians, 136
Danes, 26, 84, 117, 137, 296
  proverbs slurring, 155
Defecation in national slurs, 269
Denmark, 154
Derogatory locutions, see Ethnophaulisms,
Devon, England, 49
Dialogues of Luisa Sigea, 43
Dictionaries
  bibliography of, 347-360
  geographical references in, 248
  international references in, 247-248
  psychological references in, 248
Discrimination, 277, 319
  against Negroes, 336
Dislikes, sequence of, 252
Dutch, 264-267
  denoting German, 28, 30, 168, 265-266

rivalry with English, 265, 267
slurred in:
  Czech, 79
  Dano-Norwegian, 82
  Dutch and Flemish, 86
  English, 24, 26, 27-32, 34, 39, 64, 70, 71, (by Americans), 28-30
  French, 159
  German, 154-155
  Polish, 122
  Russian, 131
  proverbs slurring, 154-155
Dutch language, 27

Education, insufficiency of, 343
  national, 249
Ego, 249
Egypt, 31, 94, 102
Egyptian language, 77
Egyptians, 36, 94
  proverbs slurring, 155
England, slurred, 19, 36, 52
English, 261-264
  enmity toward Dutch, 266
  not self-critical, 262
  slurred in:
    Czech, 78
    Dano-Norwegian, 81
    Dutch and Flemish, 84, 85, 88, 156
    English, 21, 23, 31, 50, 52, 58, 67, 68, 156-158, (by Americans), 21, 52, (by Australians), 44, 59, (by Irish), 23, 158, (by Scotch), 156-158
    French, 34, 43, 90, 91, 93, 101, 155-157, 159
English language slurred, 135
Enlightenment, our hope, 342
Epigrams, see under Proverbs

Eskimo, 31, 40
Ethiopia, 31
Ethiopians, 76
Ethnophaulisms, 19-143; analyzed, 259; factors in, 302, German, 269-270, 306; etymology of, 251; specimens of: Albanian, 143; Arabic, 77, 142; Austrian, 103, 105, 108, 109, 112; Bavarian, 110; Bosnian, 142; Carpathian Saxon, 108, 109; Chinese, 142-143; Croatian, (see Serbo-Croatian); Czech, 78-81; Dalmatian, 143; Danish, 72, 82-84; Dano-Norwegian, 81-84; Dutch, 84-89; English, 19-72; Estonian, 143; Finnish, 143; Flemish, 84-89; French, 34, 43, 89-102; Gascon, 96; German, 102-114; Greek, 114-115; Greek (Ancient), 75-78; Hebrew, 75-77; Hungarian, 116-117; Icelandic, 117-118; Italian, 118-120; Latin, 75-78; Lettish, 143; (or Lithuanian); Norwegian, 83-84; Persian, 142; Polish, 121-126; Portuguese (see Spanish-Portuguese); Provençal, 126-128; Rumanian, 142-143; Russian, 128-132; Serbo-Croatian, 132-133; Spanish - Portuguese, 133-136, (Latin-American), 133; Swedish, 137-138; Swiss, 107; Syriac, 77; Turkish, 142; Ukrainian, 129-131; Yiddish, 138-142. See also, Slurs
Eurasians, 24
Europeans, 143
Evaluation as basis of slur, 257

Fascism, 36, 40, 271, 319, 330, 339
Feces in national taunts, 269

Fiji Islanders, 103
Filipino, 32, 36
Finland, 159
Finns
slurred in:
Dano-Norwegian, 82
English, 31
Icelandic, 117
Russian, 131
Swedish, 137-138
Flanders, 32, 95
Flemings
slurred in:
Czech, 79
Dutch and Flemish, 85
English, 21, 32
French, 95, 96, (by Walloons), 159
German, 103
Spanish, 134
Florentines, 98
Food as basis of slurs, 261
Foreigners, dread of, 254
France, 53
Franco-Prussian War, 21
Frankish, old, 102, 138
Franks, 238, 241
Free speech, 324, 332
French, 270-271
enmity toward English, 270
old, 99
Revolution, 26
slurred in:
Arabic, 160
Czech, 79
Danish, 82
Dutch and Flemish, 85, 86, 160
English, 23, 26, 27, 32-34, 36, 44, 50, 52-54, 57, 58, 67, 159, 161, (by Americans), 33; (by British), 27, 52

French, 89, 159, 160
German, 103, 104, 111, 160, 161
Greek, 115
Hungarian, 116
Icelandìc, 117
Italian, 118, 159-161
Latin, 76
Polish, 122
Portuguese, 134, 159
Provencal, 128
Russian, 129, 131, 159-161
Serbo-Croatian, 133
Spanish, 134, 136, 160, 161
Swedish, 137
Yiddish, 139
proverbs slurring, 159-161
French Canadians, 34, 51
French language, 57
old, 99
Freudianism, 338
Frisians, 86

Gaelic language, 67
Galician, 149
Galician Jews, 139, 140
Gascons, slurred, 96, 159
Genoese, 239
Gentiles, 64, 71, 304
slurred in:
Hebrew, 75-77
Yiddish, 139, 140
proverbs slurring, 204-205
Georgians, proverbs slurring, 161
German language slurred, 117, 120, 121, 123, 240
German, Low, see Low German
Germans, 148-150
national attitudes of, 267-270
slurred in:
Bosnian, 142

Czech, 79-80, 162, 165-168, 170
Danish, 166
Dutch and Flemish, 87
English, 22, 32, 34-36, 38-40, 51, 68, 70, 71, 163, (by Americans), 35, 168
Estonian, 143 169
Finnish, 162
French, 89, 92-94, 96, 97, 100, 162, 163, 169
German, 103, 109, 120, 164, 165, 167-169
Hungarian, 116, 117, 168, 174, 177
Italian, 118, 120, 162, 163, 165, 166, 168, 169
Lettish (Lithuanian), 143, 163, 167, 168, 169, 175
Polish, 121-124, 162-164, 166, 169-177
Portuguese (Brazilian), 133
Provençal, 127
Russian, 129-131, 162, 163, 166-168, 177
Serbian, 162
Slavic, 172
Spanish, 133, 166, (Chilean), 133
Swedish, 137, 166
Swiss, 169
Ukrainian, 161, 162, 165, 174-177
Wendish, 169
Yiddish, 138, 139, 141
proverbs slurring, 161-177
See also Teutons
Germany, 54
Gesta Romanorum, 315
Gibberish, 36
Gonorrhea, 306

INDEX OF SUBJECTS

English, 20, 26, 66, 67, (by
Americans), 67
French, 20, 95, 98, 101, 102,
227
German, 112, 114, 228, 229
Italian, 120
Spanish, 136
proverbs slurring, 227-229
Switzerland, 72
Switzerland, French, 148
Synecdoche complex, 338
Syphilis, 306
Syrians, 83, 195

Talmud, 330, 331
Tartar, etymology of, 312
Tartars, slurred, 67, 102, 114, 117,
124, 131, 141, 142, 189
proverbs slurring, 229
Tartary, 229
Teacher's Oath law, 343
Telugus, 229
Teutons, slurred in Latin, 78
Thebaid, 102
Thirty Years' War, 57, 112, 226,
227
Timbuctoo, 102
Tit-Bits, 320
Tolerance, 319
Trojans, 78
Trojan War, 68
Troy, 77
Turkey, 36, 63
Turkish language, 120, 140
Turkomans, 233
Turks, 291-292
hatred of, 253, 256
history of, 291-292
slurred in:
Arabic, 231
Armenian, 231

Czech, 231, 233
Danish, 84
Dano-Norwegian, 84
Dutch and Flemish, 88, 231,
232
English, 40, 44, 50, 68, 69,
230, (by British), 72
French, 102
German, 114, 231-233
Greek, 115
Hindu, 230
Hungarian, 117, 233
Icelandic, 118
Italian, 120, 232
Montenegrin, 230
Norwegian, 84
Osmanli, 230
Persian, 230, 232
Polish, 125
Russian, 232
Serbian, 231-233
Swedish, 138
Turkish, 230
Ukrainian, 231
Yiddish, 141
proverbs slurring, 230-233
Tuscan (dialect), 156
Types, problem of, 311

Ukrainians, slurred, 121, 125, 129
proverbs slurring, 233
United States, slurred, 45
Usury, 254, 273

Vandal, 69
Varna and Rutschuk Railway, 23
Venetians, slurred, 101
Vienna, 170

Wales, 44
Wallachia, 217

NOTE

Sterling Eisiminger's "A Glossary of Ethnic Slurs in American English" (*Maledicta*, Vol. III, No. 2 [Winter 1979]) contains many meanings not listed by Roback, as well as new slurs from the past thirty-five years.